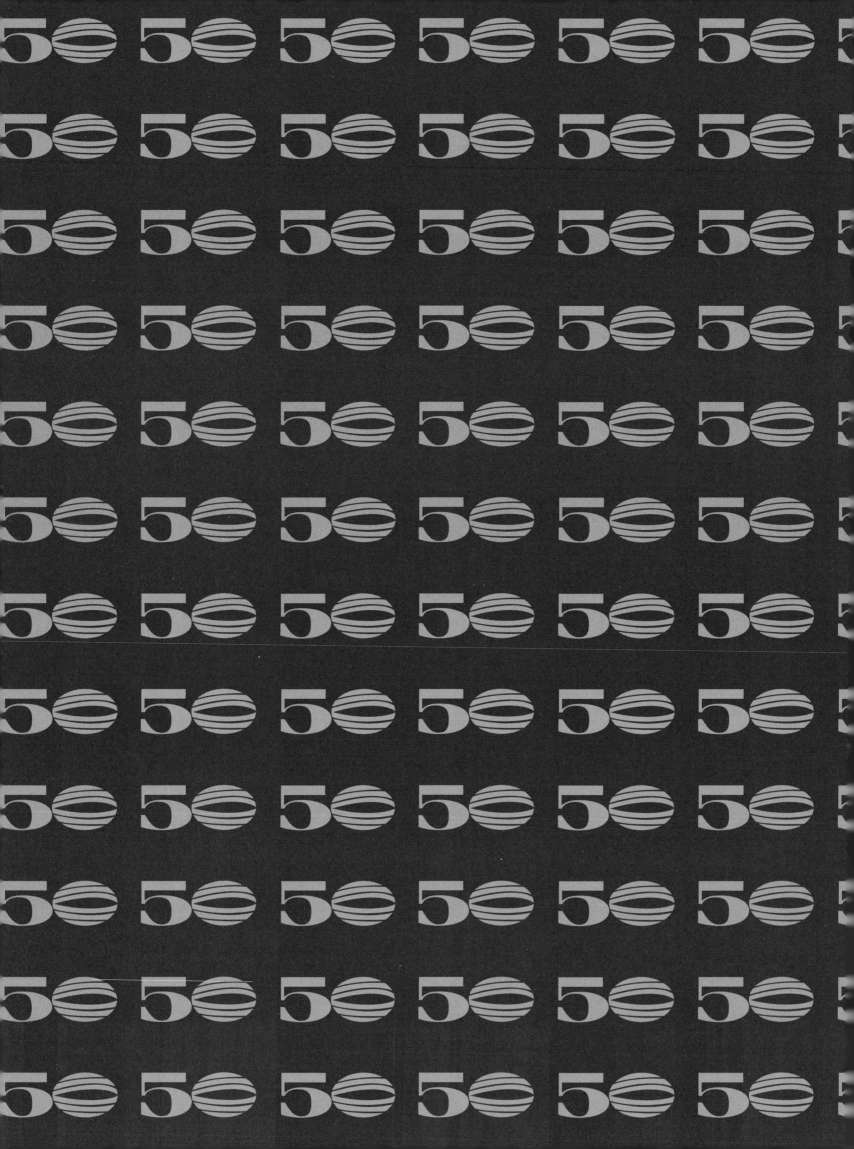

Australia's Living Heritage

ARTS OF THE DREAMING

Australia's Living Heritage

JENNIFER ISAACS

Photography
REG MORRISON
and contributing photographers

LANSDOWNE
Sydney • Auckland • London • New York

For Gertrude and Joyce

Participating communities

Amata, South Australia
Amoongana, Northern Territory
Aurukun, Queensland
Kintore, Northern Territory
Mt Liebig, Northern Territory
Nguiu, Bathurst Island, Northern Territory
Maningrida and outstations, Northern Territory
Ramingining and outstations, Northern Territory
Papunya, Northern Territory
Yirrkala, Northern Territory

Participating art galleries and museums

Art Gallery of New South Wales
Art Gallery of South Australia
Australian Museum
Macleay Museum, University of Sydney
Museum of Victoria
Northern Territory Museum of Arts and Sciences
South Australian Museum

Distributed by Gary Allen Pty Limited
15 Nowill Street, Condell Park, NSW 2200
Designer: Susan Kinealy
Editor: Jacqueline Kent

Published by Lansdowne, Sydney
a division of Weldons Pty Limited
372 Eastern Valley Way, Chatswood, NSW 2067
First published 1984
Reprinted 1987

©Copyright Jennifer Isaacs 1984
Produced in Australia by the Publisher
Typeset in Australia by Savage & Co. Pty Ltd, Brisbane, in Caslon Book
Printed in Singapore by Kyodo Printing Co. (Pte) Limited

National Library of Australia Cataloguing-in-Publication Data
Isaacs, Jennifer.
Australia's living heritage: arts of the dreaming.
Bibliography.
Includes index.
ISBN 0 7018 1497 7.

[1]. Aborigines, Australian — Art. [2]. Aborigines,
Australian — Material culture. 3. Art, Australian.
4. Handicraft — Australia, I. Title.

709'.01'10994

Half-title page: Incised boab nuts from Mowanjum, Western Australia.
Title page: Tiwi man painted in preparation for dance.

Contents page: Children playing on Tarntippi beach, Bathurst Island.
Endpapers: Strands of old necklace of quondong seeds.

Contents

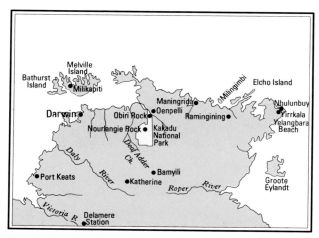

Detail of the Top End of the Northern Territory of Australia.

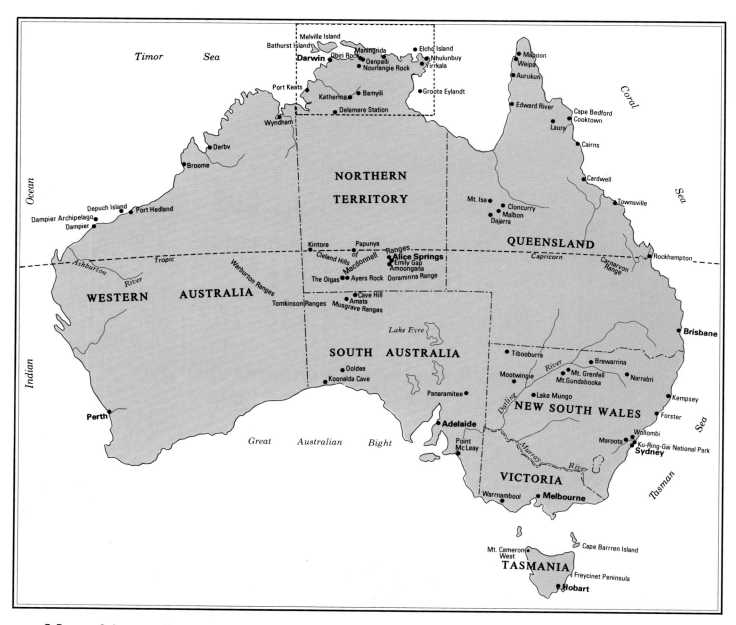

Map of Australia indicating the locations of Aboriginal communities and art sites.

PREFACE

Aboriginal art is part of a living tradition, perhaps the oldest continuous art tradition in the world. It is the visual expression of a religion which has its origins in antiquity. Serious practitioners of the ceremonies have maintained the traditional art forms throughout the deserts of Australia and in the far northern areas.

Like all forms of cultural expression, Aboriginal art is constantly adapting and changing with time. Even the traditional arts — those that express the religion, land and Dreaming — reveal the individuality of each artist, and constantly incorporate new ideas, patterns and materials.

In this book I have been fortunate to include many examples of early works now held in the collections of Australian museums and galleries. Although the styles have altered, the symbols, themes and preoccupations of the artists have not. The traditional arts have survived significant social upheaval and they now emerge as exciting, innovative expressions of an ancient and continuous philosophy and belief in the Australian landscape itself. Hundreds of Aboriginal artists in Australia may not yet be known individually, but their work is of major importance and their skills and creativity are a significant part of the unique Australian heritage.

In Aboriginal society men and women have their own parallel expressive arts. The painted or decorated body becomes a living sculpture in dance. The same designs may be transferred to many different surfaces, for different purposes — to fibre, sand, wood, bark and stone. The separation of art and craft, traditional in the Western world, does not exist in Aboriginal art. The intricacies of spinning, weaving and knotting are integrated with shells, fibre and paint, while feathers and fibre can form part of sculpture.

Since the publication of earlier books on Aboriginal arts, public perception and appreciation of the total context of creativity in the wider society have increased. Contemporary art exhibitions now include constructions, performances, fibre works and combinations of natural objects such as feathers and shells — all elements that Aboriginal artists have always explored.

I hope this book goes some way towards ensuring that the precious heritage of Aboriginal art is recognised and appreciated in all its stunning variety. The symbols that express the Dreaming continue as the living arts of Aboriginal Australia.

Aboriginal Art, Culture and Landscape

Aboriginal art is among the oldest in the world. The visual and performing arts of Aboriginal society express the ancient origins of life and the landscape, stretching back into the infinite past, the Dreaming.

Like Aboriginal oral history, the visual arts illustrate and record a monumental time span through which the Aboriginal way of life has adapted and changed. Geological changes and seasonal and weather variations over the centuries have affected food, animals, plants and vegetation, and therefore the people's way of life. Aboriginal culture developed in response to the natural environment and sometimes modified it.

In other continents of the world, environmental changes and contact with other cultures led to the spread of new technologies such as pottery and metallurgy. However, Australia was too isolated for such contact to have far-reaching effects on the indigenous people. Instead of developing a sedentary life with refinements such as agriculture, the Aboriginals used their ingenuity in intellectual and religious pursuits, expressed through elaborate art and ceremony. In the temporal sphere, techniques of physical survival were refined by the effective harvesting and use of natural resources. Men became extraordinarily skilled with the spear, the spear thrower and the boomerang: women with nets and fishing lines and in the making of utensils. In the technology of fishing alone, appropriate techniques were developed to suit every situation. Different nets were made for river estuaries, tidal waters and the sea coast. Finely honed hooks and barbs were carved for different fish; special poisons were developed for stunning fish or for bringing them to the surface.

Aboriginal exploitation of natural resources could well have drastically changed not only the Australian environment and vegetation by the use of fire, but may also account for the extinction of many animal species. Populations increased in areas that provided the greatest food resources, particularly the sea coast, rivers and estuaries. Harvesting of fish and game in heavily populated areas was intense.

At the very centre of Aboriginal culture is a rich oral mythology expressed in ceremonial life. When Europeans invaded Australia in 1788 about 200 different Aboriginal languages were spoken,[1] each representing a different people, often descended from different creation ancestors or from the same ancestors in different parts of the country. There were few general beliefs, though some concepts were common to many tribal

Opposite Tiwi men dancing on Tarntippi beach, Bathurst Island.

groups. Essentially all believe that the creation ancestors entered Australia in the creation time, when the landscape was partly formed. Some, such as the giant serpents, came from beneath the ground; as they moved, they created ridges and valleys and behind them rivers flowed to the sea. Some great ancestors, such as Baiame of the south-eastern people, came from and returned to the sky and others, such as the Djankawu of eastern Arnhem Land, travelled from distant islands across the sea. Creation ancestors caused and still cause climatic changes, the wet and dry seasons, thunder and lightning. Many Aboriginals also believe that the creation ancestors filled and fashioned the cosmos, becoming the sun, moon, stars and planets.

After the creation ancestors appeared, they began their epic journeys across the land. At times they clashed with other creatures and in the resulting cataclysm the landscape itself was formed and changed. Men and women ancestors metamorphosed into stone and rock or created rivers and waterholes. These ancestors held the first ceremonies, sang the first songs and created the designs that have continued into the living present and are painted on the body, on bark and on the ground, as well as carved on weapons.

The relationship of people to their land and to every living creature in it was well defined all over the country. Family relationships and the behaviour of each person to every other were always determined by kinship laws, generally ordained by the actions and decrees of the creation ancestors. Each clan or family grouping 'owned' its tracts of land by virtue of descent from the creation ancestors. Certain people had the duty of guarding sacred sites, visiting and retouching art, conducting ceremonies at special places or clearing unwanted vegetation from sacred rocks and trees. Intellectual life revolved around recalling complex and extensive genealogies and ceremonial songs. The ceremonies enacted the song cycles that described the travels, movements and actions of the ancestral beings at different places, and recalling genealogical information enabled all Aboriginal people to trace their relationships with sometimes distant tribes.

The songs also defined the land owned by the clan. They recounted the stories of the travels made by animal or human ancestors in minute detail and described each place the ancestors visited, thus defining lands and boundaries. Neighbouring groups shared elements of the same . mythology, and the songs they owned would extend the journeys of the ancestors across their own land, introducing new totems and describing new events that left their marks on the landscape. The ancestors have remained permanently at the sacred sites and when Aboriginal people visit them, even briefly, they often sing parts of the songs while cleaning or caretaking.

This exceptionally strong relationship with the ancestral heroes and with the landscape forms the basis of all Aboriginal art. Dance, song, ceremony and material arts all combine to form a unified whole, a complete artistic network that articulates the landscape and the Dreaming. Traditional Aboriginal culture connects the arts with every feature of religious and daily secular life. At the core of the arts is Aboriginal ceremonial life. Music, dance, song and paintings were each part of the same process of constantly connecting the life of the people with the Dreaming. On special occasions ceremonial life would be heightened. Seasonal changes produced a plentiful supply of food, resulting in a gathering of people and a flowering of ceremony, dance and art.

The arts include all facets of human creativity and need for expression, decoration and adornment. In the area of ceremonial art, the graphic arts include body decoration and ornament, paintings on rock and bark, ground designs and sculptures and special emblems of wood, stone, feathers, string or bark that may be regarded as religious sculpture.

In daily life, Aboriginal arts include the making of simple personal adornments of clothing, headbands, necklaces and pendants, as well as the carving and incising of utensils and carrying dishes. Mats, bags, mesh nets and dilly bags are spun or woven.

Painting or engraving on rock is the oldest form of Aboriginal creative expression. In Koonalda cave, beneath the Nullarbor Plain in South Australia the earliest known art in Australia has been found. The site is decorated with finger impressions made in the soft limestone walls of deep underground caverns. Archaeologists have provided evidence that the marks were made up to 20,000 years ago, which means that the art is some of the oldest known in the world.[2] Elsewhere in Australia much of the huge body of engraved and painted symbols and images has a time span of at least 10,000 years, and some sites may be almost as old as Koonalda.[3]

Rock art is predominantly magico-religious. Haunting white or red figures with dislocated limbs or with bodies pierced by spears testify to the ancient practices of malevolent magic. Paintings of animals, kangaroos, fish or turtles ensure a successful hunt, the continual reproduction of the species and a fertile land. Others powerfully evoke the likenesses of spirit ancestors themselves, such as the Wandjina in the Kimberley region or the lightning spirit in the Kakadu National Park. Living people will admit only to retouching the great spirit paintings, never to having created the original images. These came from the ancestors in the Dreaming. Legends and songs tell of places where the ancestors 'put themselves on rock' and where their painted images are their very spirits.

Legends recount that sacred objects and designs were either brought with the creation ancestors or made and painted by them and taught to their descendants. In either case, it was through the ancestors that these designs were handed down through the generations. In desert areas the exact nature of this exchange is a closely kept sacred secret, forming the core of the religious life of the older, fully initiated people; in other areas some 'outside' details have been disclosed about the nature and meaning of the designs. This limited exposure of religious belief and content only serves to indicate the true complexity of Aboriginal religion and the symbolic art that expresses it.

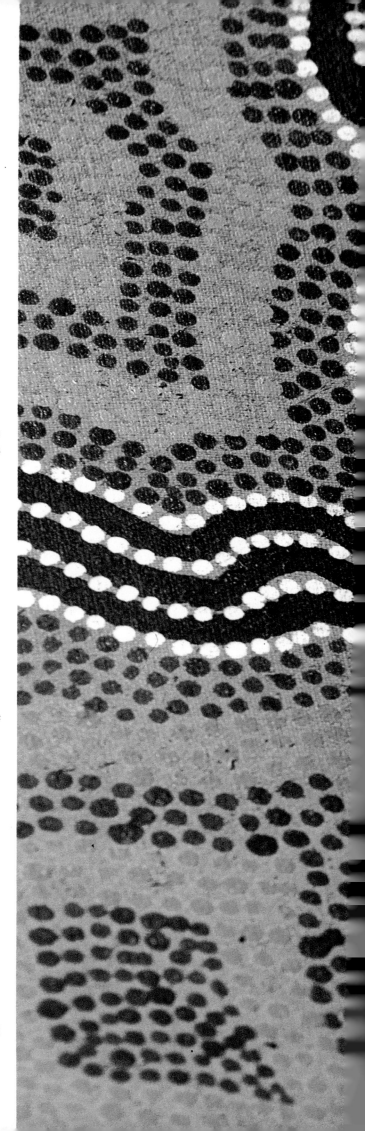

SYMBOLISM IN ABORIGINAL ART

All Aboriginal art is symbolic; much of it is geometric or non-figurative. Symbolic art is featured in body designs, carved trees, ground drawings, many rock engravings and paintings, bark paintings and designs on message sticks, boomerangs and sacred objects. Representational art showing human and animal forms exists beside abstract symbols.

Essentially, the symbols can be used for a number of purposes, and members of other groups understand them in varying degrees. For example, the Walbiri-Pintubi create magnificent ground designs from plant down, ochre and clay. These are patterns showing the land, as well as events of the creation era. A range of symbols are used, including arcs, concentric circles, circles, bars, dots and wavy lines. The meanings of the symbols vary in every painting, depending on the site shown, the religious inferences, the degree of information the authors have been allowed to convey (their ritual status) and the status of the intended audience. In a sense, some of the symbols can be used like an alphabet, but when put together they create a meaning that is totally accessible only to the creators and their immediate group. Even related clans or language groups may guess at the meanings of the juxtaposition of arcs, circles and dots, but without 'inside' knowledge of the related mythology and ceremonial information they cannot be sure of giving an interpretation that will fully coincide with the intentions of the artists.

When the symbols are used together to form the ground plan of a design, they map the landscape, showing special features with important mythological relevance to the subject matter depicted. They also tell 'stories'. The symbols, whether running feet, patterns of flowing water or fire symbols, indicate events that occurred in that landscape. For the artists — the guardians of the landscape depicted — the paintings embody their own spiritual presence. Men trace the tracks and circles and sing the songs in the process of creating the designs. Thus reproducing the designs becomes a religious act, a reaffirmation of belief in the creation ancestors and the absorption of some of their essential power.

Arnhem Land painting has a symbolic visual language distinctly different from that of other areas. In eastern Arnhem Land, each clan owns a wide range of patterns and designs that signify areas of land, natural features or specific objects. Representational figures of men, animals, fish and plants are incorporated into the art, but a full interpretation depends on the patterns and designs used in relation to the figure. For example, a turtle design painted by a young man may show the turtle swimming, with little decoration on his back and some lines flowing from his legs to indicate running water or movement. A more senior artist may include a pattern on the turtle's back, specifically denoting reeds from a special site, and another artist may show other areas of pattern around the figures, denoting the place from which the turtle has travelled and suggesting events of the creation era. Only the

Opposite Detail of a painting by Mick Namarari, a Pintubi artist from Papunya, central Australia. The circles symbolise camping sites and sacred areas.
Photograph Jennifer Isaacs

Ancient symbolic stone arrangement, central Queensland.

senior artist is permitted to paint the 'full' story, with, for example, the image of a great creation hero, Barama, in the centre, the turtles on either side and the body designs that denote this Dreaming painted on the figure.

Information is contained in the shapes of animate and inanimate objects, in the patterns painted on these, in colours used and in the superimposition of different colours in the cross-hatching. Additional information may also be conveyed in major paintings through the plan or layout of the design as it relates to the actual features of an area of land. Thus a story about the arrival of ancestors from the sea, their actions on the beaches and their travels past waterholes into the bush beyond may be painted in geographical sections: sea, sand, and bush. Interpreting the paintings is much easier if the associated mythology is known.

Symbolic markings occur all over Australia. Body decorations follow ancient prescribed patterns symbolising the totemic ancestors, weapons are carved with geometric patterns that symbolise the ownership of

specific land tracts and grave markers or coffins are painted or carved
with designs that have specific meaning to the deceased.

The giant carved trees, or dendroglyphs, of the south-east were made
to mark initiation grounds and burial sites. The patterns of spirals,
lozenges and zigzags denote territorial ownership. Ceremonies and
trading visits between Aboriginal tribes were announced by messengers
sent from one to the other. So that the messengers would be received at
their destinations and would pass unmolested through strange country,
they were given message sticks, which were sticks incised with symbols
and patterns. The patterns not only identified the carrier by symbolising
his territory, but, in some instances, they conveyed the message itself.

Symbols and signs continue to be part of traditional Aboriginal
communication. Stones are left in patterns to signify the shifting of camp;
marks are made on trees to denote the place at which a man died and
patterns of tracks, circles and lines are drawn in the sand as an aid to
conversation and storytelling.

REGIONAL VARIATIONS IN CULTURAL EXPRESSION

Throughout Australia, Aboriginal people expressed their relationships to their ancestral spirits and their lands in differing forms. Song, dance and ceremony spread and changed from group to group and aspects of ritual were shared and traded. With the sharing of ritual went diffusion of design, body decoration and technique, and in the secular sphere, changes in weapon and utensil technology.

The culture of any one tribal group has therefore never been static; it has continually absorbed influences and adapted to environmental and social change. At the time of European invasion in 1788, for example, some groups used spear throwers, whereas others held spears in the hand; the giant carved trees of the south-east were found nowhere else; the desert peoples were enacting their totemic ancestral dreamings covered in down and ochre; and the people of the south-east spoke of Baiame and made earthen *bora* ceremonial grounds. Over the centuries, the coastal people of the 'top end' had most contact with outsiders, and their culture differed strongly from that of the desert people and the people who occupied the river valleys of the south-east. Yet with these differences – in religion, language and the visual arts – there were essential similarities that still bind Aboriginal Australians together. There is a close affinity to the land and its features, to the spirits of the creation ancestors and in all communities there is a strong reluctance or total taboo about speaking of the deceased for fear of a pervading contact with their spirits. In most tribes, these two areas of belief gave rise to the fullest flowering of the visual arts: religious ceremonies of the Dreaming connected to the creation ancestors and mortuary rituals designed to send the spirit of the deceased to its final resting place.

SOUTH-EAST AUSTRALIA

The temperate region of south-eastern Australia is well watered by the Murray, Murrumbidgee and Darling River networks. The first European colonists in Australia chose this area to settle permanently and in all probability it was home to the densest Aboriginal populations on the continent. Original estimates of the population of Aboriginal people in 1788 placed the overall figure at about 300,000,[4] with perhaps 50,000 in the south-eastern regions. More recent studies, using population projection techniques in reverse, have suggested that there were perhaps three times as many people as the earlier estimates indicated.[5]

Food, particularly fish and birds, was most plentiful along river estuaries. Here the people camped on high ground, overlooking the valleys and plains that formed their hunting grounds. Shell middens or deposits of food debris and remains of centuries-old campfires are scattered throughout the countryside close to sheltered sandy areas which were favoured as campsites.

When the European settlement of Melbourne was first established, the Murray River area was well populated. Tribal areas were well defined. The southern peoples, like those of the north, guarded their territory carefully. Well-worn routes crossed the countryside, marking paths followed when visiting other peoples to arrange marriages, inviting people to ceremonies or making economic exchanges. Trespassing on lands or misuse of these routes led to battle, as did 'women trouble' and other transgressions.

Much of the tribal art that remains from these areas is embodied in the men's weapons; the clubs, boomerangs, spears and shields. Like the abstract designs from Arnhem Land or symbols from central Australia, many of the patterns on these weapons represent the country and the special sites belonging to the maker or the original owner. The design on one club in the collection of the Museum of Victoria has been interpreted as being a lagoon and a tributary of the Broken River in north-eastern Victoria, the space between two curved patterns being the country owned by the man concerned.

The weapons made throughout the south-east of Australia were actively used until perhaps the turn of this century. Warfare or fighting between Aboriginal groups was real, though sometimes it took the form of ritualised displays of aggression with few fatal or debilitating results.

The last great battle between Aboriginal tribes in Victoria occurred in Gippsland in 1856-7. The fight — between the Omeo people and the Kurnai — began because of an inappropriate marriage between a Kurnai woman and an Omeo man. The two tribes had been hostile, but European intervention had forced contact between them, resulting in the marriage. The undercurrent of tension needed only an excuse to erupt into violence, and it came when the man mistreated his wife. The Kurnai woman's relatives took revenge. The battle, waged with a combination of Aboriginal weapons and European guns, was protracted and took place in stages, each one revenging previous offences. At one point, people from a wide grouping of tribes were involved, each group calling on relatives for help. The battles ended at Bushy Creek in 1857, with great loss of life on both sides.

The beautiful and deadly weapons were also employed to great effect against the white man who transgressed the natural codes of Aboriginals; those dealing with land boundaries, sacred sites and behaviour towards women. Although heavy, deadly and deftly wielded, the wooden weapons eventually proved no match for guns and steel, and many massacres occurred. These conflicts, as well as diseases and the destruction of natural habitats of traditionally hunted animals through pastoral activities, decimated the Aboriginal population very quickly indeed.

The exquisite carved patterns on the weapons greatly impressed the European invaders, and the patterns on those they collected provide the only evidence of the wide-ranging symbolic arts of the south-eastern people. More ephemeral art objects (body ornaments or sacred objects) were usually kept hidden from the white invaders' eyes or destroyed after use. Only a handful of objects associated with Aboriginal ceremony in south-eastern Australia survive in the collections of the world.

Unlike the peoples of the centre and north, southern Aboriginals had to cope with extreme cold in winter. Most wore possum skin cloaks and wraps, often with the fur on the inside. Possum fur was also used to make fluffy headbands and the skins were used for water containers. The interior of the cloaks provided a soft surface on which designs were scratched and painted. These lovely works were fragile in the extreme and all have disappeared, except two or three in collections. One, an extremely valuable testament to the first and most ancient clothing art of Aboriginal Australians, is now in the Museum of Victoria, too fragile to travel and rarely shown to the public.

The pattern on the cloaks is divided into many vertical and horizontal rectangles, each containing an autonomous symbolic design which might have accurately reflected the artist's own mental picture of his land.

The cloaks might also have denoted individual status. There may be a link between the distinct curvilinear patterns on the cloaks and body scar decorations. However, little can be established, as few records remain of the patterns, meaning and distribution of either form of design.[6]

The most important ceremony in any tribal community was the initiation ritual known as the *bora*. Initiation ceremonies and the associated arts celebrated the great all-father spirit, Baiame, who, with Dhurramulan his son (known as Bunjil in Victoria), were the central figures in Aboriginal mythology. The rituals were conducted by large gatherings of the tribes, and for the event a large earth mound was made. These mounds ranged from long bands of patterns to simple circles of raised earth. Man-made patterns and circles of loose stones were also included in the ceremonial practice.

According to Aboriginal mythology, Baiame created the first *bora*. He is given much of the credit for shaping the world and for giving the laws of life to the people. He is a sky spirit hero who was on earth for a time in the creation era but who returned to the sky. (His voice or that of Dhurramulan his son is heard through the mouth of the bullroarer, the sacred whirling object heard in the bush at the initiation ceremonies.)[7]

Eventually the spirit of Dhurramulan entered different trees, in which he still lives except when initiation ceremonies are going on. A piece of wood cut from a tree will make a bullroarer, which may also be called Dhurramulan, as the humming sound represents his voice. He likes to live in the large irregular protuberances characteristic of many eucalypt trees, and old men say that the upper sides of these protuberances have been worn smooth by him. Like many other mythical heroes, he can change his shape from the size of a little bird to that of a giant.

A few *bora* rings remain as overgrown humps of earth close to dendroglyphs. These sites are very special to Aboriginal people today, as they provide tangible evidence of their ancestors' spiritual activities. Although dendroglyphs were made along the coast in central New South Wales and in the Dividing Range as far south as the Victorian border, they were most frequently seen on the north coast in the Kempsey and Forster areas.

Dendroglyphs were used to mark the graves of important men and in conjunction with initiations. When such men were buried, several trees near the graveside were carved with symbolic designs; the cuts were made through the outer bark to the inner layers of the trunk. Being so deeply etched, the designs became part of the tree, remaining long after the tree itself had died.

Not many of these works survive today in their original locations, though some have been preserved in the Australian Museum. Their symbolism and their precise meaning, however, are obscure. The

available information is being gathered and preserved by the descendants of these artists in the form of verbal records obtained from old men who remember trees being carved when they were children.

The thousands of rock engravings of the Sydney-Hawkesbury district remain the most tangible evidence of Aboriginal artistic activities along the New South Wales coast. These include isolated images of animals or abstract shapes and whole galleries on flat rock outcrops covered with animals, fish, bird and animal tracks, and marks. Huge ancestor figures appear at the most important places; a site upon which these are combined with other designs leading to and from an exposed flat area is most likely to have been a ceremonial site.

Stencilled paintings in a cave near Maroota, New South Wales. The cave overlooks a fern-filled valley and is a short walk from an important rock engraving site. The two places might have been used jointly for ceremonies.

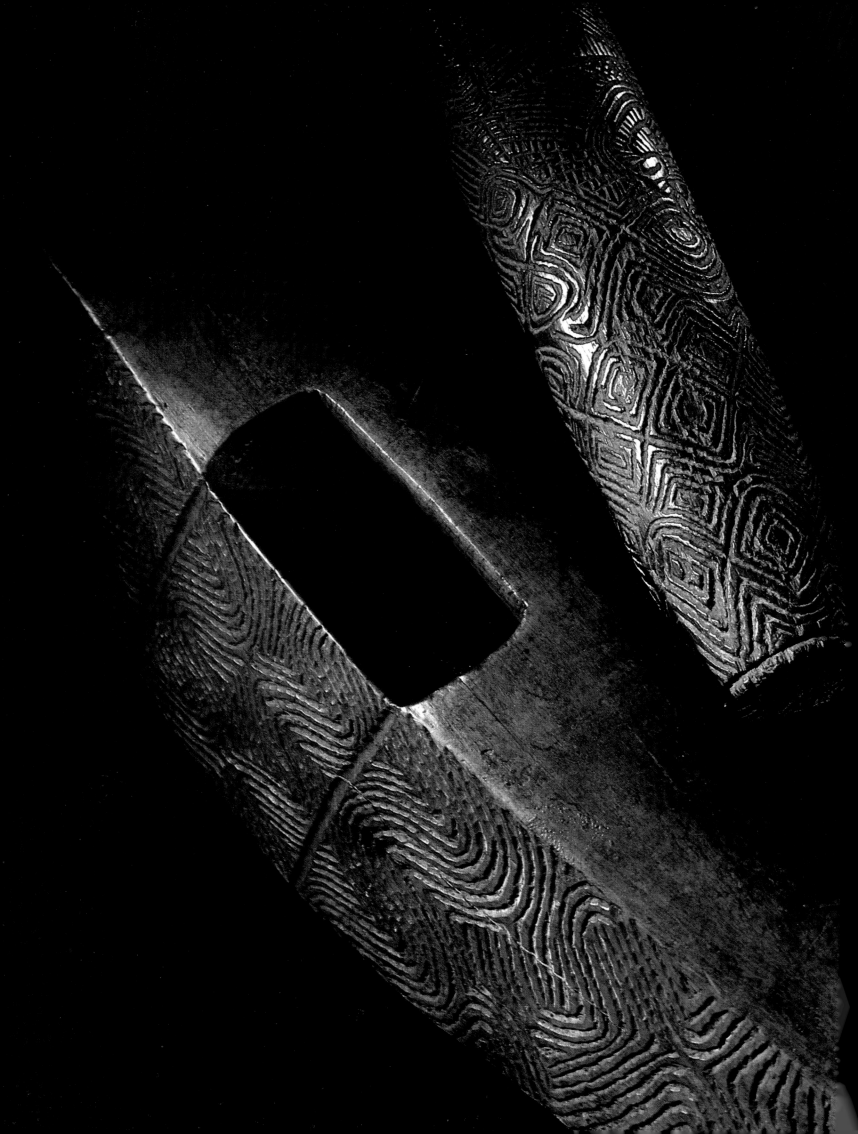

Aboriginals once occupied all parts of New South Wales; the sea coast, rivers, hills and valleys, the mountains, the open plains and the dry interior.

Large groups of people assembled at different sites along the coast to take advantage of seasonal resources. The oral history of surviving Aboriginal groups and the diary records of early white colonists mention great gatherings and feasts and archaeological excavations have corroborated these. At one site at Durras North on the south coast of New South Wales, great quantities of mutton bird bones were found; the birds were harvested on their annual southern migration. At Wombah at the mouth of the Clarence River on the north coast were large quantities of oyster shells. In fact, most references to tribal gatherings in the northern coastal riverine areas set the numbers at between 200 and 300, who occasionally met in one place and at other times travelled in smaller groups along the coast and river streams. Along the Murray River the pattern appears to have been the same, with families splitting into groups of young men going through or preparing for initiation, large groups of men, women and many children and other groups of a single family unit consisting of husband, several wives and their children.

The fertility of the northern coast made these gatherings practical, and the area is still lush; the sea and river network provided ample fish, whilst the rainforest areas yielded small animals, wild fruit and vegetables, including yams and macadamia nuts. Kangaroos were hunted on the open slopes. One of the early European settlers remarked that the young men were very muscular and athletic, some weighing up to fourteen stone (eighty-nine kilograms). The climate, food supply and general environment obviously accounted for the good health of the people.

As in other areas, men and women both collected the food. As well as kangaroos, wallabies and possums, the men hunted koala bears, echidnas and flying foxes; the birds caught and eaten included ducks, swans and scrub turkeys. To catch the birds large fibre nets were spread between trees. One report described these nets as being up to 800 metres long. The net was strung up in a semicircle and many men and women drove the birds and animals into it. There they were trapped, caught and beaten with clubs. This technique was often used when substantial amounts of food were needed before large ceremonial gatherings. When individual hunters went after kangaroos or birds, the weapons' elegant design, combined with skills learned from childhood, were highly effective. Kangaroos were run down until they tired and could be speared, while birds were knocked from trees by boomerangs, sometimes from almost thirty metres away. *Womerahs* and pronged or tipped spears were not used in the Tweed and Richmond River areas. Instead, the men used a single straight spear which they threw direct with accuracy and skill.

Most of the wooden implements they used – spears, boomerangs, digging sticks and clubs – were made from hardwood. However, the shields could be made from the green wood of a spongy tree and were elaborately decorated when dried and carved. Women made bags and nets from bark which was soaked and chewed, then spun on the thigh into string. Containers for water were also made from the hollowed-out whorls

Top, from left Right-angled boomerang, Clarence River, New South Wales, 1898; boomerang, western New South Wales, pre-1939; boomerang, Narran Lake, New South Wales, 1945.

Bottom, from left Shield, Echuca, Victoria, 1901; parrying shield, lower Murray River, 1920; shield, Wagga Wagga district, New South Wales, about 1880; shield, Lachlan River near Hay, New South Wales, 1917.

Opposite Weapons from south-eastern Australia were often decorated with geometric patterns symbolising land boundaries. *All pieces in the Collection of The Australian Museum*

21

of gum trees and from the leaves of the bangalow palm, which were bent into containers.

No description of the Tweed-Richmond people would be complete without commentary on the bunya festivals. Every three years, many people travelled north into what is now Queensland to the mountains behind Moreton Bay where grew the bunya trees (*Araucaria bidwilli*). The trees bore edible fruit that looked like pine cones, and in the right years invitations were sent to neighbouring people to gather for a feast. The nuts are about 3.8 centimetres long, thick, very sweet and nourishing.

The north coast people have strenuously held on to their cultural identity; some elders still speak the Bandjalung language, which is being revived and taught to the young.

Groups were generally drawn together for ceremonial purposes and it is more than likely that the ceremonies were arranged to coincide with seasonal food supplies. All over Australia the blossoming of certain trees or flowers heralded the movements of animal species, the spawning of fish or other changes in food resources. Small groups of people gathered together their belongings and moved to a predetermined site for ceremony and feasting.

Initiation ceremonies and the associated *bora* grounds formed the core of ritual life, but little evidence remains to show the extent of the magnificent body art that must have been such a closely guarded secret of the Aboriginal tribes during the early stages of European contact. Some early drawings, paintings and lithographs show something of the early European view but we can only imagine the context and extent of this and other ephemeral arts.

The higher ridges and mountainous areas that separate the coastal plains formed the tribal lands of different and unrelated groups, but the techniques of Aboriginal adaptation and survival in these cold and inhospitable regions are worth noting. The uplands may be divided into three regions:[8] the Southern Highlands, often snowbound for part of the year, the Blue Mountains, and the New England Ranges. Most of these areas reach altitudes up to 2200 metres. Skin cloaks kept the people from the extremes of the climate, and housing occupied choice sheltered spots.

Carved trees were much less common in the south than the north, but ceremonial life was celebrated with rich rock art, particularly in the New England area. Rock carvings from this area feature red human figures, bird tracks, reptiles and circles. To the west, the Darling River formed a natural boundary separating the lifestyles and economy of the arid centre of the continent and the more heavily populated river regions of central New South Wales.

The differences in rock art and material culture between groups west of the Darling River and the Wiradjeri to the east reflect religious differences. In central Australia, the ceremonies re-enact the travels and deeds of ancestors from the totemic past who emerged from the ground and who now live on or in it; the eastern religious beliefs concerned the creative beings from the sky, including the all-father Baiame.

Carved trees and rock paintings cease at the Darling. West of the river, rock engravings of circles and animal tracks occur near waterholes, as they do in Queensland and in central Australia.

The rainfall in western New South Wales is unpredictable and long droughts are common. After enough rain to make the river overflow, normally dry creeks that drain the surrounding plains run, stimulating growth and food supply. In times of plenty, Aboriginal groups gathered every fifty kilometres or so along the river and would fish and hunt in groups, using large nets and fish traps that needed to be operated by many people. Fishing and game nets could be up to 100 metres long, and fish traps made from stones, an example of which is still at Brewarrina, caught many fish as the waters flowed from river estuaries.

A feature of food collection that reflected the changing vegetation in the west was the widespread harvesting of grass seeds which were then winnowed, ground into flour and baked as bread or damper in the ashes of the fire. When Thomas Mitchell explored along the Darling River in 1835, the scene reminded him of a hayfield; the grasses had been harvested and stacked into hayricks extending for miles. Women used large grinding stones to grind the seeds and many of these remained behind at camp when the time came to leave the grassfields and to travel to another source of food. Until recently, the grinding stones remained scattered around the country as evidence of past campsites and Aboriginal presence in the deserted landscape. One man who spent his boyhood with the Ngemba people (whose territory was the central Darling River in western New South Wales) has commented that in this area the women harvested grass seed and other seeds of white wood, mulga and acacias to make bread. They gathered seed on the way back to camp after a morning's hunting.[9]

The same commentator has also described techniques of hunting emus and catching ducks in this area. Emus were brought close to the hunter by a decoy horn made from a piece of hollow coolibah tree (*Eucalyptus microtheca*) rubbed down with stone until it was about as thick as heavy cardboard. One end was almost stopped up with beefwood gum, though a circular hole was left. By blowing across this hole, the hunter made a sound that attracted emus from anywhere within hearing distance. A large cord net set up like a triangular palisade was used to catch the birds, which were driven into it by a small party of hunters and beaten with clubs. On the plains, the ever-curious emus were enticed close to a hunter who lay on his back, waving his legs in the air. Wild ducks were meshed by a net suspended across a narrow portion of the waterway at dusk. By imitating the whistling eaglehawk and adroitly using a returning boomerang, the hunter ensured that the ducks flew into the net, where they were captured.

Aboriginal relics in New South Wales now comprise natural sites of known significance to Aboriginal people; ceremonial sites, historical places, rock engravings and paintings and carved trees. Few carved trees are now left standing and some that remain have had the design partially or completely covered by the regrowth of the surrounding bark. The 'portable' artworks showing the elaborate pattern vocabulary are housed in museums, striking reminders of a highly developed aesthetic sense that has been used to great effect on elegant weapons.

In the lands on which Adelaide is now situated, the Kaurna people once lived. To judge from early accounts, the Kaurna had a lifestyle similar to that of other south-eastern coastal peoples, feasting on fish, birds and game during the summer months and retreating inland in the winter. They fished along the coast in groups, with several men holding long nets in a semicircle and dragging them to shore with the trapped fish inside.

The Kaurna have left their most striking art legacy in their weapons, particularly their painted and decorated shields, some of which are in the South Australian Museum. The shields are of two types, one made from the red gum, the other from bark. Both were incised or painted or smeared with ochre. Beautiful but deadly clubs were also made. *Wirris*, made from acacia wood with the root forming the knob, were hardened by fire and decorated with grooved patterns.

The use of natural fibres reached a high level of skill in the part of Australia which includes the Coorong area at the mouth of the Murray River. Here the lakes and water catchments have created a wilderness that supported fish and game all year round, and mesh nets were used for hunting and fishing. Round coiled rush mats were made by the Kaurna and used as ground mats, cloaks and support for children on the mother's back.

Body ornaments and decorations were made and used here as elsewhere. Men wore bone and reed nosepieces, often decorated with bird feathers, through pierced nasal septums. Literature and early sketches have described ceremonies in which elaborate hair and fur string constructions topped with feathers and mounted on sticks were carried and worn by dancers who were decorated with designs in ochre.

The art heritage of the people in this area is precious and deserves recognition and respect.

QUEENSLAND

The vast area of country that is now the state of Queensland encompasses a very wide range of environments and correspondingly diverse cultures.

Along Cape York, the northernmost tip of Australia, the continuous cultural influences of Papua and the islands of the Torres Strait are apparent in a unique Aboriginal culture incorporating myths of ancestral heroes who came from the Torres Strait and who returned there to die. At the end of the last Ice Age, Cape York was joined to New Guinea and the islands of the Torres Strait were part of one land mass. When the ice receded and sea levels rose, the sea gradually invaded the peninsula between the two land masses, leaving the Torres Strait Islands between Australia and Papua New Guinea.

In Cape York, Torres Strait Islanders have continued sea contact over the centuries so that some songs and dances are known to both cultures. Today, Torres Strait Islanders are present in most Aboriginal settlements and communities in the Cape and many have married Aboriginals. Their culture remains distinct and very different from that of mainland Australia and Papua, though each area has interconnected mythology. From

Opposite One of several carved trees near the grave site of Yuranigh at Molong, New South Wales. The diamond-patterned cuts made through the bark into the trunk are similar to those found on weapons in the area.

Women crabbing among the mangroves on the edge of the Archer River, Cape York. *Photograph Jennifer Isaacs*

Mornington Island in the Gulf of Carpentaria to Bamaga on the tip of Cape York and right up the west coast, people sing and praise the ancestral hero, Chivaree.

Chivaree the seagull man paddled his canoe from the Torres Strait Islands down the coast of western Cape York and then back up the coast to near Mapoon. He was camped with his brother Ee-all and they were making dances, beating drums made from hollow logs. Ee-all made a headdress of cockatoo feathers and danced the cockatoo dance.

After some time, Chivaree left his brother and went to Mapoon, where he made a big camp at Janie Creek. He made a paddle there for his canoe out of a big mangrove tree. Then he looked at the daughters of Nyungoo, the pigeon, and wanted them as his wives. Despite Nyungoo, who was against the marriage, Chivaree stole the two women and pushed off in his canoe. As he pushed his paddle in the mud it stuck there and now it marks a freshwater well at Janie Creek. The canoe, however, moved by itself and travelled north to the island of Badu. On the way, one of the pigeon women complained of a sore breast and Chivaree put her ashore. She remains abandoned there today as a rock near Verillion Point, and as the tide washes over her she cries salt tears.

In the Torres Strait Islands Chivaree continued his travels, creating waterholes and having many adventures. [10]

Chivaree was finally killed in a great fight in the Torres Strait Islands and bent trees mark the place. White cockatoo feathers, as were made by

Chivaree and his brother, are worn in headdresses for dances throughout the area.

In Cape York, a drum is also made in a form unknown elsewhere in Australia, and it is thought that this reflects Torres Strait Islands cultural influence. Around Aurukun and Edward River, a unique form of ceremonial carving is practised. The ancestral heroes are carved in their animal forms in soft light wood and painted with strong ochre colours. These carvings form an integral part of totemic dances and they include crocodiles, fish totems, dogs, birds and human effigies. Masks have also been used in Cape York ceremonial dancing. The Cape York peoples developed distinctive aspects of material culture, including spear throwers, which had fine handles made from bailer shell, stingray-barb-tipped spears, and deftly made baskets and bags, which are still made with pride in the communities of Aurukun and Weipa. The fibre arts of this area continue to exhibit a full repertoire of patterns and techniques in the twined and knotted bags and fishing nets.

The high-rainfall areas of north-east Queensland broadly extend from Cooktown to Townsville and inland to the mountain ranges. This is a rainforest area which was fully occupied by Aboriginal people until very recently. Some aspects of these people's culture have remained obscure and little understood compared to the better-known picture of Aboriginal culture drawn from the people of the open plains or the sea and river areas. In general, rainforests had minimal resources of animal protein; the

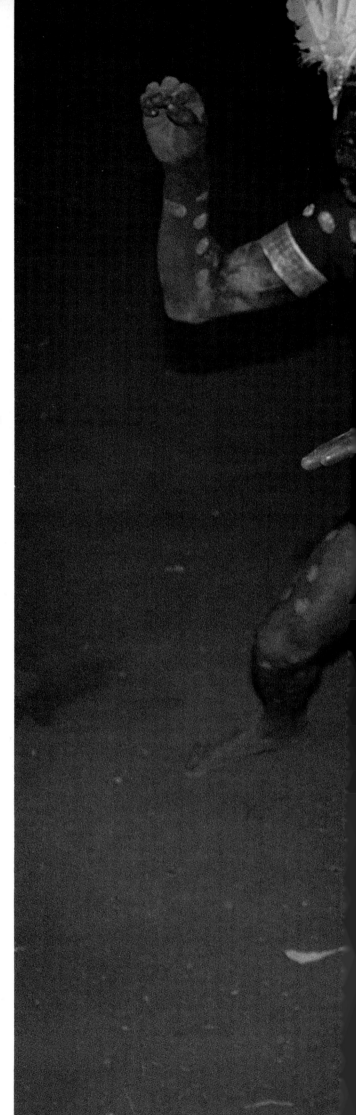

Aboriginal diet in these areas consisted mainly of vegetables. Many of the artefacts were therefore developed for processing plant products. The people developed stones and hammers for cracking the numerous varieties of hard nut, the kernels of which were processed if necessary by roasting and leaching in water to remove toxic substances. One stone, the *morah*, was a flat oval slate with transverse grooves cut into the stone. Nuts were broken on this, the grooves helping to secure them, so that they did not roll off on impact; they were also ground on the *morah*. These stones were often decorated. The most common nuts were the black walnut (*Endiandra palmerstonii*), or the yellow walnut.

Finely finished cane baskets of various sizes but similar shapes were constructed with supple lawyer cane. Fish traps were made from the same material. They took the form of long, pointed cylinders set in shallow streams. From the inner bark of the fig tree, a strong, heavy twine was made with which turkey nets were constructed. These were stretched over cane hoops that were set over turkey tracks. The nets were baited with fruit and the turkeys were called to the spot by the women.

As well as supplying nuts, fruits and seeds, tall rainforest trees yielded some animal protein in the form of possums and snakes. The people cut niches in the tall trunks and climbed to the very tops where they caught the snakes in the tree ferns or raided native bee nests for their honey.

The notable weapons of these people included rainforest shields and long wooden swords or clubs. The shields are the only ones of this type found in Australia, the soft wood and strong plaited designs making them immediately recognisable. Walter Roth has described the making of these shields in the Tully River area.[11] The wood was obtained from the buttress of the lower trunk of the native fig tree. The shape of the shield followed the curve of the wood; this accounts for the irregular kidney shape of many examples. The fully decorated shields had handles on the back. They were used in defence against clubs and wooden 'swords'.[12]

The swords could be used with one or both hands. To make them, slabs were taken from the tree, split down the centre and chipped into shape. The handles were bound with fibre twine and covered in beeswax. The swords were either naturally straight or slightly curved and could be up to 1.5 metres long. They were formed with one or two cutting edges.

The rainforests have dwindled in area, much of the lowlands having been cleared for sugar cane and maize growing. The people who once lived throughout the district have mainly dispersed to farms and reserves.

Beyond the rainforests and in the Laura-Cooktown area in the southern interior of Cape York lies one of the richest bodies of rock art in the world. Some paintings are tens of thousands of years old. Others date to within the time span encompassed by European presence. They include large humans, animals, fish, birds and reptiles and the most recent examples include horses, pigs and men with guns. There are also rock engravings that have been dated to at least 13,000 years ago and consist exclusively of bird tracks, circles, geometric shapes and meandering lines. Later engravings include humans, weapons and fish, as well as purely geometric motifs.

Opposite **Dancers from Aurukun, Cape York.** *Photograph Gunther Deichmann*

ARNHEM LAND

Arnhem Land is the name given to the 80,285-square-kilometre Aboriginal reserve that stretches from the Alligator Rivers, 150 kilometres east of Darwin, to the coast of the Gulf of Carpentaria. Although left relatively untouched by European encroachment for many years, the area is now somewhat broken up and includes mining leases. Major roads are planned and a section of the territory has become part of the Kakadu National Park.

This is the home of thousands of Aboriginal people who follow traditional lifestyles according to the laws of the creation ancestors. Most live to some extent off the bounty that the land offers. Through legal land rights claims the people have recovered as their own land much of the area previously set aside as a government-administered reserve. The mission towns and settlements are now administered by Aboriginal community councils. There is also an increasing tendency for groups of people to move back into the bush, forming satellite communities. The outstations and homelands settlements may be 50 to 300 kilometres from the nearest main supply depots and they must be serviced by truck or plane, depending on the season.

The sale of community art has become a major component of the economy; all members of the community contribute to the family income. Fibre is made into mats, dilly bags, net bags and containers, and bark paintings have assumed an important role.

In western Arnhem Land, along the ridges and rock outcrops and beside plunging gorges, large tracts of land house magnificent rock galleries that date to near-prehistoric times. The walls and ceilings of overhanging shelters display brilliantly coloured paintings in a wide variety of styles. Designs range from simple animal tracks and hand and weapon stencils to detailed images of powerful ancestor heroes associated with the formation of the landscape. Some of these sites were retouched and maintained by their guardians until relatively recently. It has been postulated that the most ancient art consists of abstract and symbolic circles and straight and meandering lines. Then came the painted red monochrome stick figures, known as Mimis in Arnhem Land and Bradshaw figures in the Kimberley area of Western Australia.[13] The most recent paintings are those of people, spirit figures, x-ray animals and other multicoloured, fully formed images.

In western Arnhem Land, Aboriginal artists paint exclusively on bark. Cave and rock painting have ceased to be practised and the last known painting was done in 1963 by the old artist, Mandarg, who still lives and makes bark paintings on an outstation near Maningrida.

Ceremony and religion are closely guarded possessions of the older men among the Gunwinggu and Maialli, the largest tribal groups. Earlier this century anthropologists were able to collect details of sacred ceremonies and rites and to publish these in learned articles, but in recent years the people have placed an embargo on continued release and discussion of their sacred lore, even by anthropologists. Because the wishes of the guardians of traditional values must be respected and their beliefs protected, the art of this area can be explained only at a very elementary level. The Rainbow Serpent, for example, figures largely in the

Bringing pandanus and dyes home to Yathalamara near Ramingining. During the wet season many outstations of Arnhem Land are isolated by water.

Opposite Aerial view of the Liverpool River south of Maningrida during the wet season.

Gunwinggu artists work on a bark painting depicting the Rainbow Serpent. Pictured are John Mowandjul and James Iyuna with their family at Maningrida. Children learn the stories and law by watching their fathers and uncles painting.

religious life of the people. It once travelled over the land making rivers, settling in remote waterholes where it waits to trap the unwary and the transgressors against tribal rules. Bark paintings frequently celebrate the power and ferocious awe that the Rainbow Serpent inspires, whilst subtle additions suggest other features of the mythology. *Maraian* or sacred ceremonies celebrate Kunapipi, the earth mother. The *ubar* drum is beaten at another sacred ceremonial series, and dances performed at these ceremonies often mime birds, animals and past events.

Looking at the rugged escarpment of Arnhem Land, only sixty-one metres up in a small plane, one can easily understand the widespread belief in evil, supernatural spirits that dwell in the remote reaches. These have been given different names such as Nyol-nyol or Namorodo and each lives at a particular site. Paintings of these frequently show grotesque features, the wildest products of human imagination.

Other spirits, such as the Mimis, are mildly benevolent and are therefore shown as inoffensive and attractive. These small creatures inhabit the sandstone escarpments near the Liverpool River; one man, Guningbal, carves and paints them exclusively. Other artists have shown Mimis in action, hunting kangaroos, travelling in family groups or having other adventures. The best bark paintings of Mimis come close to the ancient rock art that shows them in elegant red line drawings, their bodies leaping and twisting with great energy.

Women of western Arnhem Land, in common with others in the east, have retained most of their ancient fibre craft skills. The need for containers has not diminished, and traditional receptacles, single fibre baskets, string bags and conical-shaped dilly bags are made for personal use as well as for sale, even though other vessels can be easily obtained. These bags and containers are made from hand-spun bark twine or woven pandanus fibre, dyed and decorated with feathers and ochre. On the other hand, traditional weapons are infrequently made, the gun having usurped the role of the spear in hunting birds and game, although the fishing spear is still the weapon of choice. Weapons in use are seldom decorated, although of necessity they are elegantly made, strong and reliable. The core of art tradition remains ceremonial body painting, regalia for sacred dances, carvings and paintings on bark.

In eastern Arnhem Land the Aboriginal people collectively call themselves Yulngu, which translates simply as 'the people'. The term adopted for outsiders is *balanda*, an Indonesian word taken from the Macassan fishermen who made visits to the Arnhem Land coast for four centuries, collecting and processing *trepang*, the sea slug prized in Chinese cooking.[14] The rocky escarpment that houses a multitude of rock paintings falls away abruptly in the centre of Arnhem Land and there are few large rocky outcrops in the east. There is therefore no tradition of rock engraving or painting among the north-eastern Yulngu.

In eastern Arnhem Land, Yulngu ceremonies provide an opportunity to fully explore the range of art techniques and to express the relationship of the people to their Dreaming ancestors through such diverse media as sand patterns, painted or carved memorial posts, the wearing and use of feathered string and regalia in dance and the painting of ancestral clan designs on bodies of dancers and on the lids of coffins.

Paintings or designs are the central elements of Yulngu arts — the designs are sets of religious patterns and symbols owned by a clan. The designs express that clan's descent from the ancestral heroes who created their land, and because of this, some have compared them to title deeds. There are also strict rules about who can paint the designs, the context in which they can be produced and, in the case of some sacred objects, who is permitted to see them. At a ceremony in north-eastern Arnhem Land, a visitor close to a Yulngu family may be privileged to see one of the clan's ceremonies, perhaps a mortuary ceremony or the public side of an initiation. In many cases, photographs have been taken with the permission of the participants, though, when the pictures are reproduced, the people have been outraged and hurt. This reaction highlights a most sensitive issue: the objects, dances and designs may be displayed in certain contexts only. The authority to reproduce paintings and objects, whether through art works or photographs, is closely guarded.

In common with all Aboriginal art, the designs express the Dreaming and give visual presence to all aspects of Aboriginal history, including the oral legends, the song cycles and the great stories that tell the saga of the formation of the land and the creation of life by the ancestral beings. In north-eastern Arnhem Land, these creation ancestors include Djankawu and his sisters Barama and Laintjung, Wuradidi, Nyapilingu, the Wawilak sisters, Djambuwal the thunder man and many more.[15]

After the main work of creation had been finished, when the rivers, waterholes, trees, rocks, people and animals had been formed or named as totems, the ancestors passed into a state of rest in the landscape, often remaining in special rocks or trees. They can still act to influence life; ceremonial songs and dances and the painting of sacred designs bring the living into contact with the ancestors again.

At death, mortuary ceremonies reaffirm membership of the clan. Songs and dances send the spirits of the dead on a journey to the land of the spirits. In eastern Arnhem Land, the spirits of the dead, known as *mokoy*, can remain and cause trouble to the living, even killing them. These *mokoy* can take the physical forms of living animals such as the wild buffalo.

During funeral ceremonies, dancers coat their bodies with white clay to prevent pollution from the dead, which in turn could cause their own sickness and death. The body of the deceased is carefully painted with the ancestral designs of his clan; if a coffin is used, its lid may be painted instead, often on the inside. The designs guide the spirit to its resting place by representing the country where the spirit must go.

As they do in western Arnhem Land, women actively contribute to the material welfare of the family by making a range of traditional fibre bags and nets, particularly pandanus dilly bags and hand-spun fibre mesh bags. Magnificent feathered string creations feature in many ceremonies.

One of the most important ritual items is the feathered dilly bag. Made of tightly twined pandanus interwoven with white and orange feathers, and having long strings of feathers hanging from the rim, dilly bags are held or worn by initiates and hung in trees during ceremonial preparation. They symbolise the stored power from the ancestors. In mythology and song cycles, stories tell that the women once stored the sacred objects in their feathered bags, but the men stole them.

Although all Yulngu art has a religious basis, not all is made for ceremonial purposes. Fibre and net bags are made for everyday use, although their origins lie in the teachings of the ancestors. Relatively new forms of art have appeared in the carving of birds, crocodiles, goannas and other figures, and the making of the long 'Macassan' pipes that are now preferred by Aboriginal people all over Arnhem Land. The Macassans left not only their pipes and a smattering of their language, but also some influence in design. Some of the old artists, now deceased, maintained that the Macassans wore beautiful cloth which they traded with Aboriginals. The sarongs had geometric prints and the triangles and diamond patterns on some carved figures may be Indonesian-influenced.

The women work to provide additional income for their families by carving and decorating their totemic animals. The surfaces of these softwood carvings are finely gouged in the manner of wood blocks; the surfaces are then painted in natural ochres.

Throughout Arnhem Land, strong forces may affect the art in the future. At Gove, one company has been mining bauxite for over ten years and a large township is well established, and at Elcho Island the fundamentalist Christian religious beliefs of some influential Yulngu have tended to weaken the traditional ceremonies. Without casting judgment on the changes in art that have resulted, it is fair to say that the Yulngu are certainly entering a transitional phase. Many wish to retain and strengthen traditional values; others want mining, royalties and material progress'. The future will often be determined by the outcome of struggles within communities whose members hold these opposing views. There is little doubt, however, that Aboriginal artists will continue to freely express their beliefs and values through their own distinctive arts.

Carved and painted pelican by Tiwi artist Stanislaus Puruntatameri.

Opposite Group of carved and painted ironwood figures associated with the Tiwi myth of Purukapali, Bathurst Island. *Collection Northern Territory Museum of Arts and Sciences*

BATHURST AND MELVILLE ISLANDS

Bathurst and Melville Islands are situated off the coast of Darwin, the nearest point from the mainland being only twenty-four kilometres offshore. The islands form one geographical entity and are the traditional lands of the Tiwi people, whose language and culture differ significantly from those of other Aboriginal groups.

One could assume that over the centuries the Tiwi have visited the mainland and have had close contact with peoples there. However, it seems that this was never the case and the culture has developed distinct characteristics.

For example, boomerangs and *womerahs* were unknown to the Tiwi. On the mainland *womerahs* were extensively used, and the boomerangs, although not used as weapons for centuries along the coast, were traded from the central tribes and used in the north as clapping sticks during ceremonies. Conversely, the two-to-five-metres-high carved poles that the Tiwi erect during their funeral ceremonies are not found on the Australian mainland at all. The designs the Tiwi paint on their bodies, their burial poles and other art objects are strikingly different: they are boldly coloured broad geometric patterns, almost totally non-representational.

The reasons for these differences become obvious when it is understood that the Tiwi believed the mainland to be the home of spirits of the dead, and the mainland people spoke of the Tiwi as violent and aggressive enemies. This isolation ended when Europeans first came to the islands in the nineteenth century. A British garrison was established on Melville Island from 1825 to 1829. During that time, no contact was observed between the people of the islands and the mainland, although this came with increased European involvement in the area at the beginning of the twentieth century. A further reason for the isolation was that the Tiwi used bark canoes as water craft. Although the distances are small, the currents through the twenty-four-kilometre channel are rapid and dangerous. The journey was possible in such canoes, though inadvisable.

Most of the Tiwi arts are connected with the *pukumani* ceremonies. *Pukumani* is the term given to the ceremonies performed after a death, including the actual burial, as well as later dancing and erection of carved and decorated poles. It is also the term used to denote the taboo associated with the close kin and all the belongings of the deceased. They remain in a state of *pukumani*. The name of the deceased cannot be spoken; this practice extends strongly into present-day life, so that if a person who dies has a European name such as John, all other Johns in the community, or visitors, must be called by an alternative name until the *pukumani* interval has expired. Tiwi language names are carefully chosen to guard against this possibility.

The body is elaborately painted with geometric designs and decorations of cockatoo feather hair ornaments; bark and cane armbands and false beards are added. Dancers use ceremonial, larger than life carved and painted wooden spears with multiple flanges; a single-sided spear is known as the male spear, a double-sided is the female.

The decoration of the bodies and performances of dances and songs during the *pukumani* ceremonies have their origins in the decree and actions of a great ancestor figure in Tiwi mythology, Purukapali.[16] Purukapali ordered that all people make poles, dance, sing and conduct this ceremony after the death of his young child.

A Catholic mission has been established on Bathurst Island for most of this century. Although the influence of Christian values is keenly felt by the modern Tiwi, the practice of *pukumani* remains strong. Often funerals are bicultural, with a priest officiating for one segment and the *pukumani* dancers following afterwards. The grave may be marked by both a cross and a circle of *pukumani* poles.

Adaptations in Tiwi art continue, and striking carvings have been features of the last twenty or thirty years. These carvings are of ancestral figures, including Purukapali, his wife Bima and their child. Others depict birds, particularly pelicans and owls, as well as turtles and crocodiles. The pieces are chopped with an axe out of the same hardwood used for the burial poles. Metal axes were introduced in the early part of the nineteenth century and it is unlikely that the elaborations of some of the burial poles or the carved figures were made before then, as the artists used only stone tools. The grave poles reported rotting in the bush by the earlier observers were barely shaped tree trunks, perhaps with a few flanges — the emphasis had been on surface decoration. Contemporary examples include holes through the post, 'ears' on the top and other embellishments, which could probably not have been achieved without metal tools.

Above Tiwi bark baskets are stitched along the sides and rim with strips of pandanus. *Opposite* Family group at Nguiu, Bathurst Island.

CENTRAL DESERT

There are many cultural similarities among Aboriginal tribes that inhabited the dry desert interior of Australia, although particular artistic features of different people are evident. Broadly, among desert peoples the creation time or the mythological past are common, but the manner in which the earth was created and the events of the Dreaming are different from the feats of the ancestral spirits of the north and the sky heroes of the south-east. In the arid centre of Australia there is no one great spirit ancestor responsible for life as it is known, but there are numerous totemic beings who existed in the distant Dreaming and from whom each man and his family claim descent. The path of each person's ancestor as he or she wandered the land forms the individual's own Dreaming path, and at various times of the year particular rocks, waterholes, trees or caves that mark the route are visited for ceremonial purposes. During these rituals, an incredible transformation takes place. Over successive days and nights of song poetry, the dancers methodically stamp and move in rhythmic imitation of the events that befell the ancestor at this site. The men are completely decorated with feathers, ochre and grass seeds, stuck to their bodies with dried sacred blood let from their veins. Dancers at different sites embody the ancestors and become Mala the wallaby or Nintaka the perentie lizard. The designs belonging to the ancestors may be painted on the chests of dancers or, as is the case among the Pintubi and Walbiri, formed on the ground out of ochres, seeds and plants. The very existence of the people is traced to the era when the ancestors were travelling the country, forming the geography of the desert lands and making ceremonies. The pervasive belief in the desert is that before the creation times, before the Dreaming, the earth was flat and desolate. There were no hills, no desert trees or grasses, no beautiful waterholes and no animals, birds, insects or living creatures. Life did not exist above the surface, but in the depths of the earth great beings lived and emerged one by one, pushing the earth up as they came. These were the great spirit ancestors and gradually, as the ages passed, they began their journeys across the land. Although legends give them the appearance of creatures and plants, they behaved in the same manner as human beings: they made camps and fire, cooked food, dug for water, performed ceremonies, made love and gave birth to children. They differ from human beings in that wherever any event took place in their lives, their actions created the features of the landscape that remain today.

The art of the desert is rarely representational; it is generally symbolic. Ancestors are shown in sacred cave paintings and incorporated into sacred ground constructions. The symbols used include single and concentric circles, straight lines, animal tracks and curving lines. These occur in all art forms: as rock engravings, rock paintings, body patterns and ground designs, as well as decorations on weapons and utensils. Many decorative features found among the desert peoples today were also common to tribes living west of the Darling River in New South Wales and the peoples of north-west Queensland, as well as the Pitjantjatjara and Yangkuntjatjara, whose lands extend into South Australia.

View from Initiation Rock, Palm Valley, central Australia.

Opposite Winbirri waterhole in the western desert. Small water soaks occur throughout the rocky areas of central Australia and these are carefully guarded by Aboriginal people. At this soak in a rock outcrop between Papunya and Kintore, the stone lid is replaced on each visit to prevent evaporation.

41

Symbolic designs showing journeys and sacred sites are used to decorate dancing boards and carrying dishes. Don Tjungurrayi works in his camp at Papunya, and the wavy line on the dancing board symbolises a rock fissure at a women's water Dreaming.

Opposite **Coolamon or carrying dish. The painting by George Tjungurrayi is a 'women's Dreaming' showing women seated at three different sites.**

Researchers have established that this art is probably the most ancient on the Australian continent. Techniques for dating abstract rock engravings have put some at about 20,000 years old, with many more than 10,000 years old. Western desert designs are also used to decorate wooden carrying dishes and shields. These are made from finely carved quondong or mulga woods. The surface is usually coated with red ochre, over which the design is painted. Patterns and symbols are identical to those used in other art forms and convey visual information about a particular ancestral site important to the artist.

By government legislation and by traditional law, the Pitjantjatjara now own the largest area of land of any one Aboriginal group in Australia. These lands extend through north-western South Australia into central Australia, including Ayers Rock. They include the main ranges in the central desert: the Mann, Musgrave, Tomkinson, Blackstone, Rawlinson, Peterman and Warburton ranges. The climate in this area is very dry with an unpredictable rainfall and the Pitjantjatjara therefore ranged widely across the desert, following food supplies and travelling from the water supplies at soaks, waterholes or to larger trees or roots.

Since the mid-1970s, the Pitjantjatjara have established decentralised communities close to the available artesian water supplies. The groups comprising each community have special ties to the totemic sites in the area, though some mixed groups have been established pending negotiations to sink bores or establish supply routes. The people connected to the *malu* (kangaroo) have moved to Pipalyatjara, near their important sites. The Ngintaka (goanna) people have moved to Lake Wilson, where sites are found. These groups are based on mythology inherited through the father of 'Dreaming tracks', and the obligation of caring for the sites and performing ceremonies for the ancestral beings. The elaborate ground patterns are not a part of Pitjantjatjara expression, though decorations and body paintings are.

In a secular context, the Pitjantjatjara concentrate on wood carving, making exceptional weapons and utensils which are as immaculately balanced as any of the old weapons used for survival in other parts of Australia. One of the most ingenious is the leaf-shaped *womerah* or spear thrower. This particular type was once found from Barrow Creek in the Northern Territory to South Australia and across to eastern Western Australia, and is similar to others found in western Queensland. The spear thrower was immensely useful, not only to launch spears. Its curving interior and the sharp stone edge fixed to one end allowed it to serve as an adze, a receptacle and a fire saw. Multiple-use utensils ensured that during long treks, people were not burdened with a great number of implements. The range of weapons and utensils was small and versatile.

Women make three types of curved wooden carrying dish, each shaped to accommodate different functions: winnowing seeds, carrying water and possessions and digging. These *coolamons*, as they have come to be called, are also decorated on the convex surface with blackened designs burned into the wood with heated wire. This decoration technique is a relatively recent development, though women artists recall that the designs originated in their own 'women's stories' about creation times.

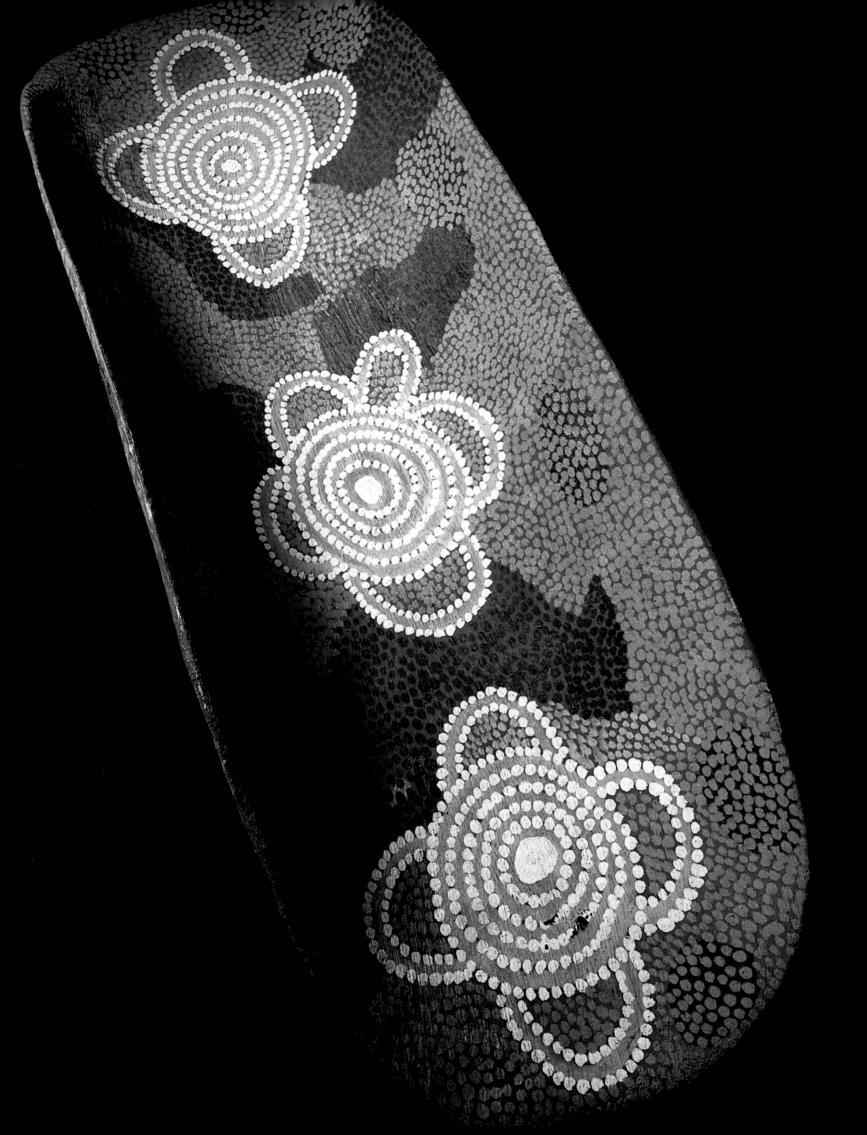

Opposite In the desert areas, a strong hard resin is obtained from spinifex grass. The clumps of spinifex are gathered when the seed is ripe and the grass is sticky.

The grass is threshed so the seeds and gum fall and the grass is then discarded.

Small pellets of resin are winnowed to separate them from the chaff.

3, 4 When heated the resin melts and is mixed with ash. It can then be padded onto a tick for storage.

When soft, the resin is used to hold slivers of stone in place on adzes and spear throwers, nd to form handles for waddies. The resin sets quite hard.

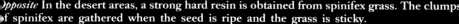

Papunya, a settlement about 300 kilometres north-west of Alice Springs in the desert of central Australia, is the home of over 1000 Walbiri, Pintubi, Anmatjera and Aranda people. The art of these people reaches its fullest expression in the elaborate ceremonial ground designs made from plant down, earth ochres and feathers. These are found only in the central, northern and western areas of central Australia. Most of this art can be described as geometric as the motifs usually consist of circles, arcs, barred lines, curved sinuous lines, dots and animal tracks. The symbols used in the ground paintings and in the body paintings of dancers performing ceremonies around the designs are similar to cave art of the same era. The people of the desert are extremely careful about telling outsiders of their secret ceremonies and rituals. Communication about ceremonial events is frequently in secret or in a code known only to the older men.

When constructing a ground painting, many people participate and the ceremony is planned for weeks beforehand. The announcement of a ceremony and the organisation and behaviour that go into making sure people are assembled at the same time and that their material and ceremonial needs are met are the most important political and social elements of community life. According to male observers the largest ground paintings can cover over 100 square metres of ground and may include, as well as the flat patterning, raised and decorated mounds of sand, several sacred objects and a large decorated pole. The ground design, the objects and the dancers are decorated with red ochre, down or feathers and leaves. The bodily shapes of the dancers may be completely obliterated; their faces, heads, hair and bodies become masses of eerie white padding as they move in the dust of the desert in time to the chanting of the song men. Although the native daisies that provide the plant down used for these constructions grew freely, in the past a great deal of time was spent in collecting sufficient quantities for a major painting. Similarly, the feathers required for a major ceremony were only available from flocks of birds, and they had to be gathered over long periods. Red and yellow ochres and white clay were gathered or traded over great distances or carried carefully in small bark containers bound with human hair string. The gathering of these things today is much easier, using modern tools, motor vehicles and suitcases as well as rifles. Occasionally new materials are used; these are not regarded as inferior to the old in any way, provided they create the same effect. Red and yellow cement mix powders, cotton wool, flour and chicken feathers are occasionally used to make the ground designs.

Groups of different people – Anmatjera, Pintubi, Walbiri and others – have for some years been establishing smaller camps away from Papunya. Each group has moved into its own lands and towards its own important sites. Here the physical proximity has helped the continued ritual performance of ceremonies to ensure the procreation of species, initiation ceremonies and manhood training rites. The ground paintings, together with body designs and ritual songs and dances, are physical manifestations of the religious process, the celebration of the meaning of life and a form of communication with the ancestors.

Song leader of a women's ceremony at Kintore, west of the Macdonnell Ranges in central Australia.

Opposite Through symbols drawn in the sand, Pintubi women discuss the journeys of their ancestors, the two sisters, as they travelled across the desert to Kintore looking for bush food. By means of such teachings, children learn about the country and gain their world view.

NORTH-WEST AUSTRALIA

The desert cultures follow the arid lands across into the state of Western Australia and cultural affinities are found right to the coast. The Western Australian people have developed a strong frontier culture associated with the early missions and cattle stations of the region. Today, mining ventures also make their presence felt and aspects of culture that might once have been sacred have fused with 'open' art practices. The contemporary image of many Aboriginal people in the west is a capable, hard-living man or woman, wearing a cowboy hat, a shirt and jeans, and riding boots. The dreams of many of the young men involve riding horses and running cattle properties efficiently; many properties are in fact Aboriginal-run, providing the greatest number of jobs in some areas.

The cultures of the far northern area are connected to those south-east of Darwin, and the Rainbow Serpent figures prominently in the paintings and ritual. Towards the Kimberley region, however, coastal cultures fuse with northern and central Rainbow Serpent mythology. The Kimberleys place great emphasis on the Wandjina, ancestral beings who came across the sea and populated their country, resting at different rocks to paint their images there.

Rock paintings at Waniliri, Gibb River, north-western Australia. The upper level is an older series of spirit, plant and animal images. The lower level is a group of Wandjina faces, spirits of thunder and lightning. *Photograph Jutta Malnic*

The images of the Wandjina have enthralled all who have seen them. Somehow, with their large white heads and staring mouthless faces, they seem to capture the timelessness of the mythology.

This is Wandjina. There was a time when this Earth — he made Earth and Sea and everything. This is Wandjina — he made people. Wandjina is Wandjina. He gave Man to live in this Earth, for this World, this Tribal Country. He put the Wandjina in the cave for him to remember this Wandjina, to follow his Laws, to go about the right ways.

Wandjina, he said. You must believe Wandjina. If you won't believe Wandjina, you won't live. This is because Wandjina gave us that Law to follow. And then he says, I give you this Land, and you must keep your Tribal Land. You can't touch somebody's land because it is your body, and your body is right here, and the Aborigines believe his body is his own Tribal Land. Aborigines believe that the Wandjina give rain. Then it says that the Earth is hot and that it breathes; the Earth it breathes — it is like live Earth. When it breathes, it's a steam blow up, and it gives cloud to give rain. Rain gives fruit, and everything grows, and the trees and the grass to feed other things, kangaroos and birds and everything.[17]

If the Wandjina are angered they will summon lightning to strike the offender or cause torrential rain. They are responsible for the wet season monsoonal rains in the area. In the past, the magnificent Wandjina paintings were retouched by men who were the traditional custodians. Now the paintings are not retouched, and many are fading or flaking, as is so much of the great rock painting throughout Australia.

One older artist who visited one of the sites in the early 1970s repainted one of the images. The words he spoke to the image hold immeasurable sadness, yet they afford us a deep insight into the relationship of the people to the painted images of the ancestors.

I don't know what happened to you, but all your spirit has gone out of you. No men or women watch over you, for the people who belong to this place — my aunties, sisters, fathers and grannies — they are all dead now. Only I, that belong to another place, came to visit you, but you were lonely for all those people who died and your spirit has gone away now. Because you are looking all dull — you're not looking bright — I'll try and draw you. I'll try and put new paint on you people . . . Don't get wild, don't send rain! You must be very glad that I'm going to make you new — don't try and get wild and don't send the rain to me . . . I made you very good now — I don't know how I did it. Very good! . . . You must be very glad, because I made your eyes like new. That eye, you know, like this my eye . . . I made them new for you people. My eye has life, and your eye has life too, because I made it new . . .

Don't try to bring rain, my wife might drown with rain. The rain might drown her.[18]

The Mowanjum people and related tribes construct elaborate string crosses and emblems known as *waninga* that they wear and carry in dances. These usually consist of crossed sticks supporting a pattern of woven string. They may have additional decorations of ochre, paint, or more modern equivalents — coloured wools.

Although the north-western peoples permit the open display of these objects, the Pitjantjatjara and other people of the desert have secret-sacred objects that are almost identical, and they have requested that the Kimberley people keep the *waninga* hidden from view. The rituals that gave rise to these constructions are centuries old; ritual, like art, was gradually dispersed along well established routes connecting the people of the centre and the west. Until pictures of these objects were published in a 1971 copy of the Aboriginal journal *Identity*, the central Australian people had no idea that these objects were made and displayed in dance in the Kimberleys. Such incidents occur frequently in Aboriginal Australia — widening communication affects all aspects of their society.

Pearl shell was traded along the same trade routes that carried other cultural and material goods between the north-west and the centre. Pearl shell was common on the north-west coast and in its natural state had little intrinsic value. However, when sacred designs were applied to the shells and they were incorporated into ritual apparel, they were accorded greater significance. That significance increased the further inland they travelled as traded objects. In central Australia the decorated pearl shells were objects of rarity and therefore of value. They became invested with sacredness in their own right and were accorded considerable respect.

As they were traded inland from the coast, the pearl shell pendants known as *longka-longka* were transformed from being ordinary objects to secret and possibly dangerous objects with power attached to their possession. They became, as *waninga* also did, links between the world of men and the world of the spirits.

Engraved pearl shell hung from hand spun hair string, the design infilled with ochre. La Grange, Western Australia.
Macleay Museum, University of Sydney

Below Shell necklaces from Cape Barren Island, Bass Strait.
Aboriginal Arts Board

TASMANIA

The Tasmanian people were effectively isolated from the changes and developments of mainland Aboriginal culture when the seas rose and cut off communication about 12,000 years ago. Evidence of Tasmanian Aboriginal art is scanty, and, although present descendants of Aboriginals practise their own art forms, there are few connections with the original religious context of the island's traditional art.

The most renowned ancient rock art in Tasmania is found at a site three kilometres north of Mt Cameron West in the north-west corner of the island. The rock engravings were discovered in 1931 by a shepherd. Sand dunes had previously covered them, but wind erosion had caused them to emerge.

The style of the engravings is non-figurative geometric, with a small proportion of animal tracks. The symbols are all based on circles, a feature of all the ancient Tasmanian sites. This style of engraving is related to the rock engravings found on the mainland in both South Australia and the centre.

Not all cultural connections with tradition have been broken in Tasmania. One skill that remains a direct link with the past is the making of delicate necklaces on Cape Barren Island off the coast. Descendants of Tasmanian Aboriginals have continuously occupied the islands in Bass Strait since the mid-nineteenth century. The Aboriginal women of Cape Barren Island make many-stranded necklaces. Descriptions of the beauty of some Tasmanian women include comments on the wearing of these shell necklaces, the most ornate worn by Aboriginal women anywhere.

A shell midden on Freycinet Peninsula, Tasmania. These are the remains of countless Aboriginal meals of shellfish.

The Body as Living Art

All people express themselves in their personal appearances; in how they groom and dress their hair, in their clothes and in their movements. By body decoration, people declare many things about themselves, including membership of a group or religion, social status and age. Individual dress and body adornment also enable society to structure and control the behaviour of its members. For example, in Western society when physical exercise and outdoor activity for women were discouraged, tight corsets and voluminous, long skirts were worn.

In the immense changes that have followed the Industrial Revolution, clothing has evolved like the societies from which it came, each change reflecting the values and mores of that society but providing the individual with a great deal of choice and scope for personal expression.

Like other indigenous tribal races, the Aboriginals had their own language of dress and body decoration. However, as their society is rooted in a history that spans over 40,000 years on this continent, and as the social changes that occurred were comparatively minor when contrasted with those of the post-industrial world, the codes of traditional body decoration and painting that have survived today are directly related to centuries-old traditions.

Individuals are not free to change social position by altering their appearance at will, but conform to the ancient and respected patterns of body decoration and adornment that mark their membership of a particular clan, their right to own and paint certain inherited designs, and that show their level of knowledge of traditional ceremony and culture.

In traditional communities throughout Australia the arts of personal adornment and body painting are inextricably linked to dances and songs. All forms of art, whether graphic, plastic or performing arts, have primarily social and religious functions. This does not mean that individual skills and accomplishments, as well as the beauty of the finished forms, are not recognised and appreciated by the community, but the function of the art is all-important. Body designs are integral to the dances performed on occasions such as the initiation of young boys, the successive stages of attainment of religious knowledge and funeral ceremonies. In a society where the addition of elaborate clothing never assumed a functional importance, the body itself was the raw material for artistic expression. The Aboriginal art of body decoration included scarring, face and body painting for ritual, the wearing of items of clothing and ornaments and the transformation of the body using added texture and headdresses to form living images of ancestral beings.

Opposite Tiwi man in full body decoration.

SCARRING

Scars were made on the body for many reasons, including aesthetic. To the outside eye, the ritual scarification practices of indigenous peoples have seemed extreme and unnecessary, largely because of the attitude that pain and mutilation are unacceptable. Yet, viewed dispassionately, many patterns and effects achieved are striking.

Among both men and women, bearing pain is part of raising status and moving from one group to another. Boys feel pain when their teeth are knocked out at the first stage of initiation, when they pass from being children to pre-circumcision young adolescents. Pain is also extreme during the more testing manhood ceremonies involving circumcision, and in some cases subincision. It is therefore not surprising that pain was easily tolerated in the secular scarification rituals that resulted in skin patterns on chest, back, arms and legs throughout Australia. In fact, pain was a small factor — the preoccupations of the surgeon artists and the subjects were correct lines, placements, technique and the finished result of a series of properly raised and pigmented welts that enhanced the appearance and status of the wearer, signified manhood and would attract women — or conversely enhanced a woman and attracted men. The technique employed varied across Australia, but it invariably involved rubbing foreign and often irritating substances into the cuts to prolong healing and to retard the joining of the skin so that prominent keloid scars resulted.

Walter Roth, a late-nineteenth-century ethnographer, made special studies of the Queensland Aboriginal customs of the time and gave an interesting account of scars being given to a young boy of the Tully River tribes at his initiation.[1] These scars, called *moingga*, were made just before sunset. The boy was prepared by his mother, who fed him an excessive quantity of *baru* nuts and water until he was bloated, his stomach distended and the skin therefore taut. The boy lay with his head in a relative's lap while the lines were marked out with charcoal. The operation was quick and adept; several straight fine cuts were made with a sharp stone flake and the words, 'Ku! Ku! Ku!' were called out. After the boy had bled, yellow ochre clay was rubbed over the belly and into the cuts. These scars were necessary before a man married and, according to Roth, much ridicule ensued if they did not heal prominently enough; this meant that he had already found a girlfriend.

Throughout Australia photographic records and written descriptions show that patterning the skin with permanent scars was common. Today scarification is rarely seen on young people, whereas on grown men and women scars remain as evidence of ceremonial status, childhood experiences and strenuous training.

Among the women of north-east Arnhem Land, one scar pattern resembled a string of beads, each one raised like a shell necklace. Some had cicatrices across their hips, on shoulders, or on the midriff. Newly made cuts were filled with clay in order to make the scars as prominent as possible. Frequently young men in particular cut and scarred themselves. The raised cords or shiny ridges stand out and gleam in the sun and are still sources of vanity to their owners.

Only in some places, such as Queensland in the Roth example given, were the scars overtly associated with initiation rituals. In most areas they were for decoration, a way to enhance the human body, decorate the more mundane and signify individual differences. Roth[2] comments that the decorative scars are often similar in men and women. On the Pennefather River the most common patterns are vertical and horizontal lines on shoulder muscles and on the upper chest.

Patterns enhance and draw attention to muscular build and to chest and arm strength. Perhaps such embellishments stress the role of the man as hunter and provider, needing strength for spear throwing, fighting, rowing and carrying meat. Certainly most Aboriginal women have commented that one of a man's most attractive assets is 'strong arms' and even the song poetry occasionally praises them.

Of the Tasmanians, Captain Cook wrote, 'They wore no ornaments, unless we consider as such some large punctures or ridges raised on different parts of their bodies, some in straight, others in curved lines . . . The women had their bodies marked with scars in the same manner.'[3] La Billardière described a group of Aboriginals as having raised points on their skin much like horseshoes. Other observers, also using comparisons from their own frames of reference, frequently describe the ridges as 'like epaulets'. Walker, an early Tasmanian settler, revealed a little of the incredulous distaste of the nineteenth-century European when he discussed an incident he observed.

When the males arrive at the age of puberty, they are deeply scarified on the thighs, shoulders and muscles of the breast with a sharp flint or glass. When I witnessed the operation, a female was the operator, and such, I believe, is always the case. The subject was a young man named Penderoine, brother to the celebrated western chief Weymerricke; the instrument was a broken bottle, and, although the fat of his shoulder literally rose and turned back like a crimped fish, he was, during the whole operation, in the highest glee, laughing and continually interrupting by picking up chips to fling at our party, in play. These scarifications are intended as ornaments.[4]

BODY PAINTING

Throughout the Australian continent, the central elements in the arts of the Aboriginal people have always been ceremony and dance. All people decorate the body in such a way that it assumes a quality and character far removed from its owner's everyday appearance. During ceremonies, all participants paint or smear their bodies with coloured pigments or white clay or build elaborate designs and constructions over the whole body frame. The number and variety of designs are extraordinarily large. Designs often differ a few kilometres apart, and even within each group, according to occasion or ceremony.

The identity of the person is often obliterated, to be replaced by a representation of his ancestral totem, frequently an animal. In Arnhem Land, complete obliteration of the features is rare, although the torso may be covered with complex painted designs that also occur in bark paintings and on other media. The effect of painted dancers performing is dramatic when accompanied by singing, percussion, and, in some places, the haunting, deep drone of the *didjeridu*. When a fire provides an indirect source of light at night, a performance becomes riveting.

The method of applying coloured earth to the body varies depending on purpose. In most areas, before hunting, the men roughly smeared their bodies with ochre. In southern areas, white settlers' journals often mention the practice of smearing the whole body with earth, coloured charcoal and animal fat, ostensibly to camouflage smell, but probably also to maintain body temperature. In tropical areas, coating the skin with earth and fat kept sandflies and mosquitoes at a distance.

Much has been said about the decorative and ritual functions of body painting. However, paint on the body has other uses less concerned with painted designs. Paint, specifically ochre, is applied to the body as a coating for protection in fighting. The Aranda covered their bodies with ochre if a fight was planned; it was not, as in other societies, 'war paint' or a signal of aggression, but rather a coating that created a protective aura for the warrior.

The belief that ochre has magical powers is widespread throughout Australia. Cape York people hold clay in special regard, keeping it in secluded storage for ceremonial use because of this power. Similarly in New South Wales, an early myth tells of the time when man's existence was threatened by giant marsupials. One old man used the strongest magic he could, and painting his body with white clay, successfully summoned the great spirit to the aid of mankind.[5] Throughout the centre, red ochre took the place of white in terms of power and deep significance because of its symbolic relationship with blood in secret ceremonies.

The association of painting with the power of sorcery is prevalent in the north even today. In a desperate outburst, one Arnhem Land man, frustrated by ten years of attempting to erect a community for his family on his tribal lands and having negotiated through what he believed was every possible government channel in the land, was finally faced with being outmanoeuvred by one of the people of his own community who had different plans. He mumbled that there was only one thing he could still do: 'I'll just have to paint myself'.

An artist using these same ochres and clays for painting designs necessarily comes into contact with their magical properties. In general, the power is not fully released without the dance and ritual songs being performed as well as the design being exposed. In some cases, however, the sight of the design itself in ochre or in other materials such as blood or down may be enough to cause the viewer to fall ill or even to die.

Both men and women paint themselves to attract lovers. Women paint themselves for ritual and sexual reasons; these paintings are designed to make them appear fatter and their breasts larger. Walbiri men also paint themselves to attract lovers. Designs in this context greatly differ from those in ritual. They generally depict through symbols men and women having intercourse, or representations of sexual organs. When viewed by women, the men maintain they make the women sick in the stomach, or 'sick with desire'. These male designs are usually done by younger men, the longing for lovers by old men being held in some ridicule by the community at large.[6]

Opposite **Pintubi child being painted for dance at Mt Liebig, central Australia.**

Colours come from a range of earth-based pigments. These give the artists a full range of tones, from white through beige and brown to yellow, rust red and black. No blues, greens or brilliant primary colours are used as paint, although, with the addition of seeds, feathers and leaves a wider choice of patterns and colours is possible. Intensity and strength of colour are very important to the artists, whether for body painting or for painting on bark. Ancient trade routes crisscross the country, following lines of exchange from one tribal group to another, as the richest and brightest red is traded from the south to the north and the brightest yellow is traded from eastern Arnhem Land across to the west. In the centre deep red ochre is considered sacred and the full initiation ceremonies are publicly referred to only as 'red ochre ceremonies'. In western Arnhem Land, a fine white paint is found in an eroded cave. This pigment, in common with most concentrated sources of colour in the earth, has a mythological origin.

During the nineteenth century, exploration was very fashionable. Pushing back the frontiers in remote lands and discovering 'primitive' untouched peoples was the goal of ethnographers the world over. Art collections were formed for English and European museums and lengthy and laborious descriptions were made of the customs of the peoples encountered. Australia was fertile ground indeed; its people were classified, studied and pronounced examples of 'stone age man'. The detrimental effect this had on the future of Aboriginal people was profound; successive governments sought to protect these 'childlike remnants of pre-industrial society'. However, if the observers had been able to step outside the ethnocentrism of their time and accept the religion and philosophy of these people, perhaps a different story would have been told.

In 1889 Carl Lumholtz published a description of his journeys through Australia, titillating the imagination of his readers with the title *Among Cannibals*.[7] Into his observations he injected the emotions and responses of his own culture and era. He described a ceremony in which the dancers shone by the firelight painted with red, yellow and white designs. Their hair was adorned with cockatoo crest feathers and some had shells glued to their beards. The women had bands of red and black painted on their faces, although the central dancers wore no ornaments. Lumholtz praised the male dancers who 'were the heroes of the day'. The lone 'middle-aged' woman dancer, to him, was merely an object of distaste, as she danced bare-breasted. 'The sight of this woman jumping up and down in the same place with her large breasts dangling was truly disgusting.' This comment causes us to reflect how little nineteenth-century observers understood about Aboriginal women's matters. Although to them naked, dancing 'primitive' males appeared splendid even in middle age, the women soon after bearing children ceased to be beautiful objects of naive and natural charm (and by extension lust), but became old, withered and unkempt, their ceremonial life being regarded as having nowhere near the relevance and importance of men's. It has taken one hundred years for this view to be challenged and refuted, as the women of traditional societies in remote parts of Australia begin to tell their story today.

Opposite Tiwi man in full face and body decoration, including a false feather beard attached to a woven pandanus band and termed *intiyintinga* or *putha*. He also wears a feather neck pendant.

A Tiwi mourner dances in the smoke to drive away the *mopaditi* or spirits of the dead during the *pukumani* funeral ceremony. Elaborate face and body decorations disguise people's identity.
Photograph Margaret West

In the south-east, we have only white men's accounts of many Aboriginal ceremonies. James Dawson wrote a broad account of the Aboriginals of Victoria, published in 1881. He described a corroboree in which the chiefs 'were painted with red in bands above and below the eyes and over the cheeks. They wore possum skin headbands, feather headdresses and kangaroo teeth ornaments. The wives of chiefs also wore red paint in stripes across their cheeks. In contrast, the performers in the ritual wore white paint, a fire was lit from dry bark, branches and leaves, and the boys and men painted their bodies, arms and legs with a clear white pattern resembling a human skeleton. Leaves were tied around the ankles in bunches to add to the decoration and to create a rustling sound during the stamping dance.'

His description of the ensuing dance could refer to any camp dance in traditional Aboriginal communities today. 'Some of the men stand beside the fire, beating time with the music sticks. After the music has begun, one of the dancers emerges from the darkness into the open ground, so as just to be seen, and, with a stamp, sets himself with arms extended, and legs wide apart and quivering, his feet shuffling in time to the music, and the twigs round his ankles rustling at each movement. He remains thus for a few seconds, and, turning round suddenly, disappears in the darkness with a rustling sound.'[8] Dawson describes other dancers who take the place of the first, appearing and disappearing in the same way. The final dance occurs with all the dancers appearing together in a line, quivering and rustling the leaves bound to their legs. They advance nearer and nearer to the fire in formation until the final song verse, a loud exclamation, and the dance is over. The bright firelight shining on the painted bodies of the dancers made a striking impression on the audience then, and it still does.

There are accounts of the Tasmanian people appearing blackened with soot or charcoal. One man in a group might have been smeared with red ochre stuck to the body with tar. The purpose of this colouring of the skin might well have been related to the environment; the additional layer of fat would have insulated the body and helped the people to survive Tasmania's cold. It was also obviously a cosmetic, according to this description by the French explorer Peron. 'Oure-Oure showed us for the first time the kind of paint in these regions, and the manner of its application. Having taken some charcoal in her hands, she reduced it to very fine powder; then putting it in her left hand, she took some in her right, rubbed first of all her forehead, and then both her cheeks, and in a moment made herself black enough to frighten one; what seemed to us most singular was the complacency with which this young girl appeared to regard us after this operation, and the confident air which this new ornament had spread over her physiognomy.'[9]

Several painting styles were practised throughout north-west Queensland. On the Pennefather River the men painted charcoal on their foreheads; a white band from either eyebrow down the front of the ear continued along the shoulders and arms. White and red bands were painted across the chest and the rest of the body was covered in red. The back was textured with a design of fine vertical lines in ochre, formed by scraping through the paint to the skin with the back of a shell.

At Cape Bedford, red, white and yellow were used in horizontal lines on the torso and vertical lines on the buttocks and legs. Along the Bloomfield River women had face designs only, and along the Tully River no patterns appeared, as an overall general smearing with pigment was preferred. In Rockhampton, red ochre was smeared in vertical streaks down trunk and limbs.

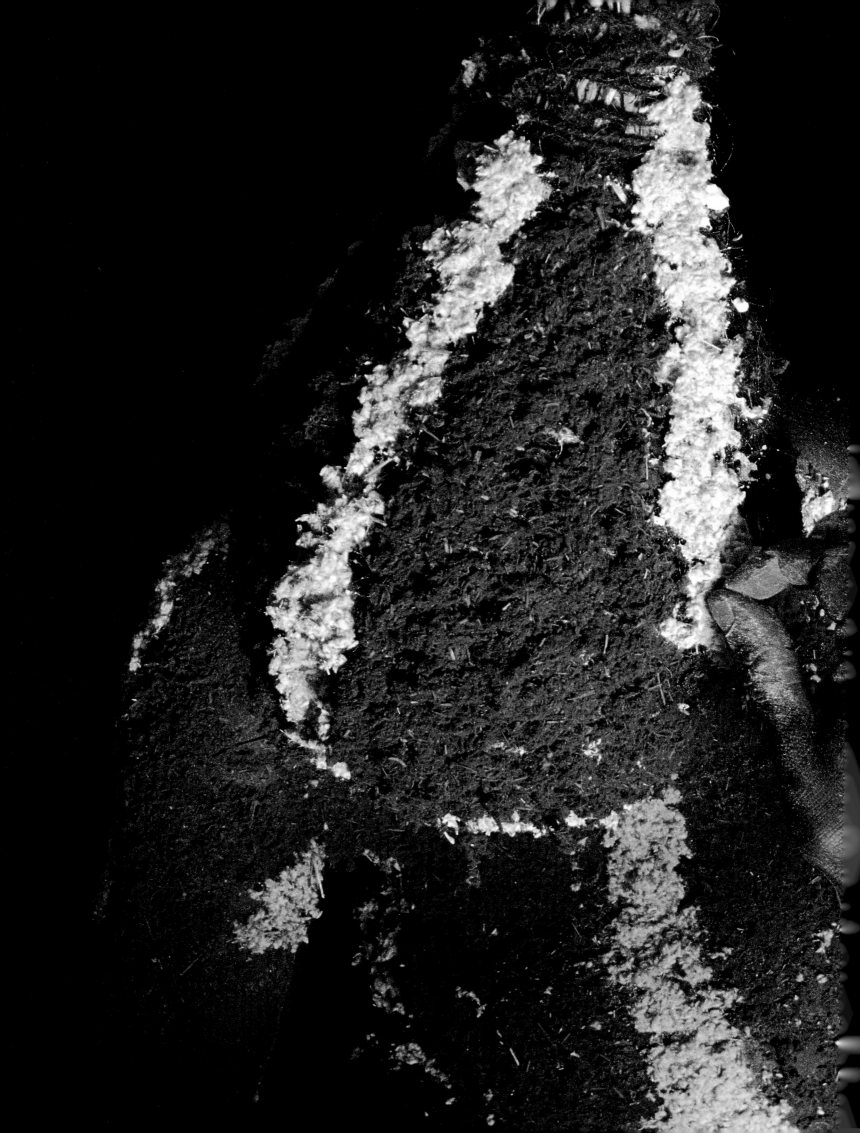

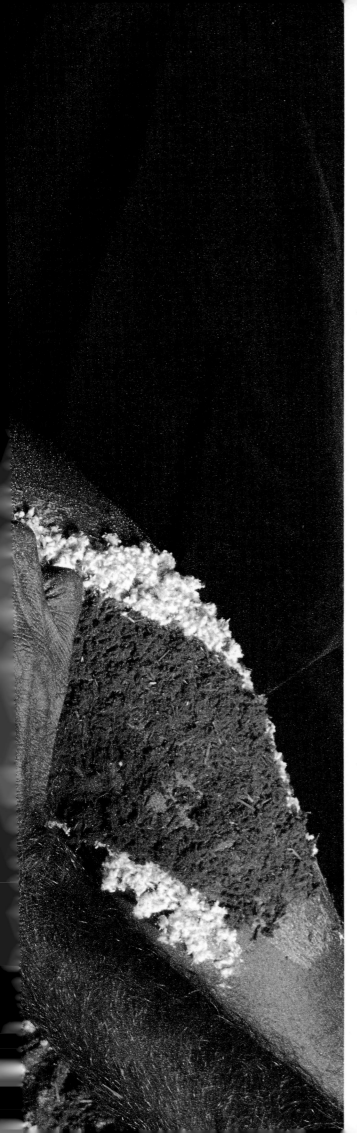

LIVING SCULPTURES OF THE DESERT

In the desert regions, the Dreaming or creation era is known by different names according to language. All the animals and living creatures are interconnected with mankind, and each group of people has its own 'Dreaming tracks' associated with the movements and actions of related animals in creation times. These tracks circumscribe land ownership and the special sacred sites must be maintained through ceremonies, including dance, song and sometimes ground paintings.

Ritual life has lost little of its intensity and during ceremonies a dramatic change takes place. Dancers completely transform their bodies with paint, down and feathers, often obliterating natural features, and taking on both the natural form and the symbolic decoration of the part danced, whether goanna, wallaby, marsupial rat or another creature. The body decorations are spectacular; they are not paintings but ceremonial designs constructed on and with the body.

Judging by accounts left by ethnographers over eighty years ago, it is remarkable how traditional body decoration techniques have been retained in central Australia. Although ceremonies are fewer and therefore occasions for adornment less common, specific designs for each dance and totem are alive and well remembered.

In 1904, Spencer and Gillen[10] described the decorations worn by men and women of the Arunta tribe for corroborees or ceremonies that they judged to be for public viewing by the whole community rather than solely restricted to men or women. Each performer wore a headdress that was usually conical in form, bound with string and topped with feathers. The headdresses were made over a frame of twigs with their bushy ends on the head and the stems pointing upwards and backwards. The string was coated with ochre and had a simple design applied in white down. The design on the headdress was integrated with the designs on the face and body and the body itself was decorated with bands and circles of 'down' made from a species of *Portulaca*; birds' down replaced plant down in sacred ceremonies. Bunches of leaves were also tied around the legs just above the ankle.

The technique of applying the down described by Spencer and Gillen is identical today. First, the body is painted in ochre and the design is worked in plant material. The flowers or hairs of the *Portulaca* and other plants used (or bird down) are a dirty grey when gathered. They are pounded in a grinding stone, sometimes with white pipeclay or red ochre. The down is held in place by human blood, the design being built up of numerous little pellets or dots. When decorating each other, the men have the left hand filled with compressed down, out of which they take little pellet-shaped masses one after the other until gradually, after hours of labour, the whole of the upper part of the body may be completely covered over with bands and masses of variously coloured down. Bird or plant down is seldom used by men or women for public ceremonies. Throughout central and northern Australia it is almost exclusively associated with the sacred ceremonial life of the people.

Opposite **In central Australia, the body and head are disguised with plant down, coloured with ochre.**

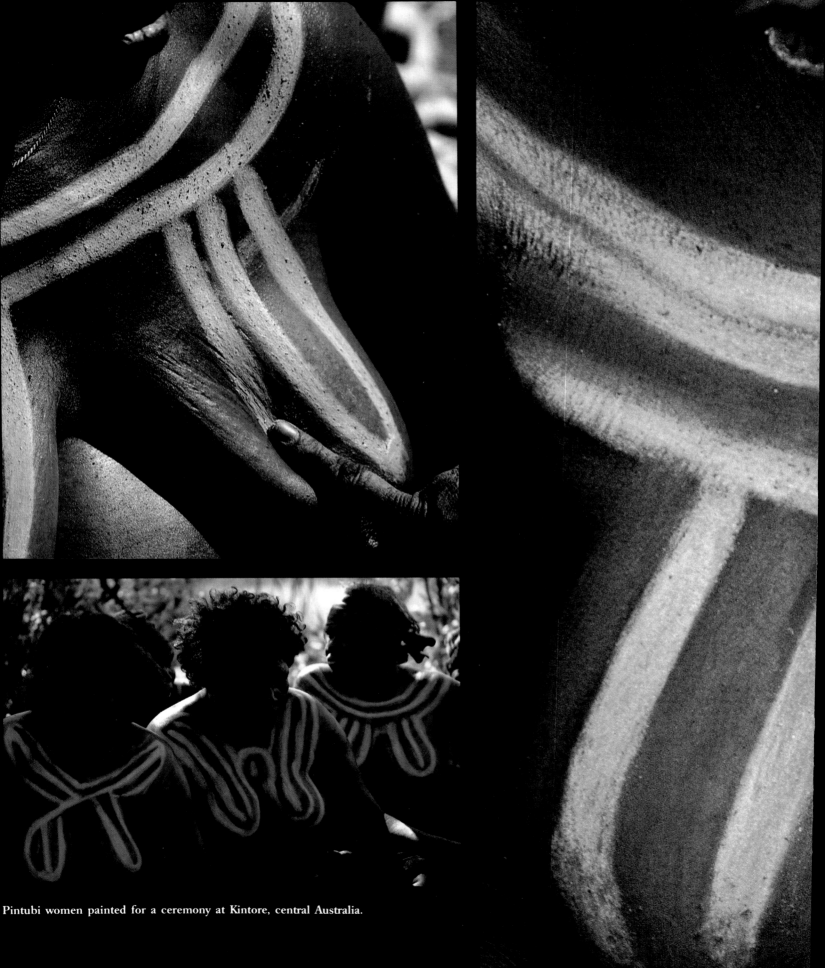

Pintubi women painted for a ceremony at Kintore, central Australia.

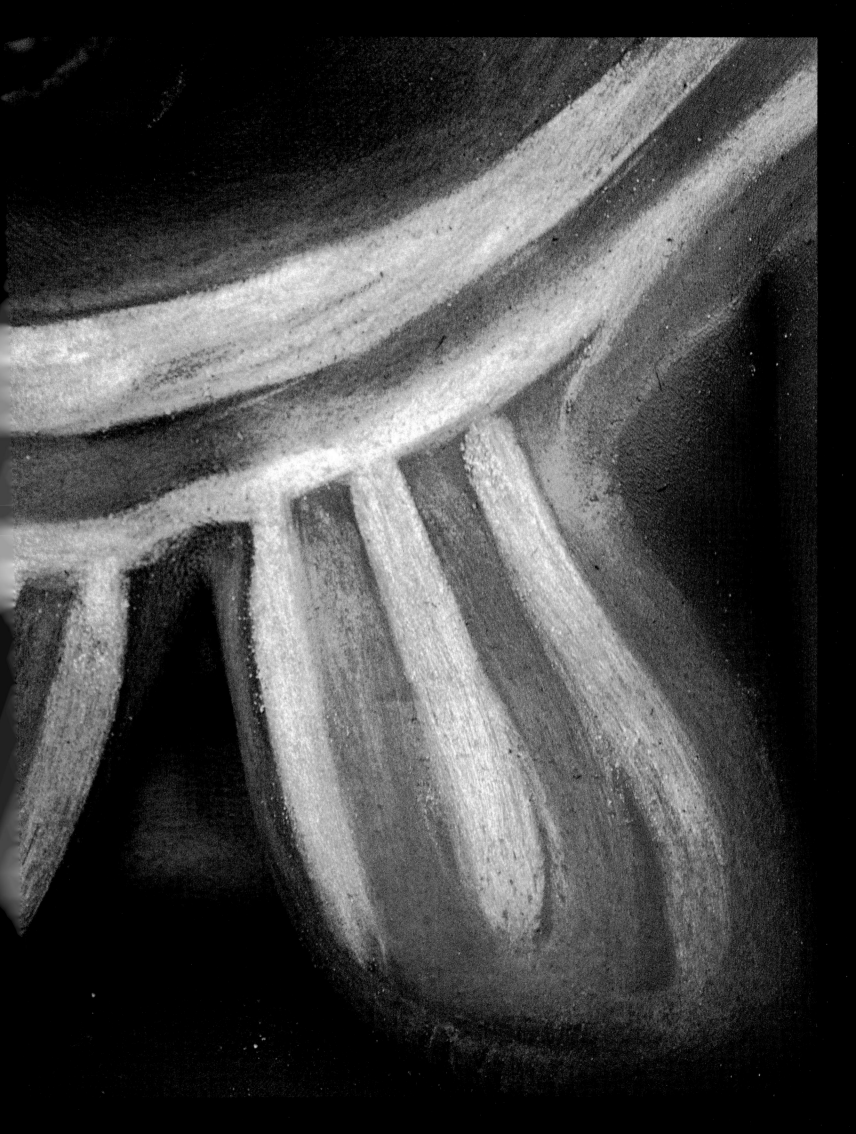

The women had their own distinct designs. They wore no headdresses in the sense of supported built-up structures, but wore headbands and fur tassels. Each woman had a double row of plant down running across the forehead, over the nose and around the eyes so that it looked as though she was wearing a mask. The designs consisted of linear patterns on stomach and thighs.

The altered lifestyles in central Australia have brought about some cultural change, although if one glances at patterns used for ceremonial dance today the only noticeable change is the physique of the people. Early this century, when all peoples walked great distances and the diet consisted of natural food, hunted and harvested, bodies were slim and lean. Today, many men and women are large; damper, billy tea and a sedentary life have had major effects on weight and health. However, larger bodies have provided bigger 'canvases' for the artists' traditional designs, particularly in the case of the women, whose full breasts are adorned with painted designs.

The intense maintenance of sacred law in central Australia includes as a prerequisite keeping advanced knowledge of ceremonial procedure and performance in the minds of the senior men alone. Information is passed on by participation in rituals from stage to stage, always in a combination of verbal and visual forms. Song poetry transfers verbal information, language names and events of the Dreaming creation era, and this information is also codified into visual symbols. These symbols are many, and separate groups are used for different purposes. In order for the designs to achieve their effect, i.e., to accurately call forth certain ancestor beings, assist in procreation, fire dreaming, water dreaming, or other purposes, they must be created in the right context that always links body decoration with dance, song poetry and sometimes making large patterns on the earth.

Among the Walbiri, special women's designs are called *yawalyu*.[11] Although the patterns may refer to an ancestor common to both men and women, the designs themselves are given to individual women in dreams. All the family members who share one camp and sleep together are thought to share the same dream. Although the woman who dreams the new design owns it, she shares it with her husband's other wives and additional women in the family (such as brother's wives and husband's sisters) and she is also expected to share the knowledge with her husband. *Yawalyu* designs may be seen by older married men and by young children.

Although often denigrated somewhat by the men as being not very 'important', not 'big business', the women's designs in central Australia form a parallel stream of art, with specifically female preoccupations in terms of function and purpose. As with the men, only the shoulders, breasts, upper arms and thighs are painted. Headbands, sometimes made of seed, may be worn, as well as other body decorations. The women carry boards in dances, but the body is the main means of visual communication. Generally sisters-in-law are expected to paint each other although this varies according to expediency and often no strict kinship rules are applied. Although the designs may represent food and other aspects of the women's role in traditional society, they are by extension associated with the renewal of life, the continuation of the species and in particular an increase in female sexuality. Designs emphasise the breasts, making them visually large and swelling them as though they are producing milk. The purpose of some ceremonies and designs and dances is to bring men, either lovers or husbands, into the aura of the women, to make the women attractive and to increase sexual desire. The paintings encourage conception during intercourse as well, and often young girls' breasts are painted when they are first married ('to make the milk come').

During Pitjantjatjara women's ceremonies, rhythmic dances are performed on a ground away from the main camp. At one ceremony held at Mimili in the early 1970s, the women alone gathered, together with some children. They danced singly or in small groups with one acting the central role. The paintings were similar to those of the northern desert women. A digging stick was used by the main dancer, who enjoyed herself and greatly amused the gathering by making sexual gestures with it. Women's gatherings such as this are generally conducted with a great sense of fun, although the content may concern ancestral characters. Women also conduct ceremonies as an adjunct to men's initiation rituals. These trace the travels of female ancestors who figure in the mythology of the surrounding land.

ARNHEM LAND BODY ART

In Arnhem Land, Aboriginal ceremony is important to every individual. The decades of mission and government intervention in the people's lives have wrought immense changes, but the basic religious orientation of the people, their beliefs about the origins of life and the land and the behaviour and obligations of each member of society necessary to maintain harmony in the universe have remained so strong that there is always some ceremonial activity. Clans may be meeting to discuss ceremonial gatherings, performing a ceremony to increase procreation, a burial or an initiation, or one old man may just be working quietly making some feathered string for a morning star ceremony. Even when an artist is painting a small work for sale, the designs he or she is painting are related to ceremonies and stories from the Dreaming. Ceremonial life is the foundation of the whole of Aboriginal society and the designs used to decorate the bodies of ceremonial participants are always part of the performer's inheritance, an aspect of his joint ownership of ritual knowledge and, by extension, of land. These he shares with other people, although specific individuals may lay claim to the right to paint certain designs from their fathers or through other kinship connections.

Body decorations in the northern coastal areas are usually chest and limb paintings, head and arm bands, with down being applied only in some areas for special ceremonies. The occasions on which down is used are frequently connected with ceremonial cycles from further south. A man or woman will be painted and will paint others many times for dancing in ceremonies and *bunguls*. *Bunguls* are general camp corroborees; they may consist of dances depicting the *mokoy* or spirits of the dead, or stories about animals, birds or other living creatures. Some are re-enacted recent events. Humorous dances have their place as well as hunting stories, and new dances are continuously introduced. The new dances are 'dreamed' by the men or the women, and in the dream the songs, dances, story and paintings necessary for the performance are transmitted for their use by the ancestors.

Body paint for these *bunguls* is quickly applied. The effect required is a roughly ochred body, usually white, so clay is patted or slapped on with the hands. Some broad linear patterns may also be painted on the face and chest with a brush. Only rarely will a full and elaborately painted performer appear in a secular public performance, as the intricate clan designs are reserved for use on more serious occasions. A *mokoy* dance is performed mainly to give children gathered around the fire a healthy respect for the dangers of the spirits of the dead that roam around at night and that have been known to take children away. The *mokoy* actor paints his body all over with white clay, leaving only his eyes bare of pigment. The white paint catches the light of the fire and the unpainted areas disappear into the blackness. What appears a living skeleton then performs a dance in which the rigid and jerky steps imitate a skeleton's movements. These dances and the emphasis on *mokoy* help ensure that wandering children return to the camp at night.

The participants vary their designs slightly for other public dances, so that something of the subjects they embody may be apparent to the audience. Leaves may be bound to arms and legs to give a rustling effect or the chest may be simply painted in rough approximations of linear patterns or sections of clan designs used for other occasions.

Now that corroborees are called for whenever an official ceremony is taking place, dancers, singers, and the owners of the 'dreamings' concerned have had to address themselves to creating a repertoire of dances, songs and associated body decorations that can be performed at non-traditional public functions. In their own tribal areas, this need may arise in conjunction with the arrival or departure of an important missionary or administrator or at a ceremony celebrating the erection of a school, museum or public building.

Aboriginal dance performances are held in Australian capital cities alongside those by other national dance companies, and several groups have travelled extensively throughout Europe and America performing their public dances. On all these occasions, the details and concern over the body painting are determined firstly by the importance of the occasion as perceived by the performers and secondly by the time allowed for preparation. Performers take elaborate care over designs in a setting they feel is sympathetic, one in which the audience is thought to take notice of such details. Every few years a major gathering is held to celebrate a festival of traditional arts throughout the Pacific region. On an occasion such as this, when groups from other traditional societies are taking great care to impress each other with the designs, dances and songs of their own culture, Aboriginal artists excel. Similarly, if visiting Aboriginal groups come to stay and perform in a northern Australian Aboriginal community, designs and dances are executed with the utmost care and interest. Like most artists, Aboriginals make greater efforts in producing a work for a knowledgeable audience. The resulting paintings

Opposite Dancer David Gulpilil from Arnhem Land.
Photograph Jennifer Isaacs

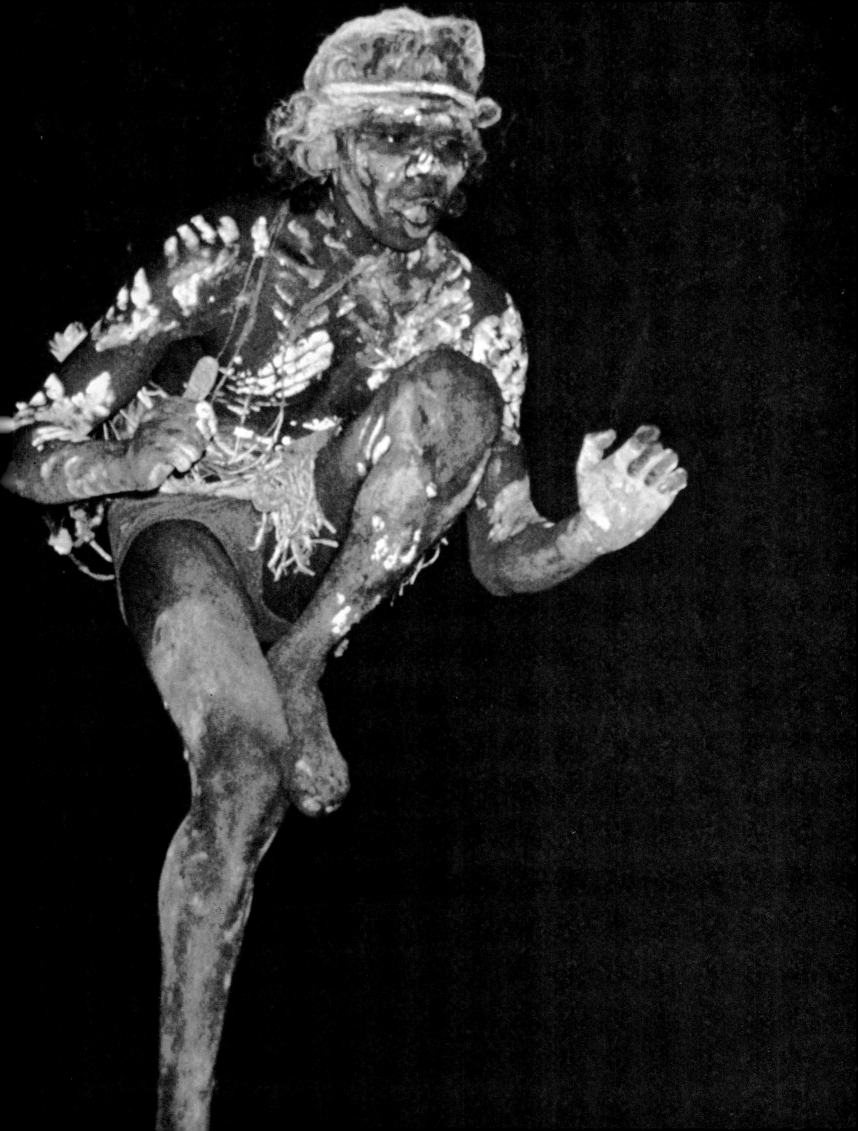

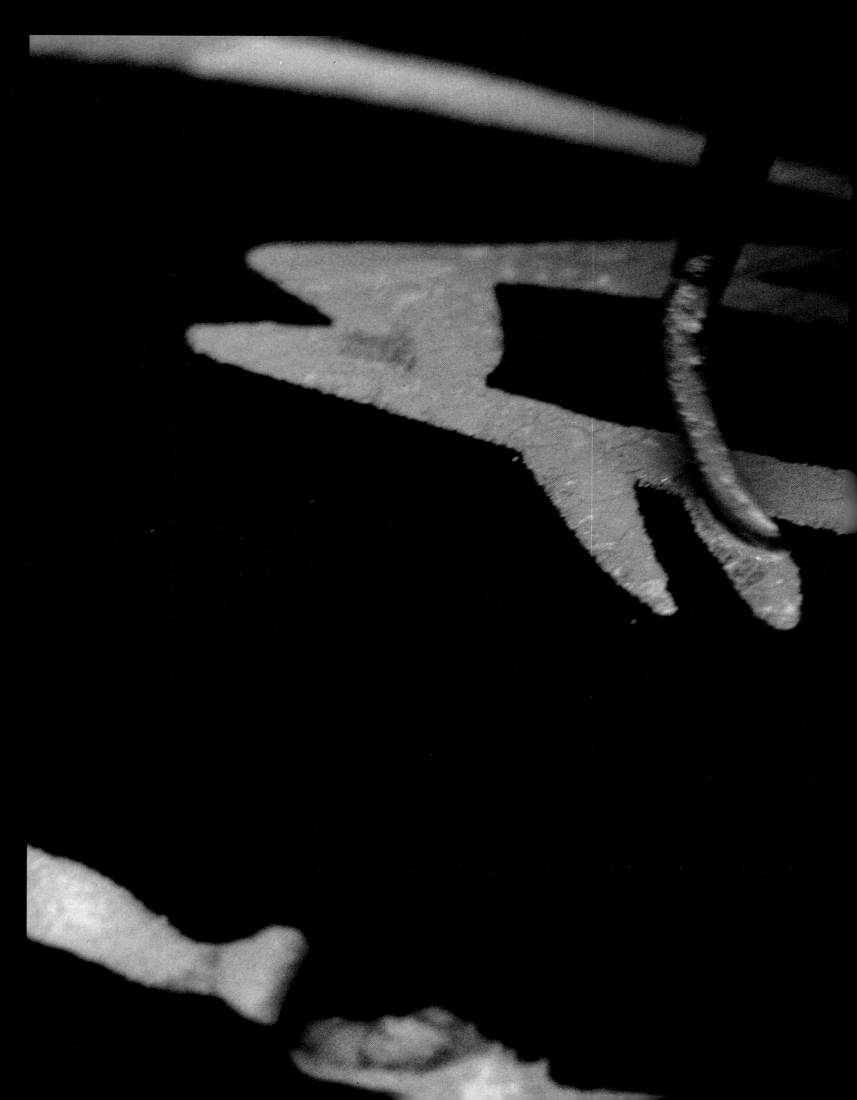

Johnny Bulu Bulun of Maningrida, central Arnhem Land, demonstrates the technique of painting designs on the chest of his nephew. Designs are painted on young boys for initiation ceremonies, and this catfish can also be seen swimming in the river on the bark painting.

and dance are outstanding if that audience contains artists who have similar skills and interests.

In the realm of ceremony, much more elaborate decorations are made, for much more is at stake than mere display. During ceremonies, the painting of the clan designs is a means of entering the Dreaming, of bringing forth the power believed to emanate from the ancestors. Through this power, the ancestors made changes in the landscape; in some cases they created the very features of the clan land. Each young boy is first painted with his own inherited clan design at his circumcision, when he is about eight years old. From time to time throughout his life he will see variations of this design painted on his brothers and cousins, nephews and other relatives. He will paint it himself with increasing symbolic content as he grows to full ritual maturity and learns more of the 'story' of which his initiation painting was one of the symbols.

To give one example, a young Riratjingu boy of north-eastern Arnhem Land may have his chest and face painted at initiation with a maze of white, yellow and red cross-hatching around the central black motif of a goanna. This is the simplest rendition of the designs and symbolic paintings associated with the great Djankawu, ancestors of the Riratjingu.

The Djankawu sailed across the sea and landed at Yelangbara, a beach on the north-eastern tip of the Northern Territory. They were the first ancestral people to come to Australia, and song cycles tell of how they travelled across the sand dunes, created waterholes, trees and rocks and produced many children. One of the first animals they saw was *djunda* the goanna, running over a sandhill. Hence the initiation design on a boy whose tribal land is Yelangbara is a composite of cross-hatched symbols of Yelangbara's natural features, such as sand and water, together with the image of *djunda*. As the young man learns more about the details of the Djankawu's travels, he gains further knowledge of the designs. They are transmitted not only in body paintings but, more commonly, through bark paintings. The paintings are usually done for sale, though they are also of immense educational benefit to the artist and his family.

The last occasion on which the clan designs are painted on a person's body is at his or her funeral. The painting may be on the body or on the lid of the coffin. The design's complexity depends on the deceased person's level of ceremonial importance. The funeral paintings reach their most important level and convey most information when the person is an elder statesman with deep ritual knowledge and great responsibility. The paintings are done by one or several men in a shelter away from the rest of the community, guarded by others to keep children from bothering them or interfering with the execution of the design. Usually outsiders are forbidden access and photographs are not permitted except as the clan's own records.

TIWI BODY PAINTING

Off the coast of Darwin lie Bathurst and Melville Islands, home of the Tiwi. The facial and body painting of the people here have been described as the most colourful and elaborate of any Australian group. Face decoration in particular is unique to every individual, permitting the full exercise of the artist's imagination. A deep red ochre is obtained from the oval polished red stones found on the beach, which are ground then mixed with water; yellow is obtained from a soft yellow ochre stone, also ground to a powder. (The Tiwi sometimes burn the yellow to produce red.) White is generally taken from a clay found all over the island, and black is obtained from charcoal.

The wonderful variety and impact of the Tiwi body paintings have led many researchers to investigate their meanings and associated rituals. The decorations essentially relate to the two Tiwi occasions for major ceremonies, the *pukumani* (mortuary or burial cycles) and the *kulama* ceremonies (initiation ceremonies associated with the harvesting of yams during the wet season). *Pukumani* ceremonies have their origin in the world of Tiwi religion and mythology and the first *pukumani* ceremony was created by Purukapali, a legendary figure of the creation time.

Tiwi stories tell of the first death, that of Purukapali's son, and the ceremony he created as a result. Purukapali lived with his wife Bima and their much-loved son at Impanali in south-eastern Melville Island. Bima and the child went out each day to gather food in the bush, returning in the evening to cook it. Tapara the moon man was attracted to Bima and sought an opportunity to be alone with her. When she was out food gathering, he persuaded her to leave her young child asleep in the shade and to sneak off with him. They stayed away too long and the sun changed position; the baby was left in the hot sun. When Bima returned, the baby was dead and she was filled with grief and remorse. Purukapali, the father, was furious. He hit his wife on the head with a throwing stick and hunted her away into the forest, where she became a curlew that still flies around, calling and wailing for her dead child.

Purukapali decreed that because his son had died, all creatures must, so death came into the world. Tapara remonstrated with Purukapali, saying he could make the child live again, but Purukapali only grew angrier. In a furious fight with Tapara, he slashed his face with his forked throwing stick. Purukapali instructed the people to create a ceremony, making grave posts, dancing and painting their bodies. The people painted their faces for hours before the dance began and put on ornaments. They put dots on their faces, wore hair belts, white cockatoo feather headdresses, false beards, dingo hair crescents, goose feather balls and cane and fibre armlets.

Purukapali himself died, too. He took the body of his son into his arms and walked into the sea until the waters closed over his head. Where he died there is now a whirlpool. Tapara the moon rose into the sky, where the battle scars of his fight can be seen as shadows across his face.

There is great personal pride in a beautiful painted face, and this is increased if the painting causes an awed reaction in the onlooker. One of the purposes of painting the face, as well as giving occasion for the Tiwi love of decoration and body adornment, is to disguise the wearer so

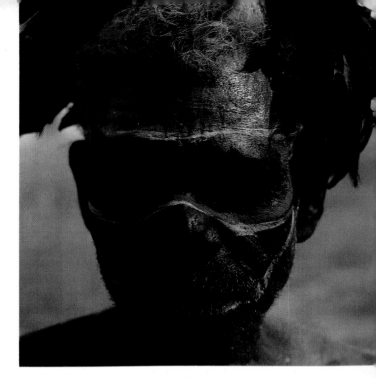

that he or she will not be recognised by the *mopaditi*. These are the spirits of the dead, and they take particular pleasure in tormenting their near relatives.

The *pukumani* face and body designs are usually more detailed than those of the *kulama*. Some of the designs' meanings were recorded by Charles Mountford[12] thirty-five years ago. As these interpretations are not mentioned by contemporary Tiwi, Mountford's work provides the only clue to the link of myth, dance and design in this area of Australia. The *pukumani* designs he describes include those associated with the shark (*tuduwala*), a design emphasising the eyes, with the use of radiating lines in order to make the face appear fierce, the fish design with facial markings imitating the fish *mungumini*, a thunderstorm design represented by cross-hatching and a salmon design said to be that of the salmon, Kumininu, who fought with the shark man at the first ceremony.

The ceremony involving the small yams known as *kulama* is the main Tiwi ritual that ensures the plentiful supply of food. When reported earlier this century, the *kulama* ceremonial cycle was a series of initiation ceremonies for mature men over thirty and included aspects no longer practised. Today the ceremonies celebrate the harvesting of the ripe yams and stretch throughout the latter part of the wet season. The first *kulama* was performed by Purutjikini, the boobook owl, and his actions are repeated in similar form by the Tiwi from January to July.

At the beginning of the cycle, groups of men go into the bush to dig the round, hairy yams. They take great care to extract them from the earth without damaging the fine root hairs, because if a yam is broken it is said to release sickness into the air, causing those nearby to fall ill. This sickness, termed *taini*, can also escape when the yams are cooking. Painting up, dancing and singing accompany the various stages of the *kulama* ceremony. The yams are soaked to remove poisons, cooked in the ashes of a fire covered with paper bark, and cut up and distributed for eating later. Everyday situations are sung about in a communal atmosphere during the early parts of this process, then during the cooking dancers re-enact the first *kulama* in dances of birds, the crocodile, the turtle, buffalo and shark. The final scenes occur after the yams are cooked and placed in a basket. Initiates are ornamented with neck rings and armbands. Senior men in the *kulama* paint their faces, bodies, hair and beards with elaborate designs in red, yellow, black and white and the yams are eaten in accordance with ritual custom.

In the past both male and female initiates would wear the ornaments and remain decorated for perhaps a month after the close of the *kulama*, then they would wash the paint from their bodies and resume a normal life. The *kulama* designs Mountford describes include a design of an initiate related to the boobook owl, in which white and red dots symbolise edible wild fruits, and another showing the barn owl (*pintoma*). A false beard is worn over the man's own beard and a headdress of white cockatoo feathers is added. Circles around the eyes symbolise the staring eyes of the barn owl that helped at the first *kulama* ceremony.

In present-day ceremonies there is a marked difference between the *kulama* and *pukumani* designs. Mountford's sketches of the designs in the late 1940s show that the *kulama* patterns were larger than the *pukumani*

Preparing for the *kulama* (yam) ceremony. The yams are seen above, cooking in the ashes. *Photographs Margaret West*

75

designs, with different colour areas more widely spaced. There were few detailed linear patterns on face or body. A similar difference remains today, and the *kulama* and *pukumani* designs used by one man, Declan Apuatimi, can be contrasted. Declan's *kulama* pattern is sombre and, using dark red and black, it divides the face into sections separated with a line of yellow. *Pukumani* design, on the other hand, consists of a totally blackened face. The eyes are emphasised with yellow ochre dots and lines of white are drawn across the forehead, along the bridge of the nose and along the upper beard line. The hair and beard are yellowed with ochre.

The technique of painting face and body is similar all over the north, although different people use a range of brushes and twigs, depending on the quality of line desired. The Tiwi designs frequently incorporate lines and dots over a base colour of yellow or white and these lines are done in a contrasting colour. The most usual implement for the lines is a paintbrush, whereas the preferred applicator for the dots is a chewed stick or, even better, a wooden comb. Tiwi make multi-pronged combs specifically for painting; the carved prongs apply rows of dots in a straight line. The combs are also used for paintings on carvings and burial poles.

The following is a fairly typical procedure for painting the face and body. The pigments are crushed onto a flat stone and mixed with water. No fixatives are added to the powder, the natural oil and sweat of the skin serving to bind the clay paint to the body for a short time only; it will soon streak or sweat off after a dance session. When the colours are prepared, the face is coated in sections with base colours, generally white and yellow. For some designs, charcoal is first rubbed across eyes and forehead so the upper face is darkly masked. This base is usually applied with the fingers and palms of the hand. Excess yellow ochre or white clay is also lightly rubbed through the hair and beard so that it sits on top of the curly hairs, greying or yellowing them and framing the face.

At this stage of the painting, the Tiwi figures very much resemble the first European descriptions of them by Phillip Parker King, who surveyed the northern Australian coastal regions in 1837. He wrote, 'The men were more muscular and better formed than any we had before seen, they were daubed over with a yellow pigment which was the colour of the neighbouring cliff; their hair was long and curly and appeared to be clotted with a whitish paint.'[13]

After the ochre is applied all over, patterns of lines are drawn across the eyebrows and around the eyes, with the lower face receiving much attention. Patterns extend from the cheeks right to the tip of the beard. These decorations are usually painted with a brush in colours that contrast with the base colour. The body is roughly coated with white clay, slapped on to camouflage the natural skin and blend with the face patterns.

The beard itself, if not decorated, may be augmented by an additional false beard made of feathers attached with beeswax to a woven pandanus band. It is termed *intiyintinga* or *putha*.

In the hair, black and white cockatoo feathers are worn. These are fastened to a bone or wood pin and twisted around into one lock of hair to stay in place. Pandanus armbands and neck pendants consisting of feather balls are commonly worn.

Top Yellow ochre dots are carefully placed over a coating of black charcoal.

Bottom Yellow ochre is rubbed through the hair and beard and coats the face before the geometric designs are painted. The body is covered in white clay.

Tiwi family group preparing for a *pukumani* ceremony.

Regardless of the function a work of art on the body may have, its essential nature is transitory. Preparation may take minutes or hours but, however spectacular the impact of the finished body design may be, within minutes of impressing its audience during the dance performance (which may also be over in minutes) heat, sweat and abrasive movements have dislodged the down, eroded the designs and substantially removed the work of art that was there. This is of absolutely no consequence to the Aboriginal artists, who have been doing similar paintings on their bodies for thousands of years. There is no need to 'record' this art or to house it in special museums in order to keep it alive. The designs live in the minds of every adult man and woman and are passed on without visual records. In fact, part of the special quality of this body art is its transitory nature, its impact on revelation in performances and its necessary immediate decay.

Perhaps a regrettable aspect of our belated appreciation of the treasure that Aboriginal art has to offer is the tardy investigation in twentieth-century European art circles of the nature of art. Questions concerning the durability of art (Can a work of art last only a minute? Can it be a living, moving work?) and other more cerebral considerations have led to the most advanced art houses showing works in categories such as performance art, assemblage art, conceptual art, installations, and so on. In this environment Aboriginal art, whether bark paintings, fibre, sculpture or body paintings, finds a ready home and easy acceptance. It is now most obvious that it ranks as a most distinctive contribution to world culture and that works by living Aboriginal artists rank among the best of Australia's contemporary art. It has naturally developed from its origins over a time span unequalled anywhere else in the world.

Tiwi men in full *pukumani* ceremonial body designs. These were executed for the funeral of an important man, and patterns extend through the beard and hair and incorporate cockatoo feather headdresses. *Photographs Tom Nell*

BODY ORNAMENTS

Wearing clothes, body ornaments and jewellery or decorations reflects individuality as well as group membership. In Australia, the traditional Aboriginal arts include a wealth of spectacular personal adornments made from shells, feathers and fibre.

Archaeological discoveries have made it clear that, just as ancient men and women painted themselves for ceremonies, body ornaments also played a significant role in personal status. People used a range of animal and plant materials to construct headbands and necklaces. Excavations have revealed cut segments of kangaroo bones that were worn as beads over 12,000 years ago in areas south of Perth; a skull from Kow swamp in north-west Victoria had a row of kangaroo teeth embedded around the forehead and linked by traces of resin.

Shell pendants were frequently worn in ancient times and fragments with holes drilled for threading have been found in New South Wales. In the recent past, pearl shell was traded from the coast of the Kimberley region in Western Australia and bailer shell was traded south from Cape York. Shell pendants continue to be used in Cape York.

So far, the most interesting ornament known to have been worn thousands of years ago is a full necklace of over 170 teeth extracted from the Tasmanian devil; this was discovered with traces of a man's skeleton in Lake Nitchie, western New South Wales, and dated to 6000 years ago.[14] Evidence of the full extent to which the everyday ornamentation of the body was enhanced and embellished in ceremony is now lost to us. These ritual occasions were only fleeting moments, whereas the body in burial remains in its final resting state for thousands of years, allowing us now to have only a glimpse of society's need for body adornment thousands of years ago.

Tribal artists sought materials to make colourful and striking objects, chosen from the natural environment and the bounty that their tribal lands had to offer. Coastal sea people chose bailer shell, nautilus, cockle, pearl shell and small sea and mangrove shells to string into necklaces and form into pendants. Along the northern rivers of Arnhem Land, snail shells were strung together and painted. In central Australia, bright red, yellow and brown seeds were strung onto hair string, or simply tied into the hair, forming a frame for the faces of young girls.

The magnificent plumage of wild birds was the source of the most decorative and colourful regalia. Usually worn for dance or ceremony, feather plumes formed headdresses and lengthy tassels of string and feathers, shimmering like the breast of a rainbow lorikeet, hung and swung from the arms and hips of dancers. Natural plant and animal fibres were twined, plaited, stitched and spun, making headbands and armbands that were often embellished with ochre designs or filled with black beeswax and embedded with bright red abrus seeds.

In decorating the person, requirements varied from the secular sphere of daily life to the flamboyance of ceremonial occasion. Forms of personal clothing ranged from possum fur rugs, bearing the personal insignias of the wearers in the form of designs scratched into the hide, to other small items of clothing such as the simple hair string belts of

central Australian nomads, pulled tight to prevent hunger, or headbands of fur, string or fibre. In many parts of the country daily wear also included nose pin ornaments made of reeds, carved wood, shell or bone.

In the ceremonial arena the art of personal adornment reached its colourful zenith. Ochres were applied in exciting and dramatic designs, headdresses ranged from simple headbands to string and feather constructions metres high, and arms and bodies were adorned with feathers or shell pendants. The lower legs were frequently encased in masses of leaves, altering the proportions of the body completely, and contributing to the rustling sound effects as the dancers performed.

SOUTH-EAST AUSTRALIA AND TASMANIA

In the colder southern climate when temperatures in the winter months dropped to freezing point, both men and women wore fur cloaks, generally suspended from one shoulder, leaving the other arm free. At other times, not only in the south-east but throughout the country, people went naked, although pubic tassels of fur and string were worn by both men and women. The southern cloaks were worn inland and along the coasts north and south of Sydney, although, curiously, not around Sydney itself. They were also worn in Victoria, South Australia and Western Australia.

A description of the manufacture of the cloaks in the central Darling region of New South Wales was given by a local European man who grew up there and who watched the process. He wrote:

> . . . cloaks were made of the skin of the doe kangaroo, murraway; this was stretched and dried in the shade, rubbed with ashes and then with some emu oil or goanna fat, and pulled backwards and forwards around a smooth-barked tree to make it a little pliable. Other than this, no attempt was made at tanning. The skins were roughly trimmed and sewn together by thread of kangaroo tail sinews, and in the very cold windy weather the cloak was worn with the fur inside. Skins were sewn together for a sleeping cover, and their manufacture was only discarded with the giving of blankets by the government. [15]

Such rugs were sewn together using a fine awl as a needle and kangaroo leg sinew for thread. The holes were made with the bone point, then the thread was pushed through these holes by hand.

The Darling River people also wore nose ornaments made from carved sticks or wild turkey feather quills that they inserted through the pierced nasal septum, and headbands of spun string. Small shells were worn as necklaces and possum skin strips were worn as headbands by both sexes. In South Australia the possum skin rugs could once be seen along the length of the Murray River; they were also worn by the people of the Coorong and the Adelaide plains. The Kaurna in the Adelaide area preferred more pliable rugs made from small animals rather than large kangaroos, whose pelts were tougher and less flexible. [16] The rugs were worn over the left shoulder, fastened under the right armpit and tied with string. Women in all these areas wore the cloaks in such a way that a pouch was created on their back in which a child could ride, supported under its bottom by a special baby harness made of netted hand-spun string. In severe cold the rugs or cloaks were worn with the fur against the skin. The inner soft surface was occasionally decorated by scratching the skin with sharp shells and then rubbing charcoal and animal fat into the surface to darken the incisions and to emphasise the decoration.

Extremely unusual items of clothing worn by the Kaurna were seaweed cloaks. None of these survive in the national collections, but the written records describe them as being cloaks worn in a manner similar to the skin rug and constructed of lengths of seaweed interwoven to form a square. Tassels hung in lengths off the lower edge.

Shell was universally used in body ornaments. Along the Richmond and Tweed Rivers of New South Wales, the people wore pendants of ground segments of nautilus shell frequently as large as the palm of the hand, which had been traded from the sea coast. Women in many areas wore

Fur cloaks were worn by men and women in the cold southern climate. They were made of possum and kangaroo skins sewn together with kangaroo sinew thread.
Collection Museum of Victoria

Opposite Detail of the designs scratched into the soft inner surface.

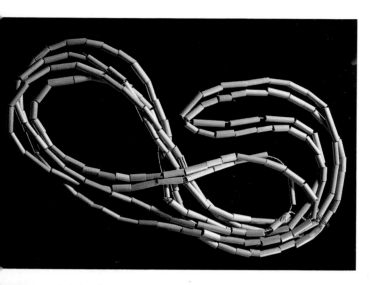

Top Necklace made from segments of aquatic reeds.
Collection Museum of Victoria

Centre Old necklace of quondong seeds, coloured with paint and ochre and threaded on hand spun human hair string.
Hogarth Galleries

Bottom Ripe quondong fruit and seeds.
Photograph Jennifer Isaacs

delicate strings of small pearls, some strung in multi-strand patterns and combinations. The shell necklaces still made by the Aboriginals of Cape Barren Island in Bass Strait are most like the early examples. These are made from tiny marine snail shells and were worn exclusively by women.

Unlocking the old drawers in the museums of the nation reveals a wealth of tiny and relatively inconspicuous Aboriginal decorations gathered by the early European settlers and by nineteenth-century collectors. Materials employed by the coastal and southern riverine peoples, as with all forms of Aboriginal artistic expression, reflect not only the locality but a joy and love of the colourful and unusual offerings of natural plants and animals that can be worked into wearable ornaments.

Emu feather waist girdles were worn along the Yarra River and referred to as *til-bur-nin* or *jerr-barr-ning*. The delicate long feathers were gathered into tufts of six or more and bound along the length of a waistband. Waistbands for men in the Lake Callabonna area of South Australia were reportedly made from strips of pelican skin attached to a cord of human hair string. Other feathered bands and ornaments were made from owl feathers (for head ornaments) and parrot feathers. One example in the National Museum of Victoria is listed as a waist belt of Blue Mountain parakeet feathers. A spectacular piece that has survived the ravages of insect attack and natural age rot is a man's pelican feather apron from South Australia, also in the Museum of Victoria.

Necklaces were strung from tiny sections of hollow reeds and worn by both men and women in Victoria and New South Wales. On Lake Hindmarsh in Victoria they were up to ten metres in length and called *jahkul*; along the Yarra in Victoria they had another name, *djarrk*. Similar necklaces are still made at Aurukun, Cape York. Quandong seeds were used to make necklaces in many parts of Australia. These delicious fruit trees grow in more arid regions, though in the nineteenth century necklaces were found in Victoria's mallee region, perhaps traded or grown locally. Must unusual necklaces were made by the people of Warrnambool, Victoria, of small sections cut out of the orange claws of a crayfish, drilled and strung together.

String, bone and teeth were combined in many variations, particularly for headbands. One elegant piece from the lower Murray, dated before 1878, used hand-spun string, probably aquatic vegetable fibre, which was then knotted into a band of about five centimetres. Two pairs of kangaroo teeth were attached at either side to hang onto the temple, forming a frame for the eyes.[17]

Descriptions by James Dawson[18] of mid-nineteenth century decoration for ceremonies in New South Wales mention that nose reeds up to thirty centimetres in length were worn by men for corroborees. When the men stood with their knees quivering in dance, the reeds seemed to connect the dancers in a continuous line. Dawson also noted the women's practice of wearing flowers 'in the slits of the ears'; it is unfortunate that he does not elaborate on this, as his is the only record of this custom.

In the south-east, the practice of wearing fur cloaks, neck pendants and other traditional ornaments disappeared with European colonisation and the issue of blankets and clothing by the government of the day. The elegant shells were replaced with brass plates inscribed to commemorate the wearer's status, such as King Billy or Queen Emma, awarded for being outstanding leaders.

Ceremonial life, including the great *bora* initiations, continued in secret away from the towns and camps, but as Aboriginal cultural values were being constantly eroded, ceremonial practice ceased early this century. In parts of the north coast of New South Wales, some descendants of the early people are beginning a planned revival. They hope this will encourage young Aboriginal people to understand the depth and quality of their ancient heritage.

QUEENSLAND

In the richly detailed records of Walter Roth[19], as well as in museum collections, is evidence of a considerable range of body ornaments and decorations. Just as the scar patterns and body paintings represented tribal affiliations and individual status, other techniques of embellishing the body were important. Necklaces, pendants, headdresses and bracelets were worn by both men and women, the substances used for their manufacture being drawn from the natural environment. Reed segments, cut small and strung into lengths, were common throughout Queensland, as well as shells gathered in quantities and strung onto threads or worn as pendants. Local mussel shells from inland freshwater rivers were used and sea shells were traded from the coast. Some of the stencilled cave

Gindjimirr of Yathalamara outstation in central Arnhem Land, wearing a reed as a nose ornament. Such decorations of wood and bone were once commonly worn.

Nose ornaments from the lower Murray area.
Collection Museum of Victoria

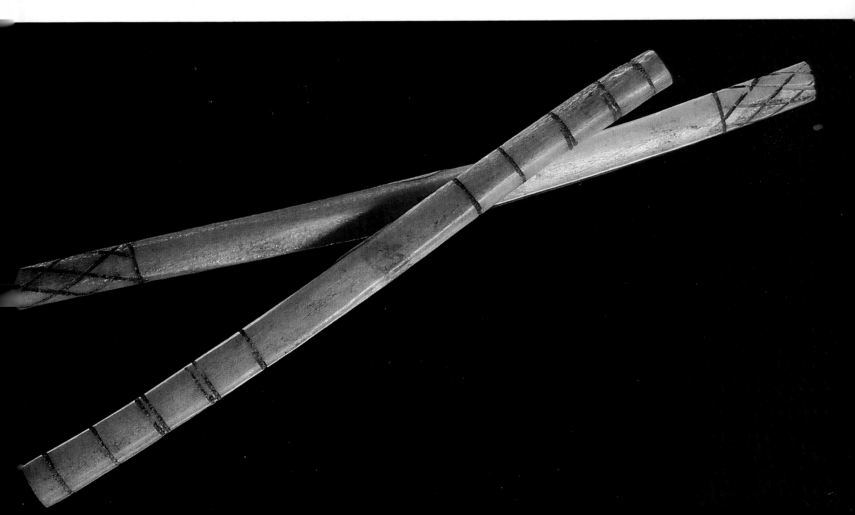

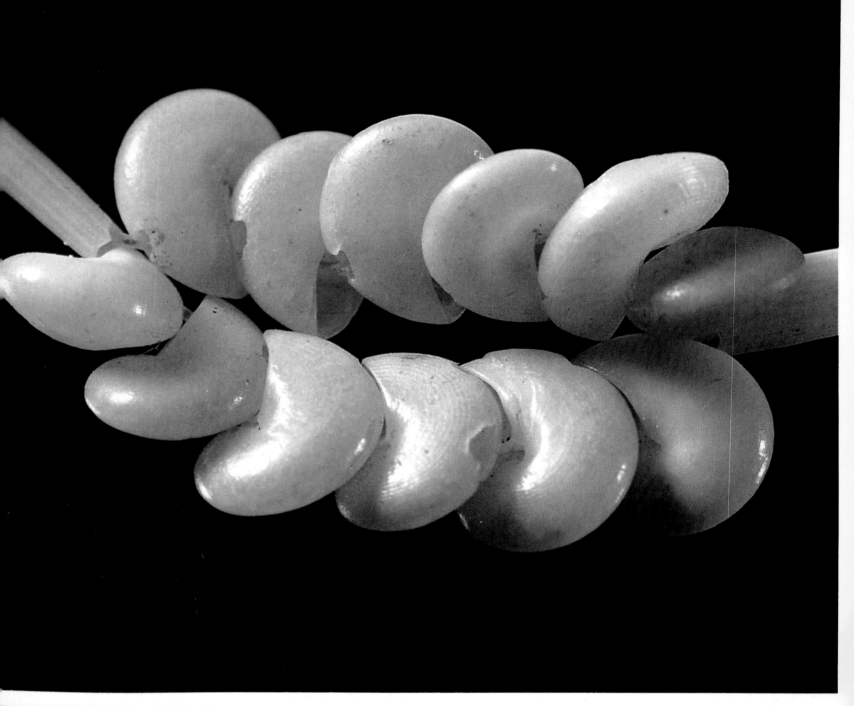

Shell necklaces from Aurukun, Cape York, with detail above.

paintings in the Carnarvon area are thought to be Melo shell pendants, suggesting the importance of such shell and its trade over long distances. Melo shells could be worn suspended from hair on the forehead; one account also tells that the beards of the men were decorated with nautilus shells stuck firmly on with beeswax. Fine flat shells were also ground into small square segments and then strung and tied into double rows to form distinctive necklaces in the Mackay area.[20]

Unusual body ornaments recorded in Queensland include eagle claw necklaces from the upper Nogoa River, a circular pendant made from the compressed cloaca of a large macropod and necklaces made from the backbone of a snake.[21] Nose ornaments were common, and the ears were occasionally also decorated with tiny carved pegs. For ceremonies, headdresses of bunches of sulphur-crested white cockatoo feathers were worn, and many other feathered variations were constructed along Cape York for dances enacting the ancestral stories.

The ancient body ornaments once worn throughout Queensland have a direct and continuous link with the secular and ceremonial decorations still made at the traditional community of Aurukun on the east coast of Cape York. String from the fibre of the cabbage fan palm is worn in different ways on specific parts of the body to signify status. It is made

into belts, widows' harnesses and armbands, as well as being incorporated into waist girdles or skirts. The tradition of making shell necklaces is strongly upheld by the women, who create simple and complex strings in pure white or combinations of white and grey or white and pink.

One of the most delicate shell necklace patterns incorporates the long white horn shell linking clusters of small, round, coloured shells. Using two strands of string (today fishing line has replaced hand-spun string in shell art), the necklace is made by passing both threads through the horizontal white linking shell, and then separating the threads to make two sections of small threaded coloured shells about 2.5 centimetres long. The threads then meet again to pass through the linker, and so on. The effect can be of a series of loops connected by eggshell-thin strands of shell. These necklaces are termed *uch* in the Wikmunkan language. Pearl shell pendants called *ongkam* are also made and worn in ceremonial dancing. The pendants gleam and bounce on the painted chests of the men as they perform their traditional dances, wearing headdresses of white cockatoo feathers. Reed segment necklaces similar to those found all over the eastern states last century are also maintained as living craft at Aurukun, where they are called *yaath*. Occasionally the seeds are mixed with the shells in regular colour combinations to make necklaces.

Termed *uch* in the Wikmunkan language, the delicate thin horn shells of these necklaces from Aurukun link clusters of bivalve and horn shells.

Top Maudie Booth of the Anmatjera people making eucalypt seed necklaces at Amoongana, central Australia.
Photograph Jennifer Isaacs

Bottom Detail of scented eucalyptus seed necklaces made by women of the desert areas.

CENTRAL DESERT

Although the desert grows very cold on winter nights, its people never had to wear heavy clothing, such as the fur rugs of the coastal and southern areas. Instead, they wore string tassels, waistbands and simple headbands. All wore nose bones and the men dressed their hair in elaborate chignons. In everyday life no other ornaments were needed, the body cicatrices denoting status and individuality. Women and children enjoyed the simple social ritual of adorning each other's hair with grass seeds, attaching them to form a fringe around the face, and occasionally little pellets of clay were added for the same decorative purpose. Women's seed necklaces were certainly made and worn, probably then, as now, for the women's ceremonies centring on sexuality and fecundity and for others that formed an adjunct to the men's separate initiation ceremonies. The necklaces are now also made as craft items for sale.

Seeds of the *ininti* tree are found in large quantities, either in their pods still on the tree, or fallen in scattered quantities amongst the sand and leaf debris below. One of the favourite pastimes of the women and children is to collect the seeds as they search for food. The seeds may be yellow, orange or brilliant red. The colours can be clearly picked out as the children and women run the sand through their hands, allowing the wind to separate it from the seeds. *Ininti* and *witchinbarara*, the small round brown seeds, are formed into long strands, generally on hand spun string made from human hair, although this is occasionally replaced by machine spun wool.

Necklaces are in fact decorative body ornaments, worn in lengthy harnesses over one shoulder, across the chest and under the arms. They are also wound around the head to form headbands to hold feather headdresses in place. These might always have been secular in nature, as very young girls are encouraged to wear the regalia when learning the dances from their older relatives. A similar *ininti* seed necklace was collected by early ethnographer Baldwin Spencer in 1912, testifying to the continuity of this ancient form of body decoration.[22]

An interesting item worn daily by Aranda men was the *chilara* or forehead band. This was a decorative headband composed of multiple strands of possum or wallaby fur string that had been thickly coated with ochre and then painted in the traditional geometric circle and line designs denoting country, journeys and land ownership. Spencer did not consider that these designs stemmed from the same source as the Dreaming stories depicted on sacred objects, but they almost certainly did, being secular versions of sacred ancestral journeys, perhaps signifying group membership and land ownership.

During ceremony, elaborate 'costumes' were made and string and feather constructions were worn on the head or carried. Such ornamentation is still an integral part of the men's sacred ceremonies in this area of the country. The costumes were part of the body itself and the method of decorating using feather or plant down has already been briefly described. As in the south-east, emu feathers were used as tufts on the apex of a ceremonial headdress or as additions to body ornamentation. On particular occasions forehead decorations were worn by women; these consisted of flattened lumps of spinifex resin or porcupine grass resin, into which rows of kangaroo incisor teeth were embedded. These were attached to a string and worn around the head on the forehead.

There is evidence that ceremonies were traded and passed from group to group. These desert forehead ornaments now have their equivalents in the *ubar* ceremonial head ornaments made and worn by the Gunwinggu of western Arnhem Land. Similarly, pearl shell ornaments were traded from the north-west coast to the centre, where they were worn suspended from waistbands.

Children from Mt Liebig in the western Macdonnell Ranges gathering *ininti* seeds for body decorations. The seeds come from the bat-winged coral tree *Erythrina vespertilio*.

Teacher's assistant Maude Peterson from Mt Liebig prepares children wearing body paint and seed decorations to perform their traditional songs and dances.

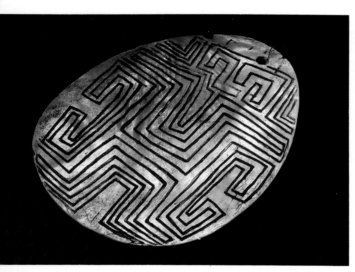

Incised Western Australian pearl shell pendant with traditional interlocking key design.
Collection Macleay Museum, University of Sydney

NORTH-WEST AUSTRALIA

The desert culture and way of life extended as far as the coast of north-western Australia with body decorations and ceremonial practice reflecting the continuity of the journeys of common Dreaming ancestors. Hair string girdles, pubic aprons and headbands were commonly worn in daily life, and for ceremonies feathers and leaves were added to the body decorations.

Bunches of yellow and white cockatoo feathers were worn at Northampton. These were attached at their base to a wooden peg that could be inserted through the headband or wound into the hair. Emu feathers were worn in the same way, occasionally rubbed with red ochre to change their colour and texture. Two bunches of emu feathers were also fastened onto the upper arms by binding them with spinifex resin and inserting the base through an armband made of fur string. For special ceremonies north-western men and women also wore waistbands with numerous tassels made from the fluffy tails of rabbit kangaroos.

On the coast near Wyndham, Sunday Island and the Admiralty Gulf, decorated bailer shells were made. These were found throughout the desert and down to the Nullarbor Plain, where they were reported by Daisy Bates at Ooldea. The shells are engraved on their shiny interiors with many different designs, and they were worn in the Kimberley region as neck pendants as well as from waist girdles. As they were traded further inland they assumed a religious or magical role and were ground and rubbed for rainmaking rituals. At the Great Australian Bight, they had been exchanged and ground so frequently they were often only the size of a flattened egg.

When made and worn in Western Australia the shells were attached to hand-spun lengths of hair or fur string and elegant complex linear patterns were frequently engraved. The designs included mazes, zigzags and the interlocking key design, occasionally featuring representational human figures or animals. Almost all the shells used parallel geometric lines to form the composition and red ochre was rubbed into the engraving to darken the design and to make it stand out against the lustrous pearl surface.

The interlocking key design, which is an angular meandering design, has been found in many parts of the world, and its presence in north-western Australia has led to speculation that it was derived from contact on the coast with fishermen from Indonesia in the last two centuries. The design has been found in Bronze Age ceramic deposits from the Celebes and was once common on Chinese ceramics traded widely in South-East Asia.[23]

In Western Australia, the pattern was most commonly used in pearl shell ornaments and it is thought that it spread for use on shields, carved wooden hair pins and sacred objects such as *tjuringa*. The pearl shells assumed an increasingly esoteric function the further they were traded from the coast, and the designs they bore developed additional power as well. Today the interlocking key design can be found on carved weapons, including shields and spear throwers made far from the Kimberleys by groups of Pitjantjatjara in South Australia.

ARNHEM LAND

Before European contact, few clothes were worn along the humid and tropical Arnhem Land wilderness. Women made paper bark and woven pandanus pubic covers. On Groote Eylandt, off the east coast in the Gulf of Carpentaria, the women were naked but carried sheets of bark as body covers when they revealed themselves to outsiders. Along the mainland coast, shells of all descriptions were gathered to make necklaces, and lovely strings are still made for sale at Milingimbi, Elcho Island and Yirrkala. Once strung on bark fibre string, they are now universally made on fishing line. Nevertheless, they show a sympathetic response to the natural beauty of the materials.

Spencer records some unusual decorative practices of the Kakadu, the original inhabitants of the lands now known as the Kakadu National Park. The pieces Spencer collected in 1912-13 included a woman's head decoration made from parrot feathers formed into the shapes of flowers.[24] Spencer described it thus before missionary settlement of the Northern Territory caused the making of feather flowers to become an Aboriginal skill. The making of feather flowers was a domestic skill admired in the sitting-rooms of late Victorian and Federation era Australian society, so Spencer might have placed his own interpretation on the imitative intentions of the feather ornament makers. Such feather ornaments, worn in bunches on strings, were widespread across the top end of the Northern Territory and they do resemble flowers. They are circular bunches with a colourful central ring, although the artists make and wear them for ceremonial purposes unrelated to flowers. Each coloured feather has both a totemic relevance (because of the bird it has been taken from) and a religious significance. Thus, *lindridj*, the lorikeet found in north-eastern Arnhem Land, is sacred to the Riratjingu; the feathers are used for ceremonial armbands or headbands. Today such feathered regalia is worn for both sacred ceremonies and for public *bungul*, camp corroborees, though exclusively by men. The feathered regalia pieces of Arnhem Land are the most spectacular and skilfully crafted body decorations made today.

Feathers, either white down or the small orange-tipped downy neck feathers of parrots, are spun into the string while it is being twined on the knee. This special string is made by both men and women, and it can be used in headbands and head ornaments, as well as handles for sacred dilly bags, or as binding on other ritual items. It is also used as a wrapping binder on pandanus armbands.

Multiple strings of feather tassels are made to hang from armbands, headbands and waist girdles, varying in composition with each local group. These are generally made from several lengths of string onto which tiered feather arrangements are joined. The feathers are attached in circular layers by binding the tips of the feather quills, beginning at the base of the string and proceeding upwards, each circlet covering the quills of the circlet below. Lumps of beeswax or soft resin are used to secure the feathers to the string at various points along the length. The resin gives some weight to the tassels, which can be from thirty centimetres to over a metre long, allowing them to swing with a pendular motion in dance.

Detail of string waistband with feather tassels worn by men of the Rembarrnga group, western Arnhem Land.
Hogarth Galleries

Top Hand spun string and kangaroo teeth headband from western Arnhem Land.

Bottom Dance fan made by Brian Yinawaya of Ramingining. The feathers are inserted into a beeswax handle and decorated with ochre.

Opposite Strings of snail shells from Maningrida, Arnhem Land, painted with ochre and used as rattles for musical accompaniment. The shells may also be worn.
All pieces Hogarth Galleries.

Birds' feathers known to be used in various ornaments include those of parrots, rainbow lorikeets, Torres Straits pigeons and black and white cockatoos, although pragmatism occasionally triumphs and the occasional local chicken feather appears in a feather string. Under local legislation the birds are now protected species, and Aboriginals are only permitted to kill them for ceremonial occasions.

Feathered regalia is best appreciated in dance performances; many strings flash and arch with a quick turn of the hips or sharp lift of the shoulder and elbow as each dancer stamps and twists his torso, acting the drama of the ancient songs to the accompaniment of the *didjeridu*. Items of ritual body adornment, which appear in collections up to eighty years old and which are still made and used, include kangaroo teeth head ornaments. Known as *lenderra* and used in the *ubar* ceremony, these consist of lumps of wax or resin in which a row of teeth has been embedded. The emblems are worn on the forehead attached to hand spun string.

Teeth necklaces and other magnificent and imaginative pieces are occasionally made, including an echidna quill necklace (now in the Maningrida Museum) and the bill of a royal spoonbill (*Platalea regia*) worn as a neck pendant and made in central Arnhem Land.

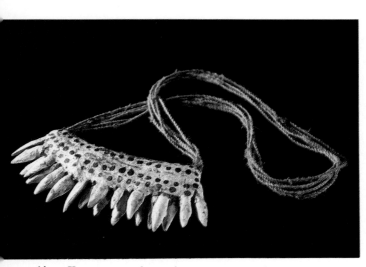

Above Kangaroo teeth pendant, western Arnhem Land. *Hogarth Galleries*
Below Necklace of kangaroo teeth attached to hide, Yarra River, Victoria. *Collection Museum of Victoria*
Opposite Echidna quill necklace, western Arnhem Land. *Collection Maningrida Museum*

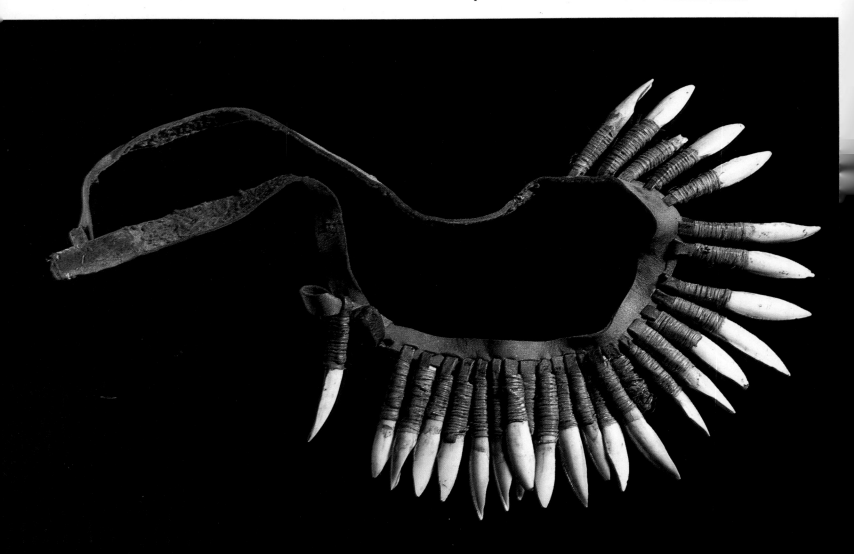

Top left Tiwi armband collected by Baldwin Spencer in 1912.
Collection Museum of Victoria

Top right Tiwi armband circa 1960. These are made of bark
and pandanus, and decorated with ochre, wax, red abrus seeds
and feathers.
Collection Northern Territory Museum of Arts and Sciences

Bottom Preparations for a *pukumani* ceremony include body
painting and wearing pandanus armbands. Dots are applied
with a multi-pronged wooden comb. *Photograph Margaret West*

Opposite Tiwi red and black feather headdress made from
black cockatoo tail feathers. These are fastened to the hair as
part of the decoration for *pukumani* ceremonies. *Hogarth Galleries*

Previous page Contemporary Tiwi armbands constructed of
woven pandanus and padded with beeswax.
Collection Northern Territory Museum of Arts and Sciences

TIWI BODY DECORATION

Tiwi body painting designs are the most colourful and detailed body art
in northern Australia. Additional ornaments of head feathers and
armbands are equally impressive, adding to the impact of the body
paintings. The Tiwi *pukumani* rituals surrounding death and burial have
already been described. Body ornaments worn for these ceremonies
concentrate on the face and arms. Head tufts of feathers are made from
the tail feathers of the black cockatoo. These have a bright orange patch
against the black base, providing a strong contrast and flash of colour.
The feathers are bound onto a small wooden peg fastened by winding
some of the hair around it to keep it in place. Headbands may be of
plaited or woven pandanus; lengthy tassels hang from both temples and
are finished with feathers.

Armbands are made of plaited pandanus palm fibre or are elaborate
constructions of bark, decorated with painted designs or padded and
filled in different ways with beeswax impregnated with the brilliant red
abrus seeds. The design of the armbands is unique to each individual. Just
as individual body painting is admired, these exceptional constructions
can assume most unusual shapes and proportions. Seams and flanges may
be stitched with pandanus fibre to form decorative edges or the flattened
bark seam can extend out from the arm for several centimetres, with red
and black feathers attached to either corner. Circular armbands of woven
pandanus occasionally appear as two thick, black, doughnut-shaped
masses of wax attached at the centre and again decorated with paint,
feathers and seeds. Such items are worn not only on the upper arm but
also suspended on a string around the neck.

Ritual beards are made and worn for dance performances as well as
tufts of feathers which are worn as a ball or pompom around the neck.
The latter are thought to increase the power of the performance and are
clenched between the teeth during the climax of the dance.

Most of the Tiwi ceremonial regalia is still made, as the *pukumani* rituals
continue to be central facets of Tiwi culture.

Fibre Craft

In the range of twined, coiled, woven and knotted objects that comprise the fibre arts of the whole continent, there is a wide diversity in techniques and materials, as well as great variety in the forms of the objects themselves. Natural fibres were used not only for baskets but for ceremonial objects, and for body adornment; in combination with other materials they were also used for clothing, for shelters, shades, fishing nets, fishing lines, sieves and canoe sails. Bark, human and animal hair, palm leaves and many varieties of vines and roots were all spun into strong twine.

The ancient and ingenious fibre arts show the balance and natural ease of the relationship between Aboriginals and their landscape and its plants. At one time, every Aboriginal woman across the north of Australia, through Queensland, New South Wales, Victoria, Tasmania, South Australia and parts of Western Australia carried her belongings in a netted bag or used twined or coiled baskets to gather shellfish, berries, roots or even wild honey. Around the camps of south-eastern Australia, it must have been common to see women sitting and making string bags, or twining reeds together; this is often seen in Arnhem Land today.

Each Aboriginal group used locally found materials. Even the men and children knew the nature of these materials and where they could be found, and the finished works reflect their areas of origin. For instance, the finest and most complex tough string for large bags appears from Cape York, where cable-line twine for dugong and turtle fishing was also made. All over the north, pandanus palm is used for making twined and coiled bags, mats and sieves for soaking fruit. At Aurukun, Cape York, women still practise the traditional craft of spinning the fibre from the shoot of the cabbage tree palm, and various barks are used for making string in all northern traditional areas.

Weaving baskets and making bags were and are essentially women's arts. Men made stronger rope for fishing and occasionally objects associated with their own ceremonies, though even in these the women might have done a substantial amount of the basic production, including spinning. Writings on Aboriginal arts have revealed a lack of perception about fibre weaving bordering on complete apathy. Given the interests of predominantly male writers about Aboriginals, it is not really surprising that the arts of carving boomerangs, spears and shields were given great attention, while the parallel women's fibre arts were not considered particularly special. This was in line with the idea that objects of value lasted for some time, and also with the idea that men's weapons and utensils provided the basis of a primitive family's survival. However, even these notions can now be overturned; modern research (frequently carried out by women, at that) indicates that the women provided about sixty per cent of the daily food, bringing it to the family in their fibre containers and string bags.

Opposite Twined ceremonial dilly bag with *yirritja* diamond designs painted in ochre on the pandanus surface and rainbow lorikeet feather pendants from eastern Arnhem Land
Collection The Australian Museum

Traditional woven bags made from natural fibres are still used to gather bush foods near Aurukun, Cape York.

In this sense, there is now a double reason for paying attention to the fibre arts of the Aboriginal people. Not only are they great works of art that originated in ancient times and are still made today, but they also had extremely important functions within the society from which they came.

In recent years, the textile arts have emerged from the shadows of craft skills courses and are now represented in art galleries. This has led to a complete change in the way in which people perceive the arts of fibre weaving and basket making among Aboriginals. Baskets have come to be respected as a form of modular sculpture, the interaction of two linear elements creating patterns in colour, light and shade. Never has it been more clearly apparent that Aboriginal fibre constructions are unquestionably fine art.

In the ritual sphere, bunched clumps of neatly shaped bark bound with woven twine are used in northern ceremonies to represent totemic animals and plants during the dances, and in many of these, the form

echoes the object represented. Some, with subtle bird heads and necks, are among the most elegant examples of fibre work that can be found anywhere on the continent.

Particularly in relation to the work of the south-eastern peoples, we have only collections of baskets once made to show the extent of this ancient art. Museums amassed their collections from government surveyors, anthropological field workers and through donations from private individuals. Stored in trays and drawers, carefully laid out and smelling of age, rot, naphthalene and other insecticides, these beautiful works have lain for many years. Although they have occasionally been taken out of their resting places to be displayed as examples of Aboriginal culture, the collections of the bags and baskets of the south-eastern peoples are largely unknown as works of art in their own right. Lying hidden, in fact, is a treasure trove of forgotten cultural heritage, unique to Australia.

Aboriginal weavers obtain a range of warm colours from natural roots and barks.
1, 2 Red *Haemodorum coccineum* roots are pounded at Ramingining, Northern Territory.
3, 4 The dark yellow outer bark of *Coelospermum reticulatum* is scraped off with a mangrove
shell at Aurukun.
5 Colours change with the addition of ash to the dye bath.

Opposite Livistona palm fibre boiling in the dye.

Arkapenya of Aurukun, Cape York, digs deep into the soil to gather roots to use for dyes.

DYEING

Before Aboriginal women had access to clay or metal containers, there were no traditional vessels that could be used to boil water. As pottery had never developed as a traditional craft, fast dyeing was impossible. Most writers conclude that weavers simply rubbed the spun string through ochred hands. Red ochre particularly has a strong tendency to stain, and many early baskets and bags show traces of ochre rubbed into the string. Other baskets, notably the traditional twined dilly bags, were painted after weaving. Using the present dye stuff, it is not impossible to achieve some colour by simply soaking the fibre and twine in the dye, but this was probably not done.

As has been documented,[1] Indonesian fishermen were frequent visitors to western Arnhem Land for at least 400 years before Europeans first visited the area. These people, from the Macassar Straits, set up villages, grew rice, built huts, made wells and planted tamarind trees and bamboo. They made pottery and their beautiful batik sarongs inspired many Aboriginal designs.

As the Aboriginals worked for the Macassans all this time, the pottery might have been used to dye fibre. The Indonesians were probably well versed in natural dyeing techniques.

However, the introduction of European metal containers meant that Aboriginal dyers could extend their skills; the effect of European missionary encouragement was also profound. Dyeing was encouraged, colours were major decorative features and prices paid for coloured weaving were higher than before. Some of the women missionaries were skilled basket makers themselves. They encouraged not only dyeing but decorative stitching and experimentation with form.

Today Aboriginal women weavers are immensely skilled dyers with new colours constantly being developed. For example, the colours that Arnhem Land craftswomen use in weaving are immensely subtle variants of several basic dye sources. The range of hues and the colour intensity depends on the time of year the dye stuff is gathered, the addition of ash to the boiling fibre and in some cases probably the type of utensil used to prepare the dye bath. Colours most frequently obtained are bright yellow from the root of a small shrub and pink through to dark purple from the bulb-like roots of reedy grasses. The bark of some trees is used for red and brown.

As well as these natural colours and others derived from plant roots and bark, an interesting greyish blue has recently appeared in central Arnhem Land string and pandanus weaving. After investigation, the colour was traced to the practice of boiling up numerous old cardboard cartons with blue ink lettering on them. The comments when the blue string appeared in craft galleries were reminiscent of the flurry of interest caused when some blue x-ray rock paintings were discovered about thirty years ago in what is now the Kakadu National Park. It seemed that Aboriginal artists had found a remarkable and unique blue pigment until the paint was traced to the use of Reckitt's Blue, taken from the laundry of friendly Europeans at the next settlement. The new string bags show that the search by Aboriginal artists for that elusive blue goes on.

The procedure for dyeing strips of pandanus palm in Arnhem Land is very similar to that used for strips of cabbage tree palm in Cape York. In Arnhem Land, the pandanus shoots are gathered from the tall palm when green, and the centre strip is carefully extracted. This is split with the fingernail into several lengths of fibre, bunches of which are spread in the sun to dry or tied and hung on a tree branch. When they have faded from green to pale green or cream, they are ready to accept the dye. Occasionally, the fresh strips will be dyed when green, but in these cases the intensity of colour is lost. To obtain yellow, the freshly dug roots of the small bush *Coelospermum reticulatum* are scraped of their outer bark. The root is pale yellow, but the inner bark is chrome yellow.

The bare roots and the bright yellow scrapings are immersed in the water to be used for dye. When dry, the bunch of pandanus is placed in a billy, old tin can or cooking pot and boiled with the dye stuff. The length of boiling will deepen the colour obtained.

At Aurukun, Cape York, the young shoots of the *Livistona* or cabbage fan palm are harvested for making into string. The bags that the craftswomen of the area most enjoy making use the natural coloured string and two other dye colours, yellow and red-brown. The yellow roots used for dye are termed *wayk*. If a rust-red colour is wanted, a special ash is added to the boiling liquid towards the end of the process. The dye and fibre immediately change colour through the mordant action of the ash. (In general, mordants assist the dye stuff to adhere to the string or cloth being dyed.) In order to make the ash, the women who are skilled in the traditional weaving of Aurukun select a particular tree which has a bark with a bright red inner surface. The bark is burned in a heap in the centre of the small fire during the yellow dyeing process, then, when reduced to ash, used for the section of fibre in which red-brown is desired.

At Ramingining and elsewhere in central Arnhem Land, the vibrant tomato red of the swollen reed roots used for dyeing (*Haemodorum coccineum*) makes one expect a brighter hue than the resulting subtle rust-maroon. The colour achieved greatly varies with the season of harvesting the reeds. The roots themselves change from brown to red from the hot dry season to the steamy wet season.

Contemporary hour-glass stitch string bag from Aurukun containing roots for dye and tree bark which is reduced to ash for a mordant.

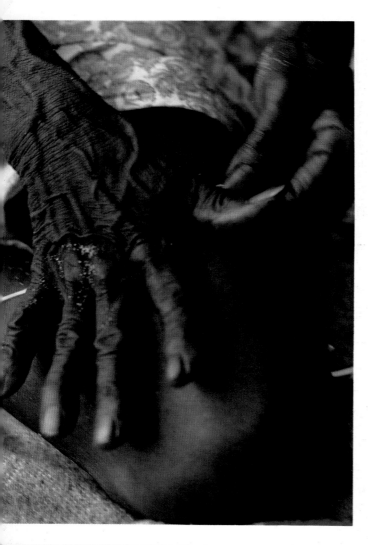

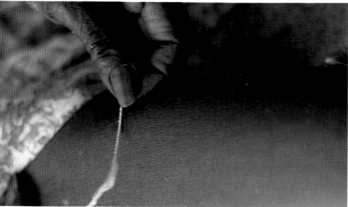

At Aurukun fibre from the cabbage fan palm is spun on the thigh to make strong two-ply string. This skill is still widely practised in northern Australia.

Opposite Nellie Patterson, a Pitjantjatjara woman, uses a traditional spindle to spin hair string.

SPINNING

The romantic longings that members of industrialised societies have for a simpler existence are intensified when we think of the ability of women in traditional societies to take some bark from a tree and spin it into thread, string or rope, make a fishing or harpoon line and catch food for survival. Many commentators have mentioned this aspect of the way in which Aboriginal people fully used the resources of their land without superfluous destruction. Aboriginal men and women knew the properties of all the plants in their environment and appreciated their seasonal changes. The medical uses of all herbs, barks, leaves and clays were thoroughly understood; softwoods and hardwoods were cut for different purposes; at certain times of the year long reeds were harvested for spears and sheets of bark were stripped for housing.

In the art of spinning fibre into twine, the deftness and ease of movement of Aboriginal spinners are exceptional. They know the tensile strength of the fibre they choose for each type of twine and the resulting strings are strong and very neat. Commenting on a variety of string bags in 1878, R. Brough Smyth stated that all the twine made was very 'durable, and well and neatly put together'.[2]

It is poignant to realise that only a century ago in Victoria, Aboriginal women were gathering the reeds (*Phragmites communis*) along the Yarra River and making them into twine. The twine for other bags in Victoria was made from bark fibre and from spun possum fur. Brough Smyth said he had observed that, in spinning possum fur the woman sat down, picked the fur off the animal and worked it into twine 'by rubbing it on the inside of her thigh'.

All over the north coast of New South Wales, bags were fashioned from hand-spun twine. This was generally made of bark, including that of the native hibiscus. Sadly, few of these bags survive in our national collections, with the exception of several in the Australian Museum. One obtained in 1896 at Nambucca shows a coarser, tougher twine than others, but its source is unknown. Possum fur string was also made in New South Wales. In the desert regions, women spun human hair and the fur of small rabbit-like marsupials known as bilbies, as well as wallaby fur. More recently rabbit fur replaced the bilbies as the introduced animals spread rapidly across the continent.

In central Australia, a simple spindle is used to spin the hair and fur into hair belts and other items for ritual use. A twig frame is formed, consisting of two crossed arms inserted through a longer shaft about twenty-five centimetres from the end. The spindle shaft (*inti*) is rolled backwards and forwards on the thigh so the thread is twisted into strong one-ply thread. As each length progresses it is wound onto the spindle. Two strands of the one-ply hair string are joined and spun in the reverse direction to the original twists, producing two-ply thread.[3]

In Aurukun and Edward River on the western coast of Cape York women spin excellent, hard two-ply string, mainly from the young unopened shoot of the *Livistona* palm, although a softer string is also made from fibres stripped from the roots of a bush fig and a wild mango.

Bundles of hand spun string from different areas of Australia. *Top* Hard, strong string from the *Livistona* palm of Aurukun. *Centre* Hair string, Amata, Musgrave Ranges, South Australia. *Bottom* Soft eucalyptus bark string, Maningrida, Arnhem Land.

In the Wikmunkan language the term for 'string' is *kuuy*, usually followed by the name of the plant the string comes from, for example, *kuuy thuuth* (cabbage fan palm string), *kuuy ngaathan* (bush fig string) and *kuuy waath* (wild mango root string).

The technique of spinning employed by the Aurukun craftswomen differs slightly from that of the Arnhem Land spinners, but it serves as a useful model of the type of action Aboriginal women use in hand spinning on the thigh to produce two-ply string from a number of strands of fibre. The *Livistona* fibre should be slightly moist when spun. With the thumbnail, several strips are peeled from the soft fibrous inner layer of the palm frond. These are held tightly with the left hand but spread out over the thigh into two groups so that they form a V, being held at the base of the V. The initial action is to roll the two separated groups of fibres away from the V join several times until the individual strands have twisted together. At this stage, there seem to be two separate strands of one-ply string. The next move is deft and fast; the left hand, which has been holding the V join taut, suddenly releases the tension just as the right hand has completed its final strong, rolling action. The result is that the two strands twist back upon themselves and twine together in a tightly twisted two-ply yarn. Fibres are continuously added to lengthen the string. A fresh grip is taken by the left hand at the point where the two-ply twine joins the two bunches of fibre waiting to be spun, and the process continues. The string thus made from *Livistona* fibre is particularly strong because of the number of fibre strands incorporated in the finished product.

The hand-spun bark of Arnhem Land is a much softer fibre. Arnhem Land twine is usually comprised of two single strands, first twisted then joined together to form two-ply string.

Throughout Australia, string has many uses: for making into knotted and looped bags in which to transport personal possessions, for carrying food and goods and for making nets in which to catch fish or game. It has been used for binding the handles and joints of weapons and utensils, for making body ornaments such as belts and armbands, for binding parts of the body for medicinal purposes or to prevent hunger and, most importantly and spectacularly, for constructing and binding ceremonial objects such as headdresses, *waninga* (massive emblems of string worn or held above the head in dances) and *rangga* (bunched paper bark wrapped in string representing yams, totemic animals and birds or sacred mythological objects).

Just as most people keep a supply of string in a drawer or cupboard, small bundles of neatly rolled spare string have been found inside many old Aboriginal bags as well as other important possessions such as stone tools, shells, plant medicine, pipes and native tobacco.[4] In the outstations of Arnhem Land today, many houses and shelters have string or pounded fibre stored in a traditional old string bag or in a plastic or canvas one. These bags of materials are like a conventional European sewing or knitting bag and they contain the craftswoman's spinning and weaving materials as well as odd lengths of string and implements to help her in her work.

Single fibre folded containers

Single fibre containers are the loveliest examples of the craftswoman's instant perception of the beauty and use of natural objects with minimal shaping and alteration. They represent both the man-made and the natural worlds in a way that other works of fibre art do not. Their essence is in their form and the simplicity of their construction.

Even in Australia today, Aboriginal men and women who need a carrier or a quickly made bucket can deftly remove a strip of bark or take a pliable palm leaf and within minutes fashion a serviceable and elegant utensil. This form of basketry — if it can be called that — is believed to be the simplest and earliest way in which people used fibre for making containers. They were used for a wide range of tasks, from carrying food and water to transporting small babies. Such containers were once common in many parts of the world. Single fibre containers were not meant to last or to be kept by the maker beyond their immediate use; string bags and twined or coiled baskets were for permanent use.

These ingenious containers are constructed from a single sheet of bark, broad leaf or plant substance which has been curved, folded and twisted at the sides and two ends to form a container shape. They are sewn, pleated or bound at each end, the shape subtly following the line of the natural grain and the texture of the fibre itself. Occasionally, a separate handle is attached, or the two ends may be bunched to form handles.

In Western Australia, the two main types of folded container are the *anngum* and the bucket, both made from bark. The *anngum* is a long semi-cylindrical container used to cradle babies and to carry food and other goods. The bark is stripped from the trees and cuts are made through the rough surface, but not right through the bark, some distance from either end. The rough bark is then stripped off from the cuts to the ends and the softened, thin bark at either end is gathered neatly upwards towards perpendicular stick handles. The ends are bound in place with hand-spun bush string. The bark has a natural tendency to return to the curved shape of the tree trunk, and it is this tendency that the Aboriginal craftswoman exploits so cleverly. The two ends are reinforced with eucalyptus gum.

Bark buckets have come to be so named because of their shape, and the vessels of early European settlers might have inspired a tradition of imitation. The bark equivalent of metal serves its purpose just as well. It even has an advantage in the hot dry climate of north-west Australia because it does not conduct heat, so the water remains cool. The bark buckets are made by cutting a circular piece of bark for the base and adding a bark cylinder to form a container. The cylinder is sealed at the side and attached to the base by means of sewn seams of strong hand spun fibre. The seams are made by first puncturing the bark with a sharp tool and then, using a needle, sewing the pieces together. The seams are made airtight and waterproof by coating them with a thick supply of resin. Handles are attached and the outer bark surface frequently provides a ground for the artist to embellish with traditional symbols or designs, or occasionally just a subtle spray of white clay paint. Bark cylinders similar to the Western Australian *anngum* are also made in central Arnhem Land and in Cape York.

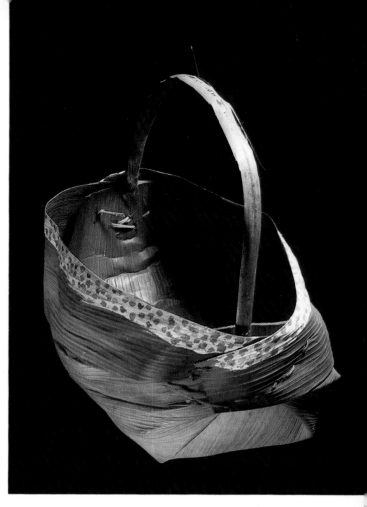

Top Folded container made from a single leaf of the cabbage fan palm, Maningrida. *Hogarth Galleries*

Bottom Single fibre folded container from the Richmond River area, New South Wales, acquired 1892. *Collection The Australian Museum*

115

In central Arnhem Land and on the west coast of Cape York, the simplest forms of folded leaf containers are made from the cabbage tree palm. The huge leaf is wetted to make it pliable and to strengthen its natural creases, then the container is roughly formed by folding the edges in at the two ends and stitching them in place. The method resembles the usual technique employed to wrap a parcel; folding up the sides and then folding the corners over to meet each other, except that in this case the top is kept open. A handle of the same material is fixed to the basket simultaneously.

The folded leaf containers were probably once found in all areas where leaves grew large enough to make them. A fine example of a folded leaf water-carrying vessel from the coastal area of New South Wales is in the collection of the Australian Museum, Sydney. This piece has strong and sturdy sticks inserted into the folds at each end, with a cross handle attached to them. The folded ends are stitched into place with cane strips.

In the preservation of these temporary containers, some of the beauty that the fresh and supple green form had at the time of making is lost, and these containers become lifeless and rigid in a way that the woven structures do not. However, the few southern examples that have survived have enabled us to understand and appreciate both their form and techniques, an opportunity that would otherwise be lost.

An *anngum* or container formed from a single piece of bark to which handles have been attached, from the Kimberley area, Western Australia. *Hogarth Galleries*

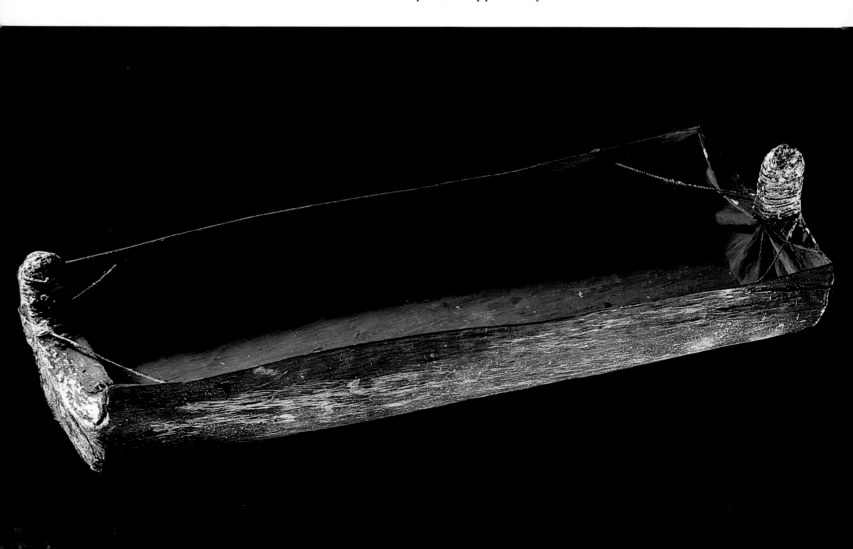

String bags

There are hundreds of string bags, nets and constructions in Australian museums. Gathered over two centuries, they give testimony to the industry and skill of the people who made them. These objects are impressive for the beauty of their forms as well as for the enormous range of techniques employed.

In a recent exhaustive study of numerous string bags in the collection of the Museum of Victoria, many examples were reconstructed, following the stitches and patterns of the originals.[5] It is clear from this patient and time-consuming analysis that the method of making them is complex. Many different knots were used and bags and nets could be constructed in many more different ways than previously assumed.
Occasionally the choice of technique was obviously influenced by aesthetic considerations relating to patterns formed by lines of loops and knots and by the placement of handles. Bags were also decorated with ochre or the thread was perhaps stained and then used in bands of contrasting hues.

At the present time, Aboriginal women of the north take great care with decorative elements in their bags, within the weave and through the use of dyes, the incorporation of feathers in the string and the addition of painted surface decorations after completion.

When the patterns used in making the Museum of Victoria's string structures were examined, several categories were established. The knots were termed slip knot half-hitch appearance, complex knot, simple knot half-hitch, clove hitch, knotted buttonhole and simple overhand knot.

The looping techniques included the simple loop, loop and twist, loop and double twist and hourglass stitch. Researcher Alan West added new looping patterns to these, calling them single interconnected looping, overlapping figure-of-eight, loop and double or triple twist.

The method of support and frame used also interested West. He was able to categorise these techniques according to the frames used, i.e., whether the bag had been made on a circular or straight support.

At Aurukun, three types of string bag are made at present. The *waangk onyan* (in the Wikmunkan language) is made by a knotted netting technique also used for scoop fishnets. This bag is made using a perpendicular stick as an anchor for the string in the early stages. *Waangk waangkam* are looped string bags made in the figure-of-eight or hourglass stitch. These bags are made on a simple frame of two upright sticks. The bag is begun on a taut string between the two posts. The looped pattern is then formed around this string, making the first circular row of the bottom of the bag. *Waangk mee* is another type of looped string bag that uses a loop and a twist technique. The knotted bag, *onyan*, is used for fishing nets and carrying large objects but is fixed in capacity; the *waangkam* and the *mee*, however, can stretch and extend as foodstuffs are inserted. Off-centre handles allow the bags to be easily filled when strung from the head or shoulder.

At both Edward River and Weipa, two other Aboriginal communities in Cape York, these three types of bag have been made in recent times. Another bag with a much closer mesh was made to soak wild bush yams.

Top String bags are used to carry foods and large bags are still taken fishing at Aurukun.

Bottom Detail of string bag, Bellingen River, New South Wales, acquired 1885. *Collection The Australian Museum*

The yams or tubers were crushed, placed in the bag and soaked in a stream. This was commonly done by all Aboriginal groups to leach out acids and food substances that were poisonous or that irritated the digestive tract.

A group of women from different families in Aurukun has been encouraged to continue making string bags, even though their daily need for them has decreased. The bags are made with pride to be exhibited and sold as works of craft. Two of the women have visited a crafts congress in the United States, and this visit has given the other women a wider perspective from which to view their traditional skills. Not only do the sales of their bags provide extra money for the family, but a very large group of people appreciate the works as fine craft as well as functional carriers.

String bags continue to be made by women throughout the coastal areas of the Northern Territory and the settlements around Bamyili near Katherine. At Ramingining, central Arnhem Land, the bags are made from a number of fibre sources. Old women who are prolific string makers but who have lost their teeth frequently give the eucalyptus bark to the young children for chewing before spinning. The bark has a delightful sweet taste, not unlike chewing gum, and the children happily co-operate.

The surprising and fascinating aspect of string bag making here is that the women still prize a pair of long, skinny legs to serve as a frame. The women sit on the ground with their legs straight out in front of them and the bag, open at either end, is made in a tubular form around the legs. One stout woman, knowing the author's interest in weaving, pointed out a young woman walking past, saying, 'She is a very good string bag maker, look at her legs.'

In south-eastern Australia, many types of string bag were made. One interesting piece held in the collection of the Museum of Victoria is known as a *beelang* and was used by the people living along the Yarra River. Most string bags were made with a long handle, suitable for supporting the bag on the head or carrying over the shoulder. The *beelang* is very wide, though not very deep. It has a short handle and it must have been carried in the hand or looped through a belt. When full, it could also have been balanced on the head rather than strung from it. Commenting in 1878, R. Brough Smyth[6] stated that these *beelang* were made in all sizes, some as small as purses, others the size of fishing nets. This desire for variation in size depending on need is still evident at Ramingining, where women make very small string bags as well as others 76 centimetres deep and 46 centimetres wide. Small string bags are made and carried by young girls.

Although string bags were once found in most parts of Australia, the area of their making and use has now shrunk to the Northern Territory and a small section of Cape York. The strength and survival of bag making as it is practised in these remote places forms a repository of skill and information that can never be replaced.

Functional string bags were made predominantly by women, but string was also spun by men, usually as part of their own hunting needs or ceremonial responsibilities. Medicine men generally carry small skin or

Top Aurukun string bags termed *waangk waangkam* are made in stripes using the figure eight or hourglass stitch.

Bottom The bag is started on a string held taut between two sticks placed upright in the ground.

Opposite Arkapenya of Aurukun working on string bags. The fibre is termed *thuuth* or string. Obtained from the cabbage fan palm, the fibre is dyed before being spun into string.

string bags made with string spun with feathers or packed with feathers after completion. Inside these the small tools and magical objects that are associated with the practice of traditional medicine and sorcery are stored.

'Feathered string', made by both men and women, is used in Arnhem Land today to make young boys' head and arm bands for initiation ceremonies; it is also used in rituals such as the morning star ceremony. For this string, the small orange neck feathers of the rainbow lorikeet and larger white feathers from other birds are incorporated into the twine during spinning. More elaborate feather constructions using string as a base are made for body adornments, such as armband tassels and head tassels. The use of feathers in spinning and weaving usually adds a magical or religious content; some properties of spirit contact or 'power' are given to the object. Early ethnographic reports of Arnhem Land describe men wearing small string bags around their necks, which hung on their chests like ties. When angered or in a fight, the men bit hard on the bags. Similarly today, men clench feathered bags (usually twined pandanus) between their teeth during powerful ceremonial dancing.

Above Feather string bag, central Arnhem Land. Feathers may be incorporated into string as it is spun.

Below Skinny legs make an excellent frame for Judy Ganinydja when weaving at Ramingining. *Photograph Jennifer Isaacs*

Opposite Gathering the new shoot of the *Livistona* (cabbage fan) palm to make into string on the Archer River, Cape York.

Top left Twined pandanus dilly bag from Milingimbi, Arnhem Land, acquired 1949. Floating surface stitches define the ceremonial designs and feathers are incorporated.

Top right Twined pandanus dilly bag decorated with ochre, from the Alligator Rivers area, western Arnhem Land, 1912. The unusual splayed neck is not seen on contemporary bags. *Both Collection The Australian Museum*

Bottom Contemporary Arnhem Land string bag painted with ochre.

Opposite Twined bicornual basket made from lawyer cane or *Calamus* palm, 1890. This style was unique to the Cairns-Cardwell district of north Queensland. *Collection The Australian Museum*

Nets

Nets for fishing and catching game were some of the most efficient
utensils that Aboriginal hunters used. They were made from hand spun
string, strongly knotted and attached to a variety of frames, as well as from
twined grasses and sticks. The nets were designed for every situation —
to span or block a river completely, to catch fish on the outgoing tide or
to scoop up fish that had been chased in by other helpers. On land, nets
were used to ensnare birds and to capture game fleeing from hunters or
from a well-placed bushfire.

In central Australia a very strong net used to be made, combining spun
fibre string with twined wallaby or kangaroo sinew. Some of these nets
are particularly elegant. The so-called 'butterfly fish nets' of Arnhem Land
comprise two knotted string nets suspended on wooden frames and
joined together at one side. They are used in a scooping action that
imitates the flapping of a butterfly's wings. If one watches a fisherman at
sunset standing to his knees in still water that reflects not only his image
but the delicate lace-like pattern of his net as he slowly guides it through
the water, one is left in no doubt about the appropriateness of elevating
a simple, hand-made fishing net to a fine work of art. Another scoop fish
net constructed from knotted string is still made at Aurukun. These are
single scoop nets of rectangular shape with rounded corners. Although
used in pairs, they are not hinged.

Hinged 'butterfly' fish nets made of knotted string (detail above) are used in estuaries in
central and western Arnhem Land. Fish are chased into the open 'wings' which trap them
when closed. James Iyuna is pictured at dusk on the Liverpool River.

Twining natural undyed pandanus strips into a traditional dilly bag, Maningrida.

Twined grass and pandanus bags

Twining is weaving in which a system of vertical warp strands are held in place by wefts or horizontal strands. Two wefts are moved together, twisted as they go, locking a warp on each twist. Australian twined baskets can be rigid or flexible, closely or openly woven. In shape they may be flat or 'collapsible', as they are in Aurukun, or conical, as found elsewhere in Cape York and in the Northern Territory.

The technique is similar in all cases and rigidity or pliability depend upon the type of materials used. In making the warps for this kind of bag, strands of grasses or pandanus are overlapped at the point that will become the centre of the base. The first rows of weft hold the strands or stakes in place and space them evenly in a circle. As the circle grows larger, more stakes may be added to avoid the stakes becoming too widely separated as the diameter of the basket increases. Many Aboriginal craftswomen block their work with screwed-up paper or clothing to keep the shape as the weaving is progressing.

The twining technique was widely used in north and south-eastern Australia. However, it was not consistently practised over the whole south-east. Twined baskets were common in Tasmania, but only a few have been reported in South Australia, Victoria and New South Wales.

In Arnhem Land, missionaries gave the term 'dilly bags' to the conical pandanus bag usually strung over the head or shoulders. The term is still in customary use and these are made today in exactly the same way as they have been for many centuries. Ancient rock paintings in the Kakadu National Park, some of which have been dated to possibly 22,000 years old, show thin red ochre figures wearing conical bags strung from their heads. The tradition is therefore timeless, for the bags have not lost their use and cultural relevance since those ancient paintings were made.

Twined bags were and are used for carrying the daily food back to camp. At Maningrida at the mouth of the Liverpool River in Arnhem Land, Aboriginal women frequently come to the arts and crafts store to purchase well-made dilly bags for their own use, and most carry one with their personal possessions inside as they move around the town.

The dilly bags of Arnhem Land are made of fibre from the fronds of the pandanus palm. Pandanus is gathered from the palm when green and the centre strip is carefully extracted and split with the fingernail or a sharp point into several lengths or bunches of fibre. These are usually set aside to dry in the sun before dyeing. Some strips are used in their natural colour. The bags can be tightly or loosely twined; the tighter the twine, the more rigid the bag. Such bags may be so tightly twined that they can be used for gathering bush honey.

Occasionally bags are made in which decorative effects are achieved by varying the weave. Areas of warp are left exposed, crossed and then picked up again by the twined weft at set intervals to make an open pattern. Decoration is also achieved by varying the colour of the warp and weft, sometimes producing horizontal stripes that may range through the full dye potential or may be limited to one or two colours. Twined bags may also be over-painted after completion. Occasionally newly created patterns in ochre clays repeat figurative designs found on similar pandanus bags early this century. Other painted patterns are simple geometric motifs. Some of the most beautiful painted dilly bags are housed now in the Museum of Victoria and in the Australian Museum, Sydney.

The most elaborately decorated dilly bags have feathers over the entire surface and appendages of spun string and feather tassels. These dilly bags are used at initiation ceremonies. They are spectacular in colour and design; the bag body is usually covered with regular patterns of orange and white parakeet feathers, arranged according to symbolic significance, and with tassels of white, orange and sometimes blue, green and black feathers. It is uncommon for such bags to be sold or to leave the possession of the family concerned.

At Aurukun, women twine two varieties of bag, a large straight-sided bag with two short handles carried on the shoulder, and a simple, conical grass bag somewhat more open than the cylindrical dilly bags from Arnhem Land. They are made with grasses gathered from the swampy low-lying areas and made when the grasses are green, before they dry out. Occasionally the discarded hard outer strips of the cabbage fan palm may be used as the warp, with grasses or hand-spun string as the weft strands. At Weipa, north of Aurukun on the western coast of Cape York, the women make similar netted bags, as well as a grass basket *wamgan* from slightly different reeds found in swampy areas. A distinguishing feature of the *wamgan* is the technique of attaching the string handles to the body of the bag using a rolled strip of ti-tree as reinforcement. This small piece of ti-tree is known as *thiig*.

Twined pandanus and grasses have many uses. They have always been made into sieves for straining foods. Many examples are still found in Arnhem Land, where the fruits of the unique cycad palm, normally poisonous, are soaked for days in specially constructed bags. The technique of twining pandanus was also used to make large ceremonial conical shades termed *ngainmira*, traditionally used to shelter young girls when they menstruate for the first time. At this time, the girls are separated from their brothers and male kin and take their place as adult females. The conical mat also has mythological significance.

A modern development of the *ngainmira* is the large pandanus mat that is beautifully woven in the same manner as the dilly bag. The circular form has been developed in more recent times as the cone-shaped mat of the past has had little appeal in the arts and crafts market. Local art advisers have encouraged a wide range of patterns, styles and colours, and they are now found in galleries and museums throughout the world. The large format has given Aboriginal weavers the opportunity to explore the whole range of their colour knowledge and technical expertise.

The mats may be tightly twined or woven with sections of bare warp in lace patterns similar to those of the dilly bags. The warp is generally left uncut as a long, uneven natural fringe around the mat.

Around the Tully, Cardwell and Cairns districts of Queensland, an open weave twined bicornual basket was made of stiff reeds, including lawyer cane. Such baskets are so named because of their upturned 'horn' at two corners of the base. Many were decorated with ochre designs.

Detail of twining and open weave pattern on a pandanus dilly bag from Elcho Island.

Details of decorative effects achieved using twined pandanus and natural dyes.

Opposite At Yathalamara outstation in central Arnhem Land, Ginjimirr and her co-wives earn income for the family by making twined mats and dilly bags.

Coiled baskets

Unlike the other techniques described, coiling is mainly a sewing process. Bunches of fibre strands are combined to form the foundation. The foundation, which is constituted as the basket progresses and is constantly being added to, forms a continuous spiral from the centre of the base to the rim. In Australian coiled baskets, the stitching or binder generally incorporates only one layer of the foundation at a time. Some baskets, however, have additional patterns created by floating the binder across two rows of the foundation.

Traditional coiled baskets were originally confined to eastern Australia and South Australia, with only a few examples in Queensland. Today, the coiling technique is found only in the Northern Territory and in Aurukun where, in both cases, it is thought to have been introduced within the last fifty years. It is fascinating to see the extent to which the modern baskets echo the beautiful baskets once made along the rivers and lakes of southern Australia.

In Victoria and South Australia, various coiled bags were made and coiling was also used for large mats worn by women to support and protect a baby being carried on the back. Flat, short-handled baskets consisting of two discs joined by rows of coiled foundation were once common in South Australia.

The southern weaving tradition continued until very recently in the Aboriginal community at Point McLeay on the edge of the Coorong, South Australia. Skills are still remembered but the impetus and incentive to continue making the baskets have gone. In Arnhem Land, contemporary baskets are made from split pandanus leaves, frequently dyed in bright colours. Purple, pink, ochre, chrome yellow and brown are all obtained from natural sources. Bunches of pandanus form the foundation, which is stitched together with a pandanus binder. Handles are either sewn onto the baskets or incorporated into the last three rows of the foundation. Occasionally, small handbag-like bags are produced in which the container is made by upending two coiled discs and binding them together, very like South Australian and Victorian examples.

At Aurukun, Gowanka Golpendun, now a woman in her sixties or seventies, has recalled her first lessons in mat making during her schooldays in a mission dormitory with other girls of her own age. 'Lydia Motlup learned it to me. She was sent from Mobiae, Thursday Island, to here for tempting a white man. Then she showed me how to make big mats from coconut leaves. After I learned that then I got the idea when I went to Cloncurry hospital. I learned myself to make the pandanus mats and bowls. Mrs MacKenzie and Mr and Mrs Owen bought them. Then I taught the girls.' The modern Aurukun pandanus weave is of the coiled style, but floated binders in decorative patterns are superimposed. Some pieces remind one of the southern style of weaving.

Perhaps in the long run the impact of individual pieces is less apparent than the patience, industry and skill that have been part of the Aboriginal presence in Australia for so many centuries. By surveying the baskets and weaving from the past to the present we can participate in the gentle, peaceful manipulation that not only produced beautiful objects, but also served the needs of the family and community, and continues to do so.

Top Old coiled cockle basket or *lokkori* from the Coorong area, South Australia. *Collection The Australian Museum*

Bottom Unique coiled basket of upended discs, joined and connected to a wide neck, made last century at Framlingham Aboriginal settlement, Warrnambool, Victoria and acquired in 1900. *Collection The Australian Museum*

Opposite Detail of a modern pandanus table mat from Aurukun.

Groups of fibres are bunched to form the foundation when making pandanus baskets, and
the basket continues as a spiral form.

Above Coiled pandanus basket from Maningrida.

Below Detail of handle attachment.

Rock Engraving

The most prolific, widely distributed and lasting works of art by Aboriginal artists are the numerous engravings on rock surfaces. These form the most ancient art of the Australian continent. Rock engravings were made if suitable rock surfaces were available and if engraving on rock was a facet of the ritual life of the people of the area. Engravings are found in most areas, except for Victoria and central New South Wales east of the Darling River, where instead the people made images in earth for *bora* ceremonies. There is also little evidence of their existence in the south-west of Western Australia. In the far north of the continent, magnificent painting galleries predominate, and, apart from grinding grooves, few rock engravings have been found. Further south are major galleries of engravings extending from Port Hedland to the Warburton Ranges and the ranges of central Australia. Galleries occur in the Flinders Ranges, South Australia and into western New South Wales, with many examples at Mootwingie and Sturt's Meadows. The engravings continue north into Queensland where many are found in the Carnarvon Ranges and others are near Brisbane and at Laura. On the Sydney coast the distinctive sandstone engravings are concentrated in and around the Ku-ring-gai National Park and along the Hawkesbury River.

Aboriginal artists invariably had some intention in mind when they engraved thousands of patterns, animals, tracks and figures on rock surfaces. We can now only guess at the purpose of many rock engravings, inferring their meaning and function through their association with contemporary ceremonial practice and symbolic art as well as through similarity of subject matter when compared to more recent paintings interpreted by Aboriginals themselves.

Although the word 'engraving' has overtones of cutting into metal, it is the most useful term to describe the range of methods used to cut into rock faces. Many techniques have been used; sometimes lines have been scratched through the surface of the rock. Other designs are pecked, rubbed or abraded. Apart from some executed after contact with Europeans, all the rock engravings were made by abrading, pounding or cutting the surface of one stone with a harder stone. The simplest marks are scratched or abraded grooves that vary in length and depth. These may be scattered over a surface, but they occasionally appear as sets of parallel or organised strokes. Some may simply be evidence that men ground their stone axe heads on particularly important rocks.

Opposite Ancient engravings cover the rock surfaces at Ewaninga south of Alice Springs. The designs are non-representational symbolic outlines similar to those found in many other sites throughout the arid interior of Australia.

Abraded grooves formed by grinding stone axes, Macquarie River, Dubbo, New South Wales.

The analysis of rock engravings by contemporary prehistorians can frequently offer no interpretations. On the other hand, some Aboriginal observers take into account not only the designs but their whole physical presence – the way in which they are grouped, and, most importantly, the natural features nearby. Because the engravings concerned hunting magic or an ancestor spirit and because all these aspects of life throughout Australia directly related to geological formations, the living embodiments of ancestral beings, all engravings must be seen in relation to their environment and religious significance. The special quality of the sites chosen by Aboriginal rock artists can best be felt at dusk when, with the low shadows of the falling sun, the engravings stand out on rock platforms, revealing hidden tracks, new signs and symbols, tantalising messages we cannot decode.

One of the problems of interpreting rock art sites is knowing what to include as part of the scheme. Scholars educated in a European tradition tend to take into account only those things that have been modified by human intervention. All the symbols have to be made on a background; however, in the past, interpretation has not included unmodified features of the environment. For Aboriginal artists such features may have great importance. Moreover, many of those unmodified features may be transient in nature, the site being used in a ritual context only at certain times of the year. Most recordings and photographs of rock engravings have concentrated on the images themselves, frequently isolating individual motifs and ignoring the combined formations that might occur over 800 metres.

For instance, photographs may include close-ups of the images while ignoring a deep, water-filled natural hole in the surface of the rock a short distance away, perhaps a sacred water pool once used in ceremony or containing life essence. Such rock holes are frequently associated with large ancestor figure engravings in the Hawkesbury River area of New South Wales. Occasionally seen between the legs of an outstretched figure, they clearly had immense significance to the artist and should, therefore, be included in the observer's perception. One Aboriginal man has said that engraved grooves at Delamere station in the Northern Territory were made to cause rain to fall. For this man, the important features were not only the abraded grooves in the rock, but the whole rock formation, which he said was 'Old Man Rain himself, or Gunbalano'. When his body was cut Gunbalano bled, thus causing rain to fall. The importance of cutting the skin in ritual, whether to obtain blood or to form scars, is widespread and therefore the rock grooves at Delamere are the physical remains of a ritual act.

Other similar grooves, about which we know little, are found on vertical rocks in relatively inaccessible places, the best known and most ancient of these being the markings in Koonalda cave. On some parts of the limestone the parallel marks were probably made by drawing the fingers across the soft surface, whereas in others a stone tool was used to cut through the harder surface.

Many engravings concern hunting or food supply – hunters with spears and kangaroos are frequently found. The designs change near the coast where sea creatures, fish, whales or turtles appear, perhaps occurring side

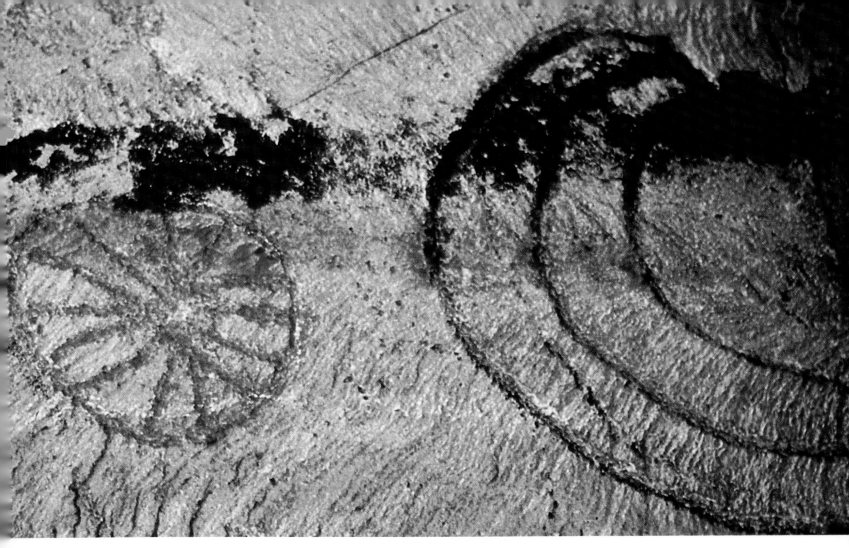

Outline engravings at Dajarra, near Duchess, Queensland.

by side with wallabies, emus or echidnas. Sometimes a hunter has prepared for the hunt by carving tracks or the image of the animal while singing songs to draw the animal to him. These engravings fulfilled the same function as 'hunting magic' paintings. More often, the engravings were intended to increase totemic species or to record great feats by ancestral beings, marking places where they changed form or merged into the rock. At sites of importance it is common to find places where the rock has been repeatedly struck or pounded close to engraved images, or where objects have been rubbed against the rock. At some sacred rock art sites in central Australia men still rub their sacred ochred boards against the rock, so releasing the essence of the totemic beings at rest there. The engravings also illustrated ceremonial life, portraying characters from oral history in human form. Human ancestor figures appear, particularly in Western Australia and the Hawkesbury River area of New South Wales, in the west as pecked intaglios and in the Hawkesbury area as deeply scored linear outlines, some six metres long.

Apart from abrading grooves, the techniques used to engrave rock included cutting or gashing an outline in the rock with a sharp stone, making an outline by pounding or pecking the rock with another, thereby removing some of the surface patina and making holes and pits by rotating stone or wooden implements in one place on a rock surface.

On coarse-textured igneous rocks, images were made by pecking or pounding a shallow layer of the surface away, a technique seen in the engravings of Dampier and Depuch Islands in the north-west of the continent. Sharper tools were needed to make deeper lines found in other areas, and it is probably that flints, which were widely traded and commonly used for cutting and affixing to weapons, were also used as sculptors' tools. Images made in this way are much more precise than the pounded designs. They might also have been produced by using a sharp pointed stone placed in position and then hit with a hammer stone; this gave a great deal of control over the line.

Over page Pecked engravings of two figures wearing rayed headdresses from N'Dhala Gorge, central Australia.

137

STYLES OF ROCK ENGRAVING

In the first attempts to organise his extensive surveys and descriptions of rock engravings, former curator of Anthropology at the Australian Museum F. D. McCarthy[1] postulated several phases in rock engraving, correlating them with possible changes in culture and art over time. He suggested that the earliest markings were abraded grooves that were scattered singly over rock faces or arranged in some meaningful form and associated with bird tracks. The second or 'outline' phase included simple representational motifs such as tortoises, circles and fish. In this category are the Hawkesbury area sandstone engravings and those in Port Hedland, Western Australia. The grooves are relatively deep and the interiors of the forms are not worked. The third phase McCarthy postulated was formal, conventionalised and symbolic. Linear and geometric designs are most commonly found, including parallel or sinuous lines, arcs, mazes and barbed lines.

The fourth phase is representational art which includes the pecked intaglios of Depuch Island. The inner surfaces of these figures have been removed; they are solid forms rather than linear grooves. They are found in the Flinders Ranges, western New South Wales and in Western Australia and they may depict mythical characters, figures engaged in rituals and men wearing elaborate headdresses.

Non-figurative engravings

More recently, archaeologists have taken a closer look at the evidence of rock art; L. Maynard[2] has proposed a style sequence that differs substantially from McCarthy's and attempts to organise both rock engravings and paintings into three styles. The first and earliest she termed Panaramitee after a site in South Australia that showed consistent characteristics. This art is essentially geometric and non-figurative, lacking human or animal shapes, although the most common features are tracks of macropods and birds as well as numerous circles. This art style is widespread, and includes many engraving sites in the central desert, South Australia, western New South Wales and a scattering in widely separate areas of Queensland.

Like many contemporary paintings, central Australian engravings are wholly non-figurative. The style is consistent, using a relatively narrow range of techniques, forms and motifs. The central desert sites are the 'classic' Panaramitee sites, though the style is very widely distributed and can exist at a site in combination with other styles. In the centre, the Panaramitee sites include N'Dhala Gorge, Ooraminna and Eucolo and the Cleland Hills; in South Australia there are many apart from Panaramitee itself. In Queensland, this non-figurative style is found in the Laura region beneath layers of paintings and also at Malbon, Danarra and other sites. In New South Wales it is found at Tibooburra and Narrabri; in Tasmania it is represented at Mt Cameron West.

The relationship in style of the Mt Cameron West, South Australian and central Australian engravings suggests that the Tasmanian examples are not recent. It is argued that the Tasmanians were migrants across the Bass Strait land bridge from South Australia, flooded 12,000 years ago, and so the cultural tradition that gave rise to the Mt Cameron West gallery was

Spiral engraving at Dajarra, Queensland.

Opposite Rock engravings at Katatjuta, the Olgas, central Australia.

141

Frieze of ancient engravings near Laura, Queensland.

severed then. The Mt Cameron West art is not necessarily the oldest in Tasmania; two other sites are just as significant and they may be older. The same range of style and subject is seen at both Sundown Point and Green's Creek. However, neither side can be accurately dated. Mt Cameron West engravings therefore stand as a benchmark for Tasmanian traditional art.

The second grouping Maynard postulated was the simple figurative, exemplified by the Sydney-Hawkesbury engravings. This coincided with a phase postulated by McCarthy. The third phase suggested was the complex figurative, including the Kurangara engravings of the upper Yule in the Pilbara region of Western Australia. Maynard also included paintings of western Arnhem Land. She included paintings and engravings in her style analysis as she considered that the two art forms should not be separated on the basis of technique.

Some of the most interesting findings have emerged from studies listing the numbers of times that certain marks or patterns have appeared at different locations. At Cleland Hills in South Australia, the most commonly published image is the now famous 'smiling face'. When discovered by Edwards,[3] these were hailed as most extraordinary; no other faces etched so clearly had been found. However, descriptions of the site indicate that there were only a handful of faces; fifty per cent of the designs were kangaroo and emu tracks and twenty per cent were circles. Yet the site is known only for its faces.

We tend to look primarily for images that we recognise and that relate to our own perceptions of the world, perhaps ignoring the importance of other evidence relating to another world view. The existence of so many tracks, circles and other marks at most of the rock engraving sites highlights an aspect of Aboriginal perception that differs from that of Europeans. Because it was so necessary for hunters to understand and relate to the tracks and marks left by every living creature, the engravings frequently showed the 'marks' made by people and animals, rather than presenting representational images of their forms. Examples are the obvious foot tracks, tail marks of the kangaroo, egg indentations to indicate a clutch of emu eggs, arcs and circles to denote seated people and a campfire.

In many cases, accurate interpretation relies on understanding Aboriginal ways of perception. Europeans are likely simply to look at an emu, admire its form and feathers, and watch or photograph it. To Aboriginal artists who hunted the bird for food or gathered its eggs from nests, tracks would always be present as a mental image sought on the ground when hunting. Straight lines engraved beside a cluster of circles indicated a bird seated on the eggs, the straight lines denoting the legs.

However, where there is no information about ceremonial life, interpretation of many other shapes is impossible. One image frequently seen in north-western Australia has been described as a 'rake' and as a 'pubic apron', referring to the hand spun hair tassels worn around the waist. Similarly, the headdresses on engraved figures are often elaborate; we can assume they illustrate ceremonial body decorations, but, without any firm knowledge, this remains conjectural. Irregularly shaped emblems are found in sacred ceremonies all over Australia and it is likely that some shapes that seem to be abstract forms relate to these. Some can be termed 'barbed spear' or 'ceremonial headdress'. The challenge to unravel symbolism is always present in non-figurative engravings, but examples show the difficulties involved. Where the art sites hold contemporary significance for Aboriginal people, the code can be broken, but only if the custodians want to provide that information. Very few engravings have been interpreted.

THE SYDNEY-HAWKESBURY AREA

The massive body of engravings found in the Sydney region and along the Hawkesbury River was first noted in 1788 by Governor Phillip, who wrote:

> In all these excursions . . . in the neighbourhood of Botany Bay and Port Jackson, the figures of animals, of shields, and weapons, and even of men, have been carved upon the rocks, roughly indeed, but sufficiently well to ascertain very fully what was the object intended. Fish were often represented, and in one place the form of a large lizard was sketched out with tolerable accuracy. On the top of one of the hills, the figure of a man in the attitude usually assumed by them when they begin to dance, was executed in a still superior style.[4]

Most of the readily found sites have been documented, and these number 600 groupings and over 4000 individual figures, the largest unified body of art so far established. The engravings are found on their own as solitary images, or in groups of over 120 images. Generally they are naturalistic engravings consisting of both deeply and shallowly etched outlines and some interior detail. Simplified silhouettes of human figures, animals, fish, birds, snakes and lizards are found, as well as numerous unidentifiable shapes and symbols.

Very little information about the meaning of these engravings has been gleaned from Aboriginals. However, in the 1840s an elderly woman named Gooseberry, a wife of Bungaree of Broken Bay, spoke of the engravings. She said they were done 'a long time ago' by the *karajis*, the clever men with knowledge of magic, and that only these and initiated men could go to the sites. In the 1930s Professor Elkin reported an interpretation of engravings north of Wollombi from a *karaji* living at Port Stephens; this man also said the engravings had religious meaning. It is therefore likely that at least the sites where large ancestor figures appear in combination with other neatly laid out sequences of engravings and tracks were related to the *bora* ceremonies, those concerned with the initiation of young men at which the voice of Dhurramulan, the son of Baiame, was heard in the whirring bullroarer.

Figures that may be Baiame or Dhurramulan occur at many sites, often with the bodies shown in frontal view but with heads turned to the side and wearing headdresses. Occasionally one large figure appears with a smaller anthropomorphic companion, and occasionally the large figure has a female companion. These are undoubtedly important religious sites. Although evidence is lacking, some conjectures seem possible, judging by descriptions of *bora* ceremonies at other places where designs were made in the soft ground. One site at Devil's Rock, Maroota, contains a series of engravings that lead one to conclude that it was a ceremonial site.[5] Two huge hero images straddle the sides of the rock outcrop, nine metres apart and linked by a line of basin-like pits. This was obviously a sacred

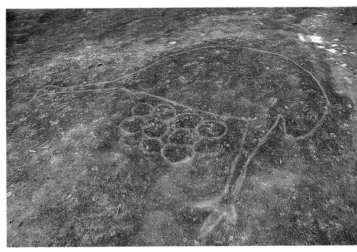

Top Engraving of a speared kangaroo and a sailing ship at Devil's Rock, Maroota, New South Wales.

Bottom An emu guarding a clutch of eggs. Devil's Rock, Maroota, New South Wales.

track between the ancestral heroes. Another significant image is a snake which has a deep and wide rubbed groove. The surprising image of a sailing ship is carved over a large kangaroo hit by weapons; was the sorcerer-artist seeking the same fate for the ship as befell the kangaroo?

At another sandstone site in the Ku-ring-gai Chase area, the giant figure of a whale forms the central image. Numerous other smaller engravings appear to radiate from it towards rock crevices and other natural features. When a bushfire cleared the outcrop of scrub and vegetation in 1980, two piles of boulders were noticed at one end of the site. These might have been 'offstage' shelters for ceremonial leaders; similar shelters are still made from bushes for central Australian ceremonies. The ridge on which the giant whale appears is a solitary and eerie place at dusk, for it juts into a valley and points straight out to sea. The ridge itself could even be seen to resemble the body of a whale. Some coastal peoples feasted upon beached whales and one engraving may represent such a feast. Whales were important ancestor figures on the north coast of New South Wales.

A story from the Gullibul tribe[6] relates that the whale and all the other animals in Australia once lived a long way from the continent. The whale had a canoe in which he planned to set off across the sea. The starfish distracted him by lulling him into a trance, picking off lice from his head while all the other animals stole the canoe and set off in it. The whale and the starfish fought, leaving the starfish in tatters on the sea bed and the whale with a hole in his head. The whale pursued the canoe through the ocean, spouting water through the hole in his head. The canoe finally came to rest at Lake Illawarra, forming an island; the animals populated Australia, and the whale still cruises the coast. The creatures in the canoe were the first ancestors of the present people.

The engravings of the Sydney-Hawkesbury region also include a wide range of hunting compositions illustrating the spearing of kangaroos and fish and the use of boomerangs as weapons. Dotted throughout the valleys from Berowra to the Colo River are many isolated figures, including paintings of stencilled hands.

The task of protecting this art heritage is immense and in the long term is almost impossible. Although a large proportion of important sites are within park boundaries and cared for by rangers, and although it is illegal to deface or damage art works, the remoteness of sites outside parks and reserves does not allow any control. It is too easy for trail bike riders or holidaymakers to find a site and yield to the impulse of leaving their own mark on history. One magnificent large ancestor hero on Wheelbarrow Ridge Road is defaced with the wheel marks of motor bikes and many others have initials carved into the rock surface.

Opposite A six-metre-long ancestor figure, Devil's Rock, Maroota, New South Wales. Two such figures straddle the sides of a rock platform and between them is another series of engravings, including rows of pits, seven kangaroos, a snake and an emu with eggs. The larger figure may be Dhurramulan or Baiame.

Simple outline engraving of an emu, Dampier, Western Australia.

NORTH-WEST AUSTRALIA

Throughout north-western Australia, extensive galleries of engravings have been made on varying surfaces, probably at different times. Most of those so far documented occur in the region between the Ashburton River, the great Sandy Desert to the north and the Gibson Desert on the eastern side.

The engravings are of two varieties. Some are of the simple figurative style showing outlines of birds, animals and figures; others are fully pecked intaglios. At Port Hedland, coastal limestone ridges provide galleries for engravings that largely reflect the people's relationship with the sea. Over 15,000 figures appear on twelve kilometres of ridges. Fish predominate and there are also turtles, dolphins or porpoises and whales, as well as human figures, boomerangs and sacred boards.

Some delightful fully pecked figures have been interpreted as Minjiburu, mythological people of local tradition. Pecked human tracks lead to them and they were probably the focus for ritual. There are both pecked outlines and pecked intaglios. The former frequently have decorative markings on the interior of their forms, including designs on engraved boards and boomerangs.

Depuch Island, less than 100 kilometres away, is a particularly interesting region with areas of diorite and dolerite boulders. Most engravings there are figurative, consisting of fully pecked intaglios in which the entire inner surface of the figures has been removed by repeatedly pecking away the crust of the rock. The dark rock surfaces thus form a background that allows the pecked inner surface of the rock to stand out strongly and for the designs to be much more easily discerned than are outline engravings. The Depuch Island engravings are miniatures, whereas Port Hedland figures are of life-sized proportions. Pecked intaglios are found there but the majority are outline engravings. Depuch Island subjects include many small human figures, often in groups showing hunting, fishing or fighting. Compared to the Sydney-Hawkesbury engravings, many distinct features are shown, enabling the species of fish or animal to be clearly identifiable.

Along the Yule River catchment area, large granite domes and boulders predominate; at one site, appropriately termed Gallery Hill, they form an immense pyramid-shaped heap. Appearing as they do over the surfaces of hundreds of rocks, the engravings form one large gallery of animated art. Some figures are anthropomorphic, others have only human characteristics. There are several kinds of engraving, some superimposed on others. Generally, the human figures deserve immediate interest as they give full range to the creative imagination of the artists. The form is sophisticated, showing flowing movement. Human bodies are given unusual heads, including that of the kangaroo. In expressing the unity of man and animal species in this way, the engravings echo the elaborate Mimi paintings of Arnhem Land.

Headdresses depicted have many shapes, possibly representing the *waninga* sacred string constructions carried on the shoulders and heads of performers during ceremonial dancing. Others show heads with antenna-like projections, including men's hair bound into elaborate and lengthy chignons, packed with ochre and often covered with bird or plant down. These engravings also exhibit exaggerated genitals and were probably associated with ceremonial life. The figures were called *kurangara* or *gurangara* by Father E. A. Worms,[7] who first discovered them at Gallery Hill in 1952. He gave the local explanation that the female figures showed Gurangara, whose consort was Djanka, an ancestral hero. These ancestors were the most important in a sacred ritual similar to the *kunapipi* of Arnhem Land, which spread westwards to the coast of Western Australia, and which is associated with the seasons, procreation and the fertility of the land.

QUEENSLAND

Queensland is a vast state in which the rock art of Aboriginal artists has only recently begun to be systematically recorded. Although the engravings occurred almost wherever there was suitable stone, detailed studies have been made only of the Mt Isa area, the central area around Carnarvon Gorge and the Laura region (south-east Cape York).

The Mt Isa area has distinctive engravings. Non-figurative elements are predominant, including circles, spirals, spoked wheels, dots, arcs and tracks. In places red ochre has been painted on to fill the inner surfaces of circles and other motifs, indicating possible use in ritual. Some figurative art is present, notably at Deighton Pass, which has a figure in a large headdress, and some facial images on boulders at Carbine Creek. These faces appear ancient with weathered and patinated surfaces and the similarity between them and the engravings at Cleland Hills has been noted by scholars. The vast distances between the two places where such faces have been found makes this connection all the more remarkable. At Carbine Creek, many surfaces can be seen with engravings extending up the slopes. The presence of a four-metre-deep rock hole in the bed of the creek suggests the importance of the site to Aboriginal people, either as a ritual centre or as a source of water supply.

Apart from a few figures and the 'Cleland faces', most of the engravings here are non-figurative. This site also contains more engravings filled in with red ochre than does any other site in Australia. Ochred motifs include split circles, bird tracks, concentric arcs and spirals. The figures that do appear at Mt Isa are simple in design. Humans are shown from the front, reptiles from above and animals in profile. Anatomical detail is minimal, although many figures can be identified as male. Headdresses are common and include radiating lines, 'branches' and grids, and the figures may vary from ten centimetres to full size. All the figures have been filled in. At Deighton Pass the main panel of engravings occurs on vertical sections of a slate outcrop. The majority are lightly pecked through a steel grey surface patina, with several showing traces of red ochre. The main figure of a pecked human figure wearing a particularly elaborate headdress and with an exaggerated penis has also been filled in with red ochre.

At Carnarvon Gorge in central Queensland, a most distinctive series of engravings exists that has been termed cup and ring designs or vulvas. These are abraded grooves and include simple pits enclosed by circles as well as other apparently more explicit carvings. Many are covered by stencilled paintings, thought to be the oldest art in the area.

Engraving on a boulder at Carbine Creek, near Deighton Pass, Queensland. The face closely resembles those found at Cleland Hills.

Engravings were discovered in the Laura region beneath layers of paintings. These occur in many of the painting shelters as well as on their own. Percy Trezise[8] who, over many years, explored and discovered the vast galleries of rock art in the area, has said that two styles of engraving, geometric and representational, are present in the area. He says that the protected rock shelters frequently housed geometric forms, while the possibly more recent naturalistic human figures, handprints and tracks are almost all on exposed areas such as the bed of the Laura River.

Along the Hann River the engravings depict boomerangs, fish and identifiable figures, and Trezise is confident that the geometric patterns are the older form of art, possibly made by tribes displaced when others took over their territory, thousands of years ago. An excavation of the early man shelter showed that a panel of non-figurative pecked engravings could be dated to a minimum of 13,000 years old, placing them in the Pleistocene era. The area, then, with its range of rock art may be unique in Australia, showing the earliest art style of non-figurative engravings as well as beautiful paintings of unknown antiquity in many layers.

Above Human figure wearing an elaborate headdress, Deighton Pass, Queensland. The engraving is lightly pecked and shows traces of red ochre.

Opposite Frieze of cup and ring engravings together with abraded grooves at Carnarvon Gorge, Queensland. Stencilled images of hands and weapons cover the engravings.

Rock Painting

Whether in Arnhem Land, Cape York, the Kimberleys or the centre, entering a gallery of rock paintings is an awe-inspiring experience. Walls are covered in layer upon layer of designs and at first the effect is chaotic, a mass of colour, texture and shapes. Perhaps a few images stand out: a barramundi here, a human figure there. Then the eye begins a process of adaptation and recognition and hundreds of animals, tracks and figures emerge from the faded outlines, filling the cave with imagery and the presence of the people who painted these works over thousands of years. Sometimes they chose the ceiling of a rock shelter and at some magnificent sites the paintings float above the viewer, taking the eye on a voyage across the cave ceiling and out into the wide valley below. Superlatives seem unnecessary. The paintings speak on behalf of their creators; for them they were the visual language of centuries of tradition and belief. Then, as the daylight changes, the interplay of images is altered; early morning light brings the colours alive in a warm yellow glow. At midday the art is flatter. Fewer shapes are clearly discernible, the recent bright paintings overshadowing the old faded red ones beneath them. At the end of the day the older paintings, perhaps ancient Mimi spirit figures, reappear, their linear, athletic red bodies showing clearly against wall surfaces blackened by the smoke of many campfires. It is difficult to convey the impact of these great art works. Their presence is sometimes intangible as the natural environment and light play a major role in the effect they create.

To Aboriginals, sites chosen for rock art galleries and for individual paintings on rock are always important in their own right, whether as camping places or, more commonly, as places of mythological significance to the artists. The natural geological formation, therefore, is fundamental to the works of art as whole entities. Although we can examine and appreciate single figures, marvel at the dexterity in execution of some of the more elegant Mimis and appreciate the use of colour and naturalistic positioning of animals such as kangaroos, brolgas and snakes, we can experience much more *in situ* than on the printed page or even in film. The artists have expressed their entire totemic and religious beliefs on these caves over many generations. Some paintings are so old that they do not relate to the living memory of any Aboriginal group, and thus are often claimed to be the work of spirits. But they are there for us to see and to appreciate. The paintings in Kakadu National Park are of such international significance that the area has been declared a World Heritage site by UNESCO, and the Australian government has agreed to protect them from destruction.

Opposite Red ochre painting of a woman, superimposed over other images at Mushroom Rock, Laura, Queensland.

Over page The magnificent frieze of barramundi on the ceiling of Obiri Rock, Kakadu National Park, Northern Territory.

Obiri Rock, Kakadu National Park, Northern Territory.

Here is a contemporary dilemma. If the magnificent heritage of Australian Aboriginal rock painting is extolled and if the necessity for viewing them *in situ* is stressed, many more visitors will go to the remote areas where they are. The paintings are, however, extremely vulnerable, not only to natural ageing and fading, to insect attack, to animal damage and to water and wind erosion, but also to vandalism by visitors. Despite educational programs designed to make people aware that Aboriginal art and culture are part of the Australian heritage of which we should be immensely proud, vandalism remains a significant problem, not just in Australia, but also at cultural sites throughout the world where tourists or holidaymakers are permitted unsupervised access. Most government bodies concerned with the protection of these galleries have therefore devised controls on visitors and have consciously chosen to open only a few galleries where an Aboriginal ranger can be in attendance.

Rock paintings were made for different reasons, depending on the nature of the site. Once every significant feature in Australia had a specific Aboriginal name, including the rocks on which paintings were made. This terminology has been recorded only in the areas where traditional people have retained their language and their traditional associations. In western Arnhem Land, for example, each site belonged to a particular group which had the responsibility of safeguarding it, retouching important paintings and conducting ceremonies. Many paintings had religious significance; they were the painted images of ancestral heroes who 'put themselves on rock' at some time during the creation era, where they are resting still. Traditional names reflected the mythological or economic importance of each site and related to the paintings at art sites. The image of Namarrkon, the lightning spirit, is painted in a cave that bears his name. Similarly, the painting of a snake appears at a site near Oenpelli regarded as the home of the snake itself. At this site procreation ceremonies were carried out to ensure a plentiful supply of snakes for food.

Many of these paintings have survived to be part of the living culture of Aboriginal people. This has necessitated frequent retouching, as probably happened throughout the continent. Aboriginal elders from as far apart as the Kimberleys, the Alligator River region and central Australia have all affirmed that it was the duty of certain people to refurbish the sacred paintings and to make the spirits 'fresh'. In so doing the artists restored the powerful presence of the ancestor at the site, they pleased him and encouraged him to fulfil his duty, to ensure a plentiful supply of food and animals or to bring rain. Most writers have clearly stated that it was the act of painting itself which was important, not the finished product. But the painted images of spirits are real and powerful, and, to judge from recorded comments made by older men visiting them, the freshness of paint and the strength of facial expression are important.

One sacred site is known as Dadbe, the name of the Rainbow Snake. When a survey team asked two men to accompany them to the place, there was much hesitation: this was the home of the Rainbow Snake and it had not been visited because it lay outside their country. They agreed to help in the survey, but would only go to some areas, not others. When the paintings were reached, the men were fearful and perspiring heavily.

The walls held beautiful images of x-ray fish, human figures and a crocodile. One image stood out, that of a doubled-up snake with a kangaroo head. One of the men refused to enter the area; the other addressed the paintings, calling out, 'I am speaking, I am talking to you, my ancestor, I have asked them. I am seeing the paintings. They are waiting for me. Maybe you are dead. I have grown up.'[1] He was possibly worried about seeking permission to come to the area and afraid the ancestral snake would not recognise him. He was quite definite that the paintings had not been done by humans, but by Jingana the Rainbow. The site is close to a sacred waterhole, the permanent home of the Rainbow Snake, and it must not be visited by anyone. The mythological importance of this area has therefore continued beyond living memory.

Paintings that were not major creation ancestors served other functions. They might have been lesser spirits, evil or benign, or they might have involved aspects of magic or sorcery practices. Also, many shelters were once used as camping places, usually galleries where hunting scenes and animals predominate. However, the major sites were seldom used for domestic purposes. In 1911, the anthropologist Baldwin Spencer observed the Kakadu people walk up Inyalak hill near the billabong in the evening. The Kakadu people had their main camp at Oenpelli, but slept at night above mosquito level in the rock shelters. The Gunwinggu people gradually displaced the Kakadu; they do not paint at Inyaluk, nor do they know who did the paintings. Spencer, who obtained bark paintings from the Kakadu that are replicas of the rock paintings, was sure the Kakadu were the artists. However, Charles Mountford, who came to the area in 1948, was unsure of this, while other anthropologists have suggested that they were done by a tribe in the area before the Kakadu. It is clear that there has been a succession of different tribal groups occupying the area where the paintings occur and that the layers of paintings in different styles reflect these changes.

Since the initial discoveries, new paintings have been made by Gunwinggu artists who occupy the area. Bobby Ngainmira, a Gunwinggu bark artist resident at Oenpelli, has claimed that some small paintings on isolated parts of Inyaluk hill are his own work,[2] and other sites have been painted by Gunwinggu in the 1960s. Spencer was an early enthusiast for the art, particularly for the way in which the painted animals conveyed the poise and distinctive body movements. He wrote, 'No artist could have expressed better the relative proportions of the body and limbs, the small head, neck and forepaws, the narrow throat swelling out of the large trunk . . . the really wonderful way in which the savage artist has depicted the pose which is always assumed by the animal when alarmed, the erect position of the body, the head thrown well up and slightly back, and the two little forepaws held forward helplessly.'[3]

Domestic shelters frequently show these animals being caught or speared; the artists were practising a form of hunting magic. Before a hunt, a man might paint a kangaroo he had seen or hoped to see; he would draw it speared through and by singing or chanting would summon it to him. In this way he hoped to ensure that his spears would find their mark. The same magical purpose may be behind paintings of turtles, fish

At many sites, rocks have uncanny physical resemblances to the creation ancestors they represent and to which the paintings refer. This is Crocodile Cave on the Gibb River, Western Australia. *Photograph Jutta Malnic*

and birds, although the actual spearing may not be depicted. Others have suggested that, as Aboriginal artists once painted simple hunting scenes on the smooth inside faces of the bark walls of family shelters, they might also have simply enjoyed giving visual expression to their mental preoccupations: to the animals, birds and fish they caught and ate, to the totem animals of their clans, which were sacred, to all manner of spirits that inhabited the bush and to the creation ancestors themselves and their great Dreaming sites.

Paintings of oddly shaped human figures with animal heads, strange limbs or non-human features are frequently depictions of spirits and they are found throughout Australia. Examples in the north include the Mimi and *namarrkain* of Arnhem Land, the Quinkans of Cape York and an enormous range of other less known individual figures, such as Nabarakbia on Obiri Rock. He is depicted with a catch of fish and is said to steal the spirits of sick people and eat them. If someone was sick, the medicine man or traditional doctor would be sent to the painting to chase Nabarakbia away.

The ability to perform love magic or sorcery was an accomplishment of Aboriginal artists, and painting images on rock was frequently an adjunct to these practices. In the case of sorcery, the intention of the artist was usually to cause an accident, punishment or even the death of a victim. From the paintings it would seem that the intended victims were frequently women, either wives who had been unfaithful or others who had spurned the attentions of a would-be lover. Direct and public punishment was a form of retribution exacted by aggrieved husbands or by the wife's brothers if the woman had been hurt or humiliated. However, if this did not suffice or if the grounds for this action did not exist, sorcery could be used. It is still widely practised in traditional communities, though its rituals have always been secret. Sorcery images frequently showed white figures in supine positions with stingray barbs protruding from their bodies. Stingray barbs are poisonous and multiple stings are excruciatingly painful. Berndt described the use of sorcery paintings to force an unwilling woman to comply with a man when he wrote, 'One drawing represents a woman with a reptile's head and two babies suckling at her breasts. Semen is flowing from her vagina and stingray nails are sticking into her body from every direction. After the woman's name is called, her whole body begins to hurt and soon she dies.'[4]

In Cape York where there are many examples of sorcery painting, the figure is inverted and painted in white ochre with an odd number of limbs, perhaps one or three. In the southern areas of New South Wales the meaning of the art and intentions of the artist cannot be established as clearly. However, since the practice of sorcery was well known and since the only recorded evidence of purpose of rock engravings linked them to the 'clever' men or sorcerers, one can guess that some paintings were used in magic.

Opposite **Inverted sorcery figure, Cape York.**

Love magic is the term generally used when the intention of the artist is not directed at harming the woman. These images may show a woman and man in coitus or a woman alone in a sexually explicit position. A man may paint and 'sing' a woman to him in this way. If he wishes to keep her affections, he must maintain the painting by retouching it. Painting a woman with a foetus or breast feeding babies was another way in which suggestive magic was employed in an attempt to cause pregnancy.

TECHNIQUES OF ROCK PAINTING

The techniques used in cave paintings done early this century and observed by ethnographers have included drawing with dry pebbles, dots of pigment, using the hand to rub large areas of ochre over the rock surface, splattering paint onto the wall, stencilling a design onto the surface by blowing paint around an object (such as a weapon or a human hand) pressed against the rock surface, finger painting and the most common technique, brush painting.

Two rock artists observed by the ethnographer Brandl[5] used different methods of making the paintings. One man, Jackie Bunggarnial, made a brush from a chewed twig. He then chewed white clay and mixed this with water in his mouth, keeping it there while he painted his design. He outlined the motif first and then filled it in. The other artist, Mandarg, painted the outline of the Rainbow Snake with a broad brush and then covered the inside of the snake by spreading the pigment with his hands. He then sprayed dots onto the surface of the serpent by mixing ochre and water in his mouth.

A number of different brushes can be used to paint on rock. Strips of bark, chewed twigs and human hair are all employed, depending whether a delicate line or a large area of colour is required. Since early Australian artists first painted on rock, the passage of time has altered the original colours. Bright red ochre has altered in many areas to black or even white, and most designs, particularly of the early Bradshaw figures and Mimi figures, once painted in bright red ochre, have now darkened to deep purple or black. Most of these changes are due to chemical interaction with the rock surface. Red ochre remains the most permanent pigment of all, permeating the rock surface in many places. Other pigments, such as yellow, white or pink, are less permanent and new paintings are subject to flaking, chipping and being washed off by water or rubbed off by animals and insects. The pigments are obtained from numerous different natural sources. Black may come from charcoal or manganese, white from pipeclay, gypsum or burnt selenite. Yellow may come from yellow limonite, red from iron oxide, laterites or burnt yellow ochre.

The same basic colours — red, yellow, black and white — are used throughout the continent. Red is the most significant colour, mythologically and ritually, though in some places other colours may predominate. For example, in the Sydney-Hawkesbury area there are many white paintings and it would seem that the strong reds and yellows are less frequently available. Blue is rarely seen but is recorded in some galleries in the Kimberleys and south to Ayers Rock.[6]

Opposite **The giant Wandjina Rowalumbin painted on a rock site at Napier, north-western Australia.** *Photograph Jutta Malnic*

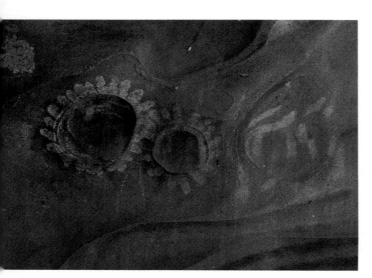

Arkaroo Rock in the Flinders Ranges of South Australia. This natural rock formation is an important site in the legend of the giant snakes of the Flinders Ranges. *Photograph Jutta Malnic*

When painting on bark, Aboriginal artists used a range of traditional fixatives, including *gurg*, a resin obtained from a bush, and wild orchid sap. The only fixative known to be used by the artists who painted on rock is human blood, most commonly mixed with red ochre or even used in place of it.

The suitability of the colours is judged by their purity and texture. White clay containing any small particles of iron oxide or sand would certainly not be considered as good as the pure white (called *delek*) found near Gudjangal, close to Maningrida.

When one looks at the range of colours in paintings on a large gallery in western Arnhem Land, it is obvious that the artists used most of the colours at their disposal. These were either available locally or were traded over long distances, and the artists might also have mixed colours. Brandl mentions that Spider Murululmi occasionally added white to red to achieve a paler shade with greater intensity of colour; Spider said he was 'making it stronger'.[7] Colours also age significantly over time, and might have once been different. When Brandl located what seemed to be some greenish paintings in the x-ray style at one site in the Deaf Adder Creek area, he found a small deposit of a green mineral called serpentine nearby. Although he had imagined that this might be the source of the paint used in the designs, upon analysis it was evident that the paintings had been charcoal and that the green discoloration was the effect of mildew on the binding agent used by the artist. Reds fade and grow dull and browns change colour over the years. These changes, plus the tendency of the artists to occasionally mix pigments, are the most obvious reasons for the range of pigments and hues that are to be found in these galleries.

STYLES OF ROCK PAINTING

Many rock paintings across the continent fit loosely into the same categories as rock engravings, although the magnificent galleries in Arnhem Land require separate and detailed analysis. Broadly, paintings throughout most of the continent fall into non-figurative (symbols and tracks), simple figurative (outlines and solid figures without embellishment or further decoration, including both humans and animals and recognisable objects) and complex figurative. In the Sydney area, for example, where there are large flat areas of rock available for engravings as well as adjacent caves in which paintings were executed, the paintings and engravings are very similar in style; the designs, scale and style of presentation closely relate to each other. It has therefore been suggested[8] that engraving and painting could have been done together.

Stencils are the simplest cave paintings and the most widely distributed. They appear to have been made throughout the continent for many centuries until recently. They were painted by holding an object against the wall so that a negative impression of its shape would remain when paint was sprayed around it. The reverse image could be obtained by dipping an object, such as a hand, into ochre, or covering the hand with ochre and pressing it against the rock surface.

Stencils are found all over Australia in association with every group of cave paintings and drawings. Hands are most commonly seen, but other parts of the body were stencilled, including whole arms and feet and, in one case, a complete body. In some areas it is common to find stencilled boomerangs and other small objects such as lizards and parts of plants.

In Queensland's Carnarvon Ranges a very diverse group of objects was stencilled, including hands, feet, axes, emu and kangaroo feet, boomerangs and other implements. Some of these were also painted using other techniques, thereby producing mixed media designs. In one cave in the Carnarvons there is a painting of an implement known as a kidney smasher. This was made of wood with a hook-like curve; the aggressor hit his victim in the kidneys with it. At Kenniff cave, a spectacular array of stencils has been found, which includes 125 red, 13 yellow, 11 white and 6 black hands, as well as 8 handprints of children. There are positive and negative stencils, and stencils of hafted axes, boomerangs and other weapons.

At another site in this area, named the Tombs, presumably because of its geological formation, a unique stencil of a complete human figure has been found. The Tombs is a cave over ten metres long, almost five metres wide, thirty to ninety centimetres high and with a sand floor thirty to sixty centimetres deep. It is in the base of a sandstone cliff. Along over 30 metres of the shelter wall stretches a frieze of ochred stencils from ground level to about 182 centimetres high. The human figure, stencilled in red ochre with outstretched arms, stands at the cave entrance; perhaps he is the guardian keeper of the sacred cave.

Stencilled hands are found extensively in galleries in the Hawkesbury region of New South Wales, in central Australia, Western Australia and Arnhem Land. In the 1960s an old man of the Kimberley area, Sam Woolagoodjah, told Ian Crawford[9] that Aboriginal people put the images of their hands on caves as a sign that they owned the territory or belonged to that place. This ownership symbol varied; it could be crooked fingers or, at Deaf Adder Gorge, the thumb and little finger had been spread but the three middle fingers were kept together to form a point.

Yirawala, one of the most significant of Gunwinggu painters, travelled back to western Arnhem Land in the early 1970s in an attempt to stop mining of his tribal lands. In a film made at the time, he spoke of a cave to which he was taken as a young man and where he was shown the hand stencils of his people. On this expedition, Yirawala found the cave in which the hand stencils had been made and those symbols convinced him that it was the cave his father had shown him.

Non-figurative paintings are found in areas closely paralleling the distribution of Panaramitee-style rock engravings. They are therefore most commonly found in the arid regions of the continent from Western Australia, through central Australia, South Australia, western New South Wales and Queensland. Designs include abstract symbols such as circles, arcs, barred lines and more complex meanders and grids. Similarities between the engravings and the paintings can be seen by comparing designs found at Trephina Gorge in the Northern Territory with those at N'Dhala Gorge.

Yalpoonaverrie rock paintings, South Australia.

Stencilled images are widely distributed throughout the continent.
Top Carnarvon Gorge, Queensland.
Centre Maroota, New South Wales.
Bottom Central Highlands, Queensland.

Opposite Laura region, Queensland.

Paintings at Maggie Springs, Ayers Rock, central Australia.

The rock paintings of New South Wales, particularly those at Cobar, fall into the simple figurative category. These generally consist of small simple human figures in white and red. These are similar in style to the vast expanse of paintings at Laura in the Cape York region. Although at first glance the Laura paintings are stunning in comparison to the New South Wales examples, the Laura ones featuring imaginative figures and compositions and layer upon layer of beautiful paintings, in execution they are essentially the same. That is, they are simple outlines filled in with one colour. They thus contrast with the more complex and elaborate polychrome paintings of Arnhem Land and the Kimberley area.

The complex figurative style is best shown in the famous x-ray paintings of Arnhem Land and the Wandjina paintings of the Kimberley area. In these, the outlines of the figures are filled in with various patterns. The older monochrome Mimi figures of Arnhem Land and the Bradshaw figures in the Kimberleys can be included in this class. These display complexity in their depiction of musculature and movement. They also portray complex headdresses, weapons and decorative apparel such as bags, armbands and belts.

CENTRAL AUSTRALIA

The art of the centre is found scattered on widely distant rock outcrops, including Ayers Rock and the Olgas and sites in the Musgrave, Mann and Tomkinson Ranges. Generally it includes a large proportion of non-figurative symbols, wandering and straight lines, animal and bird tracks. Side by side are images of human figures and of simple painted animals, including snakes and other recognisable creatures.

At Uluru, or Ayers Rock, the paintings are one aspect of the immense significance of the great desert tor for the Pitjantjatjara and related peoples. The whole complex illustrates the mythology of the Kunia, or carpet snake ancestors, the Liru, the poisonous snake ancestors and Wanambi, the great serpent. Each feature of the rock, its surrounding outcrops and the stands of trees and waterholes, are the metamorphosed remains of the battles that took place between the ancestors in the *tjugurpa* or creation era. Near the spot where people generally start climbing Uluru, the rock is pitted with round holes. These are the results of the Liru spears. In another place, the lizard ancestors were camped, eating an emu they had killed. Another group of hunters who had been chasing the emu approached and asked for some of the meat, but the lizard men refused hospitality and hid the emu away. The other hunters left but returned to set fire to the lizard men. On the rock at this campsite, the lichen is said to be the burned bodies of the lizard men. The emu's leg metamorphosed into a natural feature of the rock. At the base of the rock, below the campsite at which the lizard ancestors were killed, is a

Paintings at Emily Gap, central Australia. The design symbolises the Yipirinya caterpillar ancestors of the Aranda people.

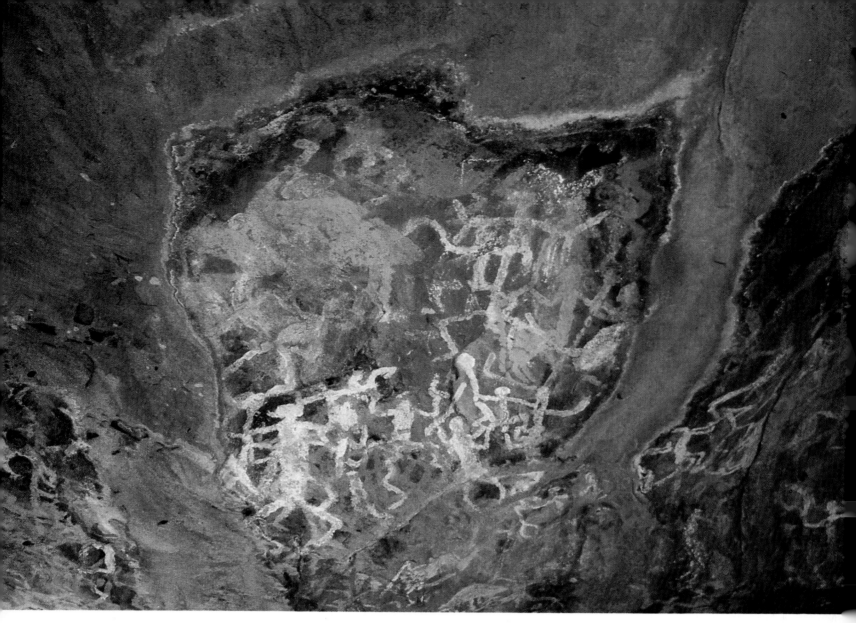

Hunting scenes with numerous small stick figures are common at sites in the central west of New South Wales, such as this one at Mt Grenfell. A large yellow emu can be clearly seen against masses of superimposed figures. *Photograph Jutta Malnic*

large sleeping lizard rock, now a site for the lizard and an important food resource. The great serpent Wanambi is related to water and now lives in the area known as Maggie Springs. If the waterhole is dry, Wanambi can be called upon to bring rain. After rain he rises into the sky as a rainbow.

The paintings at the twelve Ayers Rock sites are all related to mythology, and many of Pitjantjatjara origin are part of initiation rituals. They were used to instruct young initiates in the moral law drawn from the creation events at the rock. The paintings are in the simple figurative style, combining abstract symbols and figurative elements, including circles, concentric circles, arcs, grids and meandering patterns. They also include animal and bird tracks, snakes, dingoes and human figures. Many abstract symbols represent the ancestors in a sacred form or sacred poles, *waningas* and body designs worn or carried during initiation ceremonies. The exact age of the paintings is unknown but they are evidently deteriorating quickly. The galleries at Ayers Rock are variable in size. Most are relatively small with several very large exceptions, one being thirty metres in length with emu tracks over a metre high.

The principal mythology of Katatjuta (the Olgas) concerns the Pungalung ancestors. In the creation time the Mingarri or mice women camped at the Olgas. Pungalung, a giant man and a women chaser, was hunting in the vicinity with Mudjura his companion, the red lizard of the sandhills. The two men came into the women's camp where Pungalung made advances to them. When he found they were all virgins he raped them. Changing into dingoes, the women chased Pungalung from the camp and Pungalung used Mudjura as a shield against the women's assault. After a while, Mudjura tired of this and leapt from his back, changing into a tor. Using a heavy boomerang, Pungalung defended himself from the dingoes' attack. He knocked out their teeth, which can now be seen as the shining quartz rocks in the area. Pungalung and the Mingarri women also became tors. The paintings at the Olgas are sacred representations of the Pungalung story. Dingo tracks are common in the designs, although the precise significance of the paintings has not been revealed.

The mythology at Katatjuta and Uluru includes many minor characters. For example, at Katatjuta, Wanambi, the corkwood sisters, mice women, curlew man, kangaroo, dingoes and possums all have stories. At Uluru there is a similar list of ancestors whose activities are remembered, including hare-wallabies, dingoes, the marsupial mole, the sand lizard, the blue-tongued lizard and the snake.

SOUTH-EAST AUSTRALIA

Paintings are found in western New South Wales and in the Sydney coastal region. Those of the west occur in the Cobar pediplain, Mt Gundabooka and Mt Grenfell being major sites in low, hilly ranges. More than forty rock shelters display galleries of small stick figures from ten to forty-five centimetres in height, which have been painted in groups, all in the one colour, predominantly white or red and occasionally yellow. Many are shown holding weapons, including boomerangs and stone axes. The art of one period is superimposed over another. Apart from white human figures, mazes and tracks, emus and kangaroos can be seen.

At Gundabooka a large white maze is painted beside a small fish silhouette. The maze may represent the stone fish traps once made in river estuaries, one of which survives at Brewarrina, New South Wales. White is the most commonly used pigment on the newer paintings, whereas red ochre has survived best on those which have been superimposed. White was obtained from pipeclay in creek deposits and red was ground from ironstone in formations known locally as 'bombs'.

On the Cobar pediplain the red ochre was called *kubbur* by the Wongaibon tribe. It came from a cave that was a mythological camping place of the ancestral spirit Baiame. The site is now occupied by the town of Cobar (derived from the word *kubbur*).[10]

Many of the paintings at Mt Grenfell, Wuttagoona and other sites in the central west of New South Wales depict hunting scenes. The evidence of the paintings accords with ethnographic reports of hunting methods which were still being used in the nineteenth century. Small groups or families hunted over a restricted area of country and figures are shown in the paintings, surrounding, holding or chasing animals into nets. The main prey are kangaroos and emus, although other animals such as koalas, birds, fish, snakes and lizards, tortoises and frogs also appear. It is likely that the practice of painting such scenes was part of widespread magic to ensure successful hunting. Along the Darling River, Ngemba tribesmen chanted 'spells', and songs and other incantations were used over nets. Many of the paintings show a figure in profile sitting or standing and singing with clapsticks. This is probably the sorcerer or magician,

Painting of a kangaroo hunt at Mt Grenfell, New South Wales. Figures are grouped in lines surrounding the animals and pursuing them with boomerangs and stone axes.
Photograph Jutta Malnic

Malbon rock, in the bed of the Cloncurry river.

also known as the 'clever man' who can perform magic. Such figures are also shown touching the hunters or the nets. Further evidence of the paintings' magical qualities was the finding of quartz crystals in an archaeological excavation at a Mt Grenfell painting site. Quartz crystals were prized and only used by Aboriginal 'clever men' in magic.

In the alps straddling the New South Wales-Victoria border, similar simple figurative paintings have been found, though in smaller numbers than in the Cobar or Sydney regions. The alps were inhabited only during the warmer summer months, and it is therefore to be expected that there would have been fewer art sites. These painting sites have only recently been discovered, but they confirm the consistent occurrence of the simple figurative style in the south-east of the continent. In Victoria only a few cave art sites have been found; in style the art resembles that of New South Wales. The sites include caves of hand stencils, a bichrome painting of an ancestral being that could be Bunjil, an important spirit, and other scenes with human figures.

QUEENSLAND

The study and photographic recording of rock painting galleries in Queensland may not be complete for some years. Further discoveries are unlikely to change the primary importance of the area around Cooktown and Laura in south-east Cape York, where numerous impressive galleries rival those of western Arnhem Land in colour, imagery and impact. This region has one of the largest bodies of prehistoric rock art in the world, including paintings, stencils and engravings. Although the existence of some galleries has been known since early European travellers first reported them in the late nineteenth century, most of the sites were discovered in the last twenty years by pilot and artist Percy Trezise.[11] When flying domestic routes, Trezise would frequently fly low into the valleys to gaze along the escarpments, searching for a flash of colour that signified a painting site. Back on the ground, he followed up his sightings on foot. Later he bought his own plane and continued his quest to document all the sites of the area.

Paintings in the Laura-Cooktown area are distinct from those of other areas. Figurative motifs comprise eighty-four per cent of the images, which include colourful paintings of humans, animals, fish, birds and reptiles, intermingled with stencils of hands, feet, boomerangs and adzes that often appear to have been deliberately superimposed over particular images rather than scattered at random. The most distinctive figures are human-shaped images of spirits with various names but most frequently termed Quinkans. These wear a variety of headdresses and often have some non-human features with distortions of body, limbs, head or genitals. One important gallery is thought by Trezise to have been an initiation cave. This Quinkan gallery is probably a very old sacred cave. Large male figures are shown with rayed headdresses; other figures depict dingoes, kangaroos and emus. Most of the men have one leg raised, suggesting the dingo dance in which dancers mime lifting one leg to urinate. Aboriginal people living locally suggested to Trezise that this could have been the cave in which boys of dingo or wallaby totems were initiated. There are twelve small red hand stencils, perhaps of young boy

The most dramatic feature is the relationship of the large 'open' Quinkan cave to another in the same rock outcrop. A smaller cave nearby contains several dark red older figures of Quinkans that have no images superimposed on them. The figures stretch from the ground onto the ceiling above with their hands above their heads, staring down at the viewer. This cave has a small, low tunnel leading to it and connecting it to the other site and this probably had a significant function during ceremonies.

All the Laura-Cooktown paintings fit broadly into the simple figurative classification. Few show any body mobility and most are simple outlines filled with colour. Sorcery paintings are frequently found, and the notable giant horse gallery may well fit this category if the intentions of the artist could be gauged. Death sorcery paintings usually depict a man or woman lying down or inverted. They are often white. Known throughout Cape York as *puri-puri*, sorcery survives still.

The giant horse gallery has an extraordinary series of images that obviously post-date European settlement, or at least record the first sightings of explorers with horses. There are three shelters in which large horses appear, dwarfing and superimposing on other images. In one shelter about 18 metres long, a white and yellow horse 3.35 metres long by 1.83 metres high is shown with red reins extending forward over the head to the hand of a red horizontal image of a man who appears to have been thrown from the horse. A pig is also shown. Pigs were first released in Cape York in 1770 by Captain Cook, who hoped they would multiply to provide food for shipwrecked sailors. The pigs thrived and were incorporated into local Aboriginal legends as 'little hairy men'. Trezise suggests that the horses were painted after a man named William Hann and his party passed about three kilometres below the gallery in 1872. Mann recorded that he had 'had occasion to disperse the natives' by firing at them with rifles. The sight of the giant animal and the attack must have had a profound effect on the Aboriginal people. In another shelter, Trezise and two elderly Aboriginal men found an old, worn horseshoe, as well as a painting that the men said depicted a hafted axe with a horseshoe head. Horses were later killed and eaten by Aboriginals and their horseshoes prized for weapon manufacture.

Rock paintings in other areas of Queensland differ from the Laura examples. Around Princess Charlotte Bay approximately 120 kilometres north of Laura, the figures are mostly less than 30 centimetres long and the colours more restricted. The paintings depict coastal marine creatures: turtles, dugong, fish, sea slugs, crayfish and human figures.

South of Laura the painting becomes less figurative; around Townsville it is geometric and non-figurative. In the central highlands, notably around Carnarvon, the art consists almost exclusively of stencils and abraded or painted geometric patterns. The stencilled art of Carnarvon is most impressive, with huge caves and cliffs forming stencilled frescos up to 137 metres long.

To the west at Mt Isa, the art is predominantly engravings, but it also includes two notable painting sites that are very different in style: Malbon in the bed of the Cloncurry River and Sun Rock at Charley Creek. The Malbon rock painting is unique in Queensland; in style it resembles some

Giant horse gallery near Laura, Queensland.
Photograph Jennifer Isaacs

of the cave paintings of the central desert regions. If one walks along the usually dry Cloncurry River, the site looms as a massive quartzite outcrop with vertical sides rising twenty metres from the river bed. The main panel has a base colour of yellow pigment, onto which a red ochre design has been painted. The design is composed of thick red U shapes, parallel short strokes and other non-representational shapes that together form one complete painting. Comparison with the desert paintings such as those at Emily Gap near Alice Springs lead to the conclusion that this was probably a totemic centre and that the painting represents the symbolic journeys of spirit ancestors to this site. The most intriguing aspect of the painting is its solitary nature and the evidence that it has withstood the continual ravages of flood. Debris deposited by the river in flood can be found up to two metres above the paintings, yet the paintings are excellently preserved.

At Sun Rock the paintings are mainly red ochre figures on a rock face adjacent to water. As at Malbon, the fine ochre has penetrated into the minute cracks of the quartzite surface and a 'bonding' has developed that should permit the paintings to survive. Over thirteen human figures with elongated penises are depicted, some wearing headdresses as though for ceremony. A snakelike pattern suggests that they are associated with Rainbow Snake mythology.

Above Quinkan spirit figure from the Laura area, Queensland. *Photograph Jennifer Isaacs*

Opposite Layers of paintings extend the length of the sheltered rock face at a site named Magnificent Gallery in Cape York, Queensland. *Photograph Jutta Malnic*

Snake Cave on Gibb River, Western Australia.
Photograph Jutta Malnic

NORTH-WEST AUSTRALIA

The giant staring faces of the north-west known as the Wandjina have fascinated people interested in Aboriginal rock art for 150 years, ever since the paintings were first discovered by Sir George Grey in 1837. He commented, '. . . they appeared to stand out from the rock; and I was certainly rather surprised at the moment that I first saw this gigantic head and upper part of a body bending over and staring down at me'. Looking at a group of Wandjina figures he wrote, 'I imagine them to represent females . . . each had a very remarkable headdress coloured with a deep bright blue, and one had a necklace on . . . Each of the four faces was marked by a totally distinct expression of countenance, and although none of them had mouths, two, I thought, were otherwise good looking'.[12]

For some time, the popular view was that the Wandjina had been painted by foreign visitors to Australia, possibly shipwrecked sailors from Borneo or Indonesia. Recently, some made the exaggerated claim that they depicted visitors from outer space.

The Wandjina are actually extremely important creation ancestors of the Kimberley people, and these images on rocks represent them in places where they changed their physical form and became spirits, leaving their imprint on the rock. The Wandjina travelled across the country, creating plants, animals and the landscape. They increased spirits of babies, animals and plants and created thunder and lightning in the wet season. The mythology of the Wandjina is closely linked with that of the Rainbow Serpent and several sites include paintings of both. Associated legends tell how they met and interacted in the creation era.

If the Wandjina are angry, it is believed that they will call up lightning and strike the offender dead, or send rain to flood the land and drown the people. Aboriginal informants recount how the repositories of the spirits of children are kept by the Wandjina in waterholes, particularly freshwater pools. When a woman eats fish, turtles or crocodiles from the pool, she may simultaneously become pregnant with the child spirit.

The importance of the Wandjina to Aboriginal traditional owners is immense. They are the original ancestral spirits and their images, until very recent times, were faithfully retouched and kept fresh to ensure the continual reproduction of species and renewal of life.

The paintings are startling in impact largely because of the scale of the faces and the way in which a white background has been used. Large areas of the rock on which they appear have been filled with thick white pigment, providing a clear and stark backdrop for bright yellow, red and black ochres. Large-scale paintings of complete human figures are found, as are those showing head and shoulders only and images of faces or groups of faces by themselves. The dense white background has been painted first and the outline of the ancestral heroes delineated in red. The effect is somewhat like a halo, making the faces shimmer in the heat. The eyes and nose are joined and generally painted in black, frequently with a circle of spoke-like eyelashes, and the mouth is never painted. A range of decorative features appears around the head, including radiating headdresses. Occasionally the body is decorated with stripes and a solid black oval is sometimes painted in the middle of the chest; this obviously

Opposite **Serpent and figure, Manning Gorge, Western Australia.**

White figure from the Cannon Hill area of Kakadu National Park, Northern Territory.

had some ceremonial significance. The shape of the body and limbs, when compared to the scale of most other rock paintings, is massive. In many of the caves other images appear, including kangaroos, wallabies, echidnas, goannas, crocodiles, birds and a wide range of plants.

In the same area as the Wandjina paintings are other ancient red ochre figures known as Bradshaw figures. They have been compared to the Mimi paintings of Arnhem Land and were obviously done much earlier than the Wandjina, for the latter overlie the Bradshaw images where they appear together and some have lost clarity of outline. The elegance and form of the Bradshaw figures remain distinctive, however, and they provide tantalising glimpses of the Kimberley culture of the past. Many are faded as a result of extreme ageing.

Although contemporary Aboriginal artists retouch the great Wandjina and custodians of the various sites are responsible for maintaining their aura, they do not admit to being the original artists of these or the Bradshaw figures. All the art of the Kimberley region was thought to have been done by spirits.

WESTERN ARNHEM LAND

Western Arnhem Land houses the most magnificent galleries of all. In recognition of the extent of the art and its importance in human history, the Kakadu National Park was proclaimed a World Heritage site by UNESCO in 1981. Numerous galleries extend along the escarpment areas throughout the Alligator Rivers region and towards the Liverpool River.

The paintings are in many styles, superimposed in layers. The earlier red ochre figures have been loosely grouped together and are known as Mimi, whilst the more recent polychrome figures and animals that show internal anatomical features have been called x-ray art. These two major categories of painting differ in style, subject matter and technique.

Mimi art is the older of the two, and Aboriginal informants have indicated they believe the paintings were put on rock by the Mimi spirits themselves; they were not done by human hands. Mythology concerning the spirits is an important part of contemporary Gunwinggu belief. The Mimi are small, delicate spirits who live in the rock crevices of the escarpment area in western Arnhem Land. They are so light and fragile that it is thought a strong wind can blow them around. They are nocturnal and generally regarded as benevolent, though children are often told not to wander too far from the camp at night or the Mimi might steal them. Mimi as subject matter in paintings have continued in contemporary bark paintings by the Gunwinggu. They are thought to have taught Aboriginals how to hunt and many paintings show them with a variety of weapons. Some stories tell of how they transgress tribal laws, and their deeds are the subject of numerous cautionary tales.

Mimi figures are generally small, always painted in red ochre. They are predominantly human figures, though animals and plant forms also occur as well as elaborate hunting scenes. X-ray artists, on the other hand, used a range of colours with much more emphasis on animals and fish, as well as large figures. These feature elaborate internal decoration, including the depiction of the animals' known physical features such as the backbone, gut and intestines. Mimi paintings frequently appear in groups, composed as scenes with interrelated parts such as a group of figures spearing or fighting or another group hunting or making love. X-ray art tends to consist of separate, juxtaposed images, often superimposed over others of similar style. (One notable exception to this is the group of x-ray figures that appears at Nourlangie Rock, Kakadu National Park.)

The x-ray style is a descriptive term applied to all Arnhem Land paintings in which some internal anatomy is shown. Intestines, heart, liver, lungs and skeletal form appear in animals, while human figures show only vertebrae but are decorated in geometric patterns. Both animal and human figures are subdivided, each section being treated with pattern and colour. Figures may be outlined on a white background or they may be outlined in red and filled in with white. An extensive palette is obtained using natural ochres, as well as by juxtaposing these to form changes in optical colour effects. Cross-hatched fine lines occur in several images. The x-ray paintings have continued from about 9000 years ago to the present. However, because of the common practice of painting these over a background of white ochre which is very unstable, they are at great risk of disintegration. In many galleries these relatively recent paintings have worn off the walls, to reveal the much older dark red paintings beneath.

X-ray paintings also show more contemporary subjects such as ships, horses, rifles and pipes, indicating that the art continued up to the present and postdates contact with other cultures. Some galleries show that the people were recording events in their daily lives, including the coming of white men and the visits by ships to Arnhem Land.

Mimi paintings are animated and agile, showing a great deal of musculature and flexibility. Weapons are depicted, including barbed and multipronged spears and returning boomerangs. Some weapons shown in Mimi paintings are not known or used by Aboriginal people in Arnhem Land, so examination of the subject matter may therefore provide an interesting social history of the area unobtainable from oral records.

A study by George Chaloupka[13] of the subject matter in rock paintings of the Kakadu National Park has already significantly added to our knowledge of the ways in which Aboriginals adapted to immense climatic changes over the centuries. During the late Pleistocene era, from 20,000 to 9000 years ago, major changes in sea levels occurred along the Arnhem Land coast, flooding the Alligator Rivers and subsequently producing tidal flats, salt pans and later freshwater wetlands. Saltwater animals gave way to freshwater species, and the eating habits as well as the social and cultural practices of Aboriginal people changed.

Adopting the approach of an art historian, Chaloupka also assessed the objects depicted in context, whether they were under or over others and what subjects predominated in each sequence. The sequences Chaloupka found were the pre-estuarine (most are known as Mimi art), estuarine, freshwater and contact. The pre-estuarine period covers the time span from up to 20,000 years ago to 7000 years ago, and includes the art styles and subjects painted before the development of the freshwater river systems. This category includes stencilled objects, large naturalistic animals and figures, numerous agile dynamic figures and yam images in many forms. The large naturalistic figures may be stippled or filled in with

Top Frieze of running Mimi figures on Obiri Rock, Kakadu National Park, Northern Territory. Mimi-style paintings are the oldest on the continent and the detail of Arnhem Land's agile, elegant figures may provide historical evidence of changing weapons and animal species at different times.

Bottom Bradshaw figures from the Kimberley area of Western Australia.

Group of figures painted in the x-ray style at Nourlangie Rock, Kakadu National Park, Northern Territory. Top right is the figure of Namarrkon, the Lightning Man, shown with important male and female ancestors of the present-day people.

other lines; they mostly represent species of kangaroo and wallaby, many of which are extinct. Extinct animals identified include the thylacine, Tasmanian devil, numbat and long-beaked echidna (which has been extinct in Australia for 18,000 years).[14] Human figures are grouped according to certain characteristics: the degree to which they exhibit great elegance, animation, the wearing of headdresses, hair belts and skirts and the types of weapons being used. The human form changed from relative naturalism through stylisation to further elucidation into linear stick figures. The presence of boomerangs can also indicate time phases in the art.

One of the most fascinating aspects of this new analysis is that it postulates a connection between the ancient cultures of Australia and New Guinea. The evidence for this is partly logic, since the land masses were once joined, and partly the presence of the numerous different yam images in the earliest phase of pre-estuarine Kakadu art. Many faded red paintings of yams appear with partly human, partly animal features. Aboriginals identify the yams as *mankinjdjek* (water yam) or *karrbada* (long yam). The yams are shown as bumpy tubers with plant tendrils or vines, and many have human characteristics. Yams are transposed over other animals, including flying foxes, and they occur frequently with images of the Rainbow Serpent. The occurrence of the Rainbow Serpent for the first time in this 'yam phase' of Kakadu art is evidence that it is the oldest and most consistent religious belief of the people, continuing into the present throughout northern Australia.

Chaloupka has selected the yam paintings for particular attention. He suggests that during the last glacial age they were probably absent or dormant on the Arnhem Land plateau and that they then became apparent after the rise in sea levels 10,000 years ago. They began to figure in the art at the same time the grasslands were submerged and yams became an important food substitute. The people of New Guinea regard the ritual accompanying the cultivation of yams as important. Chaloupka also suggests that the humanoid features of the painted yams might have been associated with some extension of New Guinea pre-cultivated yam rituals derived from contact between the two areas when the seas were lower.

The x-ray paintings began to flourish with the emergence of freshwater estuarine culture. Barramundi predominate in this art phase, with whole galleries such as Inyaluk, near Oenpelli in western Arnhem Land, being devoted to the giant perch, the prized food of the riverine peoples. According to Chaloupka, the x-ray style did not completely take over, but existed alongside naturalistic images of hunting figures, flying foxes and other animals. In this period the boomerang ceased to be painted, spears changed in design and the spear thrower was introduced. There were immense climatic changes and the beginning of wet seasons, and at this time images of the still feared lightning man, Namarrkon, began to appear.

Two major sites, Obiri and Nourlangie Rock, are accessible within the Kakadu National Park. Both are now freely available to visitors, who may travel in the comfort of coaches and cars, and they contain very fine examples of the major art styles in the Arnhem Land area.

Obiri Rock, one of a large number of outliers in the escarpment area, houses one major gallery, with about thirty-six smaller sites close by. The main gallery, fifteen metres long and two metres high, is situated under a large, deep overhang and is protected by a high shelf along the base which forms a guard against abrasive damage from stock and animals. The paintings are predominantly in the polychrome x-ray style with some examples of red monochrome art of the Mimi style. The designs are large, including several different species of fish. The gallery also includes a small number of turtles, kangaroos and other animals.

Opposite the main gallery on another outlier is a frieze of five men painted in the Mimi style. This has become known as the running man gallery due to the composition of the figures. All are equipped with pronged spears, spear throwers, goose wing fans and elbow ornaments, and they have string bags on their shoulders. All are painted running except the last one, which is standing stationary on one leg. Other images painted over the top of the frieze include an x-ray tortoise and two triangular-faced spirit women. The paintings concentrate on species of fish and animals that have been hunted for food in the area's lagoons and creeks. Some interesting individual paintings include an Archer fish with water droplets blowing out of its mouth. This fish is unique in that it captures insects for food by shooting water from its mouth, knocking them into the water.

The paintings at Nourlangie depict ten male and female figures surrounded by polychrome figures of ancestral heroes and fish, possibly showing the birth of the tribes. One of the major figures is Namarrkon, the lightning man, responsible for thunder, lightning and associated storms. The lightning man is feared by Aboriginal people for his power and his violence and this is reflected in the paintings. These paintings, which were last repainted in 1962-3[15], continue to play an important part in the lives of Aboriginal people.

Female spirit figure pregnant with twins, one male and one female, from the Cannon Hill area of the Kakadu National Park, Northern Territory.

Bark Painting

If asked to name Aboriginal artistic achievements, most Europeans would firstly say boomerangs, followed, after prompting, by painting on bark. In fact, the art of bark painting has flourished over the last two decades and has become the most widespread form of Aboriginal artistic expression throughout northern Australia.

The origin of the practice of painting on bark cannot be determined, although it is clear from scant references in the writings of explorers and nineteenth-century settlers that Aboriginals have painted on bark for over a century, probably much longer.

Bark paintings are designs painted in earth ochres on the smooth inner surface of sheets of bark from stringybark eucalyptus trees, usually *Eucalyptus tetrodonta*. The bark is stripped off in the wet season; a sheet is cut off the tree and the outermost layer of rough bark is removed with an axe blade. After further stripping back to the point where only the inner layer of smooth fibre is left, the bark is placed over an open fire, outer side down, and it slowly uncurls in the heat. This also chars the outer bark and stripping can then be completed. The bark is then laid in the sun and compressed with heavy stones. Once flat and dry, the bark surface is ready and painting can begin. The materials used for painting on bark are red, brown, rust, yellow, black and white earth pigments, fixatives as well as a range of brushes and applicators.

The source of the ochre varies with each area. At Yirrkala the cliffs along the sea coast are multicoloured, providing ample supplies of red, yellow and white pigments. At Oenpelli, on the other hand, brown and white are readily available, but other colours, notably yellow, are obtained by trade from other areas. Black, apparently difficult to obtain, is seldom seen in the bark paintings of this area.

Throughout Arnhem Land, the pigments are ground with water on rough, flat stones and a fixative is added. One of the stones may be reserved for the white, or if the clay is sufficiently friable, it may be mixed with water to a slip in a tobacco tin or other receptacle. The painters do not mix their primary colours to obtain secondary colours; the different colours of the ochres account for the varying shades in the bark paintings. The resulting tones are as many as the natural colours of the earth itself. When the intense primary ochres, deep red and brilliant chrome yellow, are not to hand, artists use the nearest colours found locally. The colours therefore include pinks gathered from the ground where seams of dull red ochre meet white, and orange-brown where yellow ochre meets red. Deep rich brown, natural pigments are also used, notably at Ramingining

Opposite 'Black-headed python and fruit bats at Ngalyindi' by Milpurru of the Ganalbingu group, central Arnhem Land. During the *dhuludur* or flowering season in September, flying foxes are attracted to the blossoms on certain trees. When they roost, their droppings fall to the ground and smell as sweet as the blossoms they feed on. The black-headed python waits nearby to eat the old and sick if they fall. *Hogarth Galleries*

Close view of the technique used by Jimmy Galereya at Manmoyi outstation south of Maningrida. The bark is first covered with red ochre, then the body of a kangaroo is outlined with white clay and filled in using a stick and a frayed piece of bark as brushes.

The artists use a variety of simple brushes: a narrow strip of bark chewed at one end and held in the hand is used for the broader lines, and a thin stick about seven centimetres long and softened at one end is used for the dots. The fine lines are drawn with a brush made from a few straight human hairs seven to ten centimetres long, bound onto a thin twig. This brush is held delicately between the fingers, coated with ochre and then laid onto the bark and drawn away from the body. Fine crosshatching is achieved with this brush.

Up until the last few years, older, more skilled painters preferred to use the traditional fixatives from plant sources, notably the wild orchid. The sticky wet stem of the orchid was rubbed across the surface of the background colour and also pounded and mixed with the ground colours used in the designs. Modern fixatives have now usurped these natural binders. When used sparingly, these chemical fixatives have ensured a longer life for the paintings by lessening the degree of flaking.

It is very likely that wherever bark was available for shelters, ornaments and utensils, Aboriginals used it as a painting surface. The simple bark shelters still used by Aboriginal families in Arnhem Land outstations once had designs painted on their smooth interior surfaces, and occasional examples can still be found. Sketches of animals, birds and hunting scenes were also observed on bark shelters in Victoria. Bark paintings were seen on ceremonial grounds in western Arnhem Land, and their use in ceremonies in south-eastern Australia has also been noted in early literature. Bark painting has disappeared in the southern areas but it still flourishes on Bathurst Island, throughout Arnhem Land and the islands off the coast of the Northern Territory.

The themes in Aboriginal art are expressed in a complex system of symbols and patterns given to the first people by the creation ancestors. Each clan has its own Dreaming or mythological origin and its own symbols to express this. Through the act of painting sacred designs on the bodies of ceremonial dancers, on cylindrical coffins or on specially constructed ritual emblems, the participants, both painters and dancers, can receive some of the ritual power inherent in these designs. The ancestor is somehow present in them and by restating them the artist is reaffirming his Dreaming and his connection to and ownership of lands. The designs are owned by clans, not by individuals.

In traditional Aboriginal society there was no separate group of men or women classed as artists by virtue of their occupation; all adults were expected to remember and to reproduce correctly the clan designs appropriate to their level of ritual training and knowledge. Therefore, when speaking of the artist in Aboriginal society, one is simply referring to the person who is performing the task, creating the work. Very little of Aboriginal material art was done to last for long periods of time – it was in the act of painting itself that the spirit power came to be activated. Most of the ritual items, including emblems, *rangga*, *waninga*, sacred dilly bags, feathered string and headdresses, were usually disposed of or hidden after the rituals requiring them were over. Body designs were erased or covered. The only permanent Aboriginal sculpture could be seen in the form of burial poles among the Tiwi of Bathurst and Melville

Islands, and in the *lorrgon* hollow log coffins of Arnhem Land; even these were left to the elements after ceremonial use.

Body paintings range from crude ochre smearing to the most finely detailed clan designs. The detailed body designs are very often exactly the same as those painted on bark or on wood coffins. These fine clan designs may be painted on a man's chest on several occasions in his life: at his initiation as a young man, at a major ceremony during his life, and at his death. At other times, elements of them, or sometimes the whole design, may appear in bark paintings. Young men therefore have ample opportunity to learn and to view these clan patterns. Every line and mark within the design has symbolic meaning. Not only the patterns and visual symbols are learned but the complex and detailed meanings and song cycles that go with them. These meanings are conveyed to initiates by degree according to their status and it is only after full integration into the deepest secrets and knowledge of the clan that a man (usually by then middle-aged) is permitted to know the sacred meanings and allowed to paint them. The 'art' objects themselves, whether bark paintings, ritual emblems or painted log coffins, may perish, but the designs live on in the memories of the clan. It is of fundamental importance to each clan that the designs be passed intact from generation to generation and by constant use in ceremonies remain a source of cohesive strength.

It is common to observe in the camp of Aboriginal painters that their sons, daughters and other relatives are shown the barks as they are painted. It is clear that the mature artists use the European demand for bark paintings to provide an important traditional educational aid. This educational function often also determines the subject and the amount of sacred symbolism in the paintings done. For example, if a young man is about to participate for the first time in an important ritual, the artist responsible for his education and instruction (whether father, uncle or other kin), could certainly ensure that he sees the bark paintings that illustrate the level and stage of knowledge he is expected to attain. The duty of teaching the young men therefore directly influences the choice of subject matter by the artist making bark paintings for sale.

Wandjuk Marika, a senior painter and ceremonial leader from eastern Arnhem Land, recently spent six months in a southern city quietly painting, away from the distractions of home and the pressures of life on the settlement. During that time he completed ten paintings in a ceremonial sequence comprising many of the important symbolic revelations of knowledge about his creation ancestors. He put these on display in a major art gallery, but, before the public was invited, he personally paid for several members of his family to fly south. One of the men who came was at that time preparing to go through and learn the deepest series of ceremonies concerning these ancestor figures. For two days the artist and the 'student', a man in his forties, studied the works. The artist and his apprentice returned to Arnhem Land where the song cycles and memory feats began again, this time secure in the knowledge that the visual elements had already been taught. (Fortunately, the paintings were purchased by the Australian National Gallery and will remain together.)

Johnny Bulu Bulun rests during the demanding process of applying fine white lines over the birds in his painting at Maningrida, Northern Territory. *Photograph Jennifer Isaacs*

In many families of eastern Arnhem Land today, it is also common for the women to paint on bark. Often the father or husband will 'sketch' the outline of the design, and it is then left to the family members to fill in the detail in order to complete the painting. The 'owner' closely supervises the work. Women also paint their own designs, which commonly represent aspects of life related to their traditional role as food gatherers. Subjects along these lines include paintings of food plants and vegetation or occasionally weaving. In some cases, where there is no man in the appropriate position within the clan to carry on the painting of major designs, a woman is selected, and she holds the designs until others are old enough to receive the knowledge.

Having considered the religious and educational aspects of bark painting, it is also important to mention the way in which the designs function as clan property, with myth and song cycles and the land. In traditional Aboriginal society, a person's most important possessions are the clan's sacred objects, designs and knowledge of the accompanying ritual song cycles. Anthropologists have recorded[1] that in order to please another or to initiate a relationship in which goods or labour were to be exchanged, a man might offer to share his designs on another man's chest. The sharing of the design and the recital of the story were considered important. The man who was painted did not in any sense regard himself as the new owner of the painted design, and the body painting soon wore off. He would be expected to give goods, food or labour in return or perhaps share his designs in the same way. When Aboriginal bark painters sell their art to local craft buyers, art galleries or the public, they never feel they are selling their designs to a purchaser who will then have a claim on them. They are simply sharing the paintings in exchange for money, in the same way as they might have expected other reciprocal favours before Europeans became involved.

When an artist sells his work, he usually gives a brief 'story' to go with it. This is generally the simplest explanation of the designs, such as he might give to an uninitiated child. The deeper levels of meaning, the actual references to sacred symbols used and other details reserved for tribal elders who have reached ritual maturity, are never passed on at the sale of the painting.

There is, in a sense, an unspoken understanding on the part of the artists that the buyers will act as responsible custodians of the paintings. When this is obviously not the case, the reaction is generally deeply felt anger and outrage. For example, the Riratjingu leader Wandjuk Marika has spoken publicly many times about his anguish and anger when he saw his designs on a tea towel.[2] He claimed that his lack of desire to paint over the preceding five years had been due to the 'stealing' of these designs, much as a sorcerer 'steals' something that belongs to his would-be victim to use it to cause him harm. When official copyright action was taken against the offenders, Wandjuk began to paint again, having found the cause of the draining of his powers.

MAJOR COLLECTIONS IN AUSTRALIA

All the Australian state museums and some art galleries, notably those of New South Wales and South Australia, have acquired large collections of bark paintings. European penetration of the remote northern areas came relatively late in the history of contact across the continent. Early accounts record bark paintings in the Darwin area from 1834, and on Melville Island painted barks in a geometric style were reported by Major Campbell. Sporadic collecting began in the late nineteenth century. Small collections of these remain in southern museums, including Field Island paintings in the South Australian Museum and Port Essington paintings in the Macleay Museum, Sydney.

The most notable early collection was made in 1912 by Spencer and Cahill. It was from the Kakadu tribe at Oenpelli and is now housed in the Museum of Victoria. These paintings were acquired over a period when Spencer, then Special Commissioner for Aborigines, visited Paddy Cahill, who had commissioned them for Spencer from the local people. Cahill is remembered as a colourful character in the history of Arnhem Land. The first white settler to take up a pastoral lease, he spoke several Aboriginal languages and lived at Oenpelli, running a dairy, orchard and garden from 1906 to 1916.

Pieces acquired on the American-Australian Scientific Expedition to Arnhem Land, 1948.

Top 'Bangudja the shark attacking a porpoise' by Kumbiala, Groote Eylandt.

Bottom 'The mud crab Unwala and his wife' by an unknown artist, Groote Eylandt.
Both pieces in the Collection of the Art Gallery of South Australia

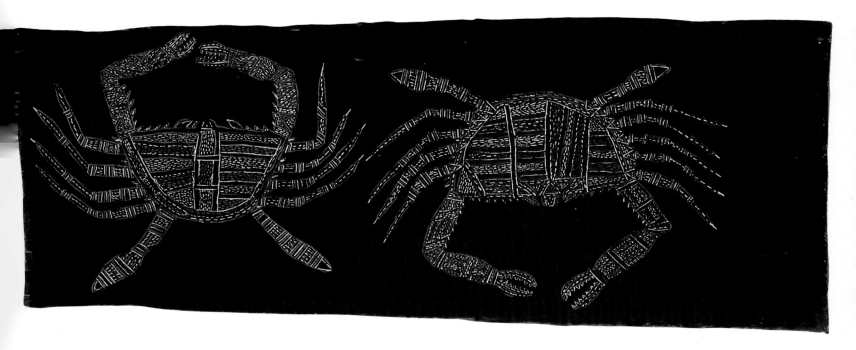

183

Two of the oldest bark paintings in existence, collected in 1878 at Port Essington, an aborted military outpost on the Coburg Peninsula, Northern Territory.

Top Goanna.

Bottom Cassowary or emu.
Both pieces in the Collection of the Macleay Museum, University of Sydney

Between 1920 and 1930 the Reverend Dyer collected paintings on Groote Eylandt and between 1938 and 1945 F. Grey and F. Rose continued collecting in this area. Other records and collections from a variety of locations began in the mid-1920s. In 1926 and again in 1929, the Reverend Wilbur Chaseling began collecting at Yirrkala in north-eastern Arnhem Land, and it was he who later began the marketing of eastern Arnhem Land paintings. During the 1930s, Miss M. Matthews collected paintings on Croker Island in western Arnhem Land.

The most comprehensive and significant early collection of bark paintings was made by the American-Australian Scientific Expedition to Arnhem Land in 1948, sponsored by the National Geographic Society and the Australian government under the leadership of C. P. Mountford. The attention of the National Geographic Society had been caught by two of Mountford's films, *Tjurunga* and *Walkabout*, both of which were made in 1942. They made the possibility of further research in this remote part of north Australia seem enticing. During a lecture tour of the United States Mountford proposed a scientific research expedition to Arnhem Land, and the National Geographic Society agreed. Seeing a good opportunity to further scientific research and to extend amicable relations with the United States, the Australian government offered to pay for a comprehensive group of American and Australian naturalists and ethnologists to participate.

Although the expedition included many more natural scientists than ethnologists, to those interested in art the collections made by Mountford have become perhaps the most important and significant. The expedition throughout the north of Australia lasted eight months, leaving Darwin in March 1948 and returning in November. The logistics of moving a team of ten scientists and their supplies and equipment across Arnhem Land in the 1940s were extremely complex. Twice the Australian Air Force was asked to help with the delivery of supplies when barges broke down.

Three major camps were made: at Groote Eylandt, Yirrkala and Oenpelli. At Groote Eylandt, the first base, the lengthy but unplanned delay in the arrival of supplies allowed Mountford to make an extensive collection of Aboriginal art from Umbakumba. The paintings on Groote Eylandt were soon to diminish and change in style when the manganese ore mine began, and this collection made by the 1948 expedition is now an invaluable record of the area's unique art style and mythology. At Yirrkala the expedition commissioned paintings and carved figures.

The third camp brought the group back 960 kilometres west to Oenpelli on the East Alligator River, where the abundant flora and fauna in the lagoons excited the naturalists. The team excavated a series of cave floors at Unbalanja Hill, and Mountford and Basset-Smith, a photographer, made films of the environment and recorded extensive galleries of the area's magnificent cave paintings. To the Australian public searching for a national identity, these paintings became the ideal symbols for 'authentic' Australian design. The simplicity and immediacy of the x-ray kangaroos as painted at Oenpelli became in the 1950s the universal symbol of Aboriginal art and hence of Australia. Several hundred bark paintings, thousands of implements and weapons and hundreds of string figures as well as numerous drawings and photographs of cave paintings were collected during this expedition.

It is refreshing to look at some of these early paintings once again. Although some have cracked and deteriorated with the years and the delicate ochres have faded, their beauty remains.

Just before the American-Australian Scientific Expedition was in Yirrkala, anthropologists Ronald and Catherine Berndt completed two years' field work there. They had made a detailed study of the religion, ceremonial practices and art of the clans gathered in the small community. The works they collected included many by the great Riratjingu artist Mawalan and his son Wandjuk, both of whom worked with Berndt. The Mountford and Berndt collections of these artists' works are the most extensive of any works by individual artists and provide a broad illustrative view of the mythology of the Riratjingu. The Berndt collection is now housed in the University of Western Australia's Anthropology Museum.

The art community's burgeoning interest in Aboriginal art and the particular sympathy and interest of Tony Tuckson, then Deputy Director of the Art Gallery of New South Wales, led to his expedition through Arnhem Land in 1958 with Dr Stuart Scougall. Tuckson and Scougall made a small but striking collection of work that formed the basis of an exhibition which then toured Australia — the first of its kind.

By this time, the paintings collected were showing some significant adaptations and developments, due to European influence and contact. In her succinct and interesting account of the European influence on bark paintings in Yirrkala, Williams[3] indicates that eastern Arnhem Land bark paintings in their present form apparently originated in the second half of the 1930s after the visit of anthropologist Donald Thomson, who requested some paintings on stringybark. Evidence from missionaries tells us that the insides of bark dwellings were painted with designs and that pieces of bark were cut from these, painted and then discarded. In 1936 the marketing of these paintings was introduced by Wilbur Chaseling, the first missionary in the area, who in turn sold all goods produced to museums in the southern cities. In western Arnhem Land bark paintings were collected by early explorers and ethnographers well before this time, but the marketing of the art was delayed. For a brief period during the war, the work was encouraged by missionary officers whose criteria for payment were the amount of time they involved and the degree of 'workmanship' — European judgments one still hears applied to Aboriginal works of art.

The marketing of bark paintings in eastern Arnhem Land did not significantly increase until the mid-1950s. At this time another missionary art officer introduced innovations that significantly affected future bark paintings of this area. He aimed at making the work more saleable so that it would fetch higher prices. He introduced barks in shapes other than rectangular, encouraged 'miniature' barks and introduced the technique of incising fine parallel lines on ochred surfaces of carvings. In response to his complaints about the bark paintings 'curving' to the shape of the tree, split stick binders devised by the artists were fixed to both ends.

Pieces acquired on the American-Australian Scientific Expedition to Arnhem Land, 1948.

Top 'Garkain, the evil spirit' by an unknown artist, Oenpelli, western Arnhem Land. Although the evil spirit appears clothed, the extensions on his arms and legs are loose flaps of skin with which he smothers people in the night.

Bottom 'Wili Wilia, the Mimi, spearing kangaroos' by an unknown artist, Oenpelli, western Arnhem Land. The figure is positioned at the thinner end of the bark sheet while the kangaroos leap at the wider end. The artist has used space in the irregular bark to suggest the secrecy needed for hunting animals.
Both pieces in the Collection of the Art Gallery of South Australia

Above 'Long-necked turtle' by an unknown artist. Gunwinggu group, western Arnhem Land.

Two pieces acquired on the American-Australian Scientific Expedition to Arnhem Land, 1948.

Below Hunting scene by an unknown artist from Yirrkala, eastern Arnhem Land. Three men in a canoe have harpooned a large turtle.

Opposite 'Totemic creatures at Yelangbara, Port Bradshaw' by Mawalan of the Riratjingu group, Yirrkala, eastern Arnhem Land. Animals include the devil ray, goanna and octopus.
All pieces in the Collection of The Australian Museum

From the early 1960s, art dealers and collectors began showing interest in barks and commissioned older artists to do major art works for them. Jim Davidson collected Yirrkala paintings, Dorothy Bennett collected art from all over Arnhem Land and Sandra Holmes began her interest in and patronage of the great Gunwinggu bark painter Yirawala. American ethnographic collectors also began to take notice and bought either from Australian collectors or direct from missions and settlements. The paintings became larger and more complex, both in their patterning and in the degree of mythological information conveyed.

Most Australian museums bought direct from the artist's communities and from private collectors. The beautiful Yirawala series on the *ubar* and *maraian* ceremonies of the Gunwinggu is now in the Australian National Gallery and the Bennett collection forms the core of the national ethnographic collection of the Museum of Australia.

In 1973 the Aboriginal Arts Board was established and the next decade substantially altered the sporadic purchase and display of Aboriginal art. The Board began to commission the artists to make pieces specifically for exhibitions to be shown in Australia, America and Europe. It provided funds for Aboriginal councils to employ people who would help the artists produce and market their work, and a national company was established to market Aboriginal art in all states.

The 1980s have seen the emergence of individual artists in the north who have their own direct contacts with private Australian galleries. Having personally observed the private gallery system of the wider art world, these artists have benefited from the increase in status and economic returns when paintings are hung in these venues rather than the usual small ethnographic outlets.

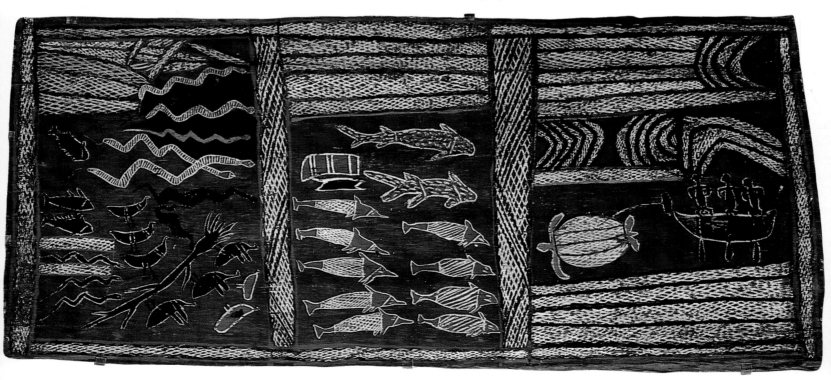

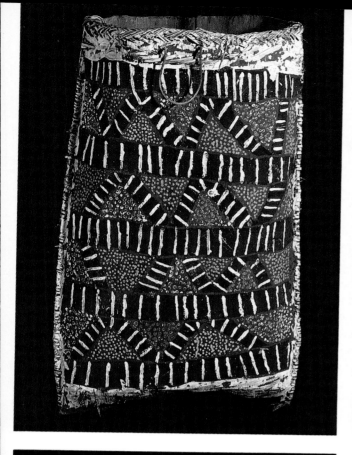

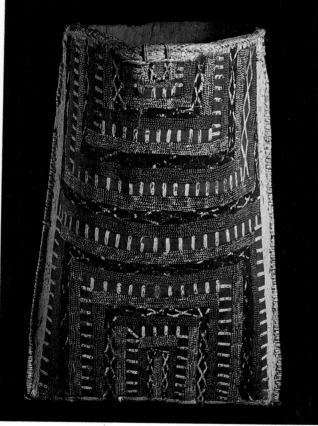

Tiwi bark paintings and baskets from the Bathurst and Melville Islands, Northern Territory.

Top left Bark basket made by Polly Miller from Pularumpi, Melville Island, 1979.

Top right 'Moon and stars in their heavenly cycle', bark painting by Deaf Tommy Mungatopi of Milikapiti.

Bottom left Bark basket from Pularumpi, Melville Island.

Opposite Bark painting of the full moon by Deaf Tommy Mungatopi, Milikapiti.

All pieces above in the Collection of the Northern Territory Museum of Arts and Sciences

REGIONAL STYLES OF BARK PAINTING

Although in some areas paintings have altered since the early collections were made, stylistic differences in each region are still clearly discernible.

TIWI PAINTING

The Tiwi people of Bathurst and Melville Islands must have been isolated for an unknown length of time from all influences of mainland Aboriginal culture. Tiwi mythology refers to the mainland as the Home of the Dead. The Tiwi, therefore, did not have intensive contact with the mainland peoples or their artistic traditions and the art that developed is quite unlike any other in north Australia. Here the simple paintings, human figures and animals familiar in Arnhem Land are absent; many paintings contain no recognisable forms but are symbolic designs. The style of painting is vigorous, with broad, strong linear patterns; Tiwi paintings have less intricate detail than those from other areas. The use of dots applied with a Tiwi invention, a multi-pronged comb, is also integral to the work.

A Tiwi woman gathers stringybark to make baskets or *tunga*, as well as bark paintings and armbands known as *jukuti*.

Much of the art of Bathurst and Melville Islands revolves around the *pukumani* funeral ceremonies described more fully in Chapter 1. A short burial ceremony is held after a person dies, and two months later another more complex ritual takes place, sometimes lasting for several days. A few weeks before this, specific people are commissioned to make grave posts: many posts if the dead man was old and important, one or two for a woman or a man of lesser status. Using a simple axe, the posts are cut and shaped from the round trunk of an extremely hard tree. They may be 90 to 250 centimetres high, always abstract in shape. Often they are pierced with rectangular or circular holes, with other sections cut out from the round pole in powerful asymmetrical forms. The surfaces of the posts are completely covered with painted designs. When erected for the ceremony, a group of these grave posts of different heights and thicknesses and vividly painted in the characteristic patterns is very impressive against the quiet grey-green of the bush. After the funeral has finished, the posts are left by the grave and gradually weather in successive bushfires and wet seasons.

Also associated with the *pukumani* rituals are bark baskets, armbands, feathered and painted ornaments and ornately carved and decorated spears. In more recent times, the original meanings of some of the designs seem to have been forgotten, but the bark baskets hold an important place in the *pukumani* ceremonies. Frequently containing possessions of the deceased, they are placed at the grave, leaning against the poles. On completion of the dancing they are inverted over the top of the poles to mark the end of the ceremony so that the spirit will stay quiet and not trouble the living.

A most interesting aspect of Tiwi art is the fact that many of the painters are women, practising their art as individuals in the same way as men. The women paint the remembered patterns of their heritage, derived from their family and the things they see around them, in the prevailing geometric style. All bark painters the author recently observed on Bathurst Island were women, the men confining themselves to carving and painting on carvings.

Painting on bark occurs on single flattened sheets, two-sided baskets and bark armbands. Most of the Tiwi bark painting was traditionally associated with bark baskets, formerly used as the principal carrying bags. These baskets, called *tunga*, are constructed from one long sheet of flattened and scraped stringybark bent double at the base. The interior is blocked with sticks to support its shape and the two sides are sewn together by threading strong pandanus strips through punched holes. The upper rim of the basket is frequently decorated with pandanus stitching. Typically the baskets were painted on one side with a central circular design with radiating spokes, or with a geometric pattern, the decoration on the other side being limited to a few simple lines. When asked what the patterns on the bark paintings mean, the usual reply is, 'body paintings'.

C. P. Mountford's[4] descriptions of the beautiful bark paintings he collected in 1956 give details of the complexity of symbolism involved in each circle and dot. Circles may be camps, fires or trees, and small dots may be fallen flowers.

WESTERN ARNHEM LAND

Western Arnhem Land encompasses the communities from Oenpelli to Maningrida, including the outstations of the Liverpool and Alligator River regions. The art rests now mainly with the Gunwinggu, Mialli and related people, the Kakadu people who painted many of the paintings collected by Mountford having since, sadly, dispersed and died. Croker and Goulburn Islands must be included in this area, as the Gunwinggu and related groups are also resident there. The people of these areas are united in ceremonial chains and most speak or understand the Gunwinggu language. Great artists from Croker Island have included Yirawala and Mijau Mijau.

In western Arnhem Land, the bark paintings are closely related in style to the ancient cave art of the escarpment area. Here during the long wet season when the rivers overflowed, Aboriginal families retreated to higher ground and camped in sandstone shelters, where they created innumerable ochre paintings. These provide a magnificent historical record of the continuous occupation of the area by successive generations of Aboriginals for possibly 30,000 years, as well as the importance of art in the lives of the people. The subjects of these rock paintings are many and varied.

Many bark paintings collected by Mountford in 1948 and reproduced here are very similar to the cave art of the same area and these artists probably also painted on rocks and caves. Today cave art is no longer practised in western Arnhem Land; bark painting has taken over as the major art form. The bark paintings still strongly resemble the cave art and include x-ray animals and figures, Mimi spirit paintings and strong images of powerful ancestral spirits. These are painted finely, usually in white pipeclay on a dark, plain background. Interiors of figures are cross-hatched or reveal x-ray features.

In the 1940s the art of western Arnhem Land consisted predominantly of single figures or groups of isolated figures on a plain ground. Unlike the painters of eastern Arnhem Land, the artists of Oenpelli did not fill the background with linear patterns but concentrated instead on the interior of the figures. Here the famous x-ray features can be seen in which the intestines, heart, liver, lungs and spinal column are shown, along with the external form of the animal. However, few paintings of this era show the fine cross-hatching the Gunwinggu now prefer.

The older paintings have an immediate appeal, with their rough texture and simplicity of design. The bark has been hacked from the trees and left untrimmed, the shape then determining the placement of figures. The figure of Garkain straddles the uneven lower edge of the bark, while Wilia Wilia hunting the kangaroo is positioned so that the movement of the hunt is captured on a most irregular piece of bark, with Wilia Wilia hidden behind a tree on the narrow end and the kangaroos leaping prominently in the foreground at the wider end. The positioning of the hunter at the cramped end of the bark gives the work another dimension and suggests the stealth and camouflage necessary when spearing game.

Some of the natural appeal of the unselfconscious older art has given way in the newer examples to precision in execution and minuteness of detail. The background is prepared perfectly, the bark edges are neatly

X-ray 'crocodile' by Yirawala, Gunwinggu group, Liverpool River. *Collection The Australian Museum*

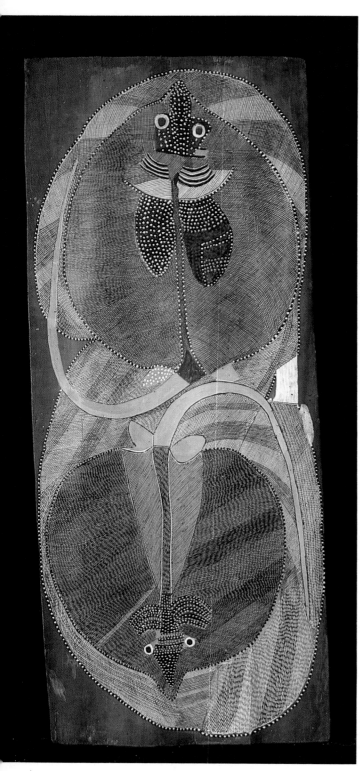

'Nawilah, freshwater stingray Dreaming' by Maralwanga of the Gunwinggu group, western Arnhem Land.

Opposite 'Darhlu spirit woman' by Maralwanga of the Gunwinggu group, western Arnhem Land.

Both pieces Hogarth Galleries

squared and fine lines are painted over the entire surfaces of the figures. The simple patterns of the old paintings have been replaced by complex and elaborate cross-hatching.

At the time of Mountford's visit, Oenpelli was a mission station run by the Church Missionary Society, active there until very recently. As well as creating training opportunities for the local people and running stock and agriculture projects, by the 1960s the mission was concentrating on reinforcing the traditional values of Aboriginal society through bilingual literary programs and the encouragement of traditional paintings which it sold through its own retail shops in Sydney.

Many paintings were accumulated by the Church Missionary Society in Sydney from the 1950s to the early 1970s. The paintings had been set aside for many reasons, both Aboriginal and European. The Aboriginals said that some were sacred paintings that should not be seen by women; the missionaries thought others were distasteful, grotesque or sexually explicit and unsuitable for public display. The Aboriginal Arts Board purchased all these paintings and mounted an exhibition that toured Australia and Europe for six years, from 1977 to 1983.[5] A survey of these paintings, together with others acquired by galleries and museums from the 1950s to the present, indicates some clear changes in the art.

The hatching on the early figures is seldom polychrome and layered as it is today and until the late 1960s there were still paintings with interior patterns comprising strong geometric blocks of colour areas filled in with dots, and generally a greater range of decorative patterns. Some artists continue the x-ray style of painting, mostly depicting the animals hunted for food; others occasionally paint more important works that incorporate complex patterning with cross-hatched lines imitative of body paintings and termed *rrark*. The sequence of application of each colour in the *rrark* is most significant. The paintings are of animals and bush creatures, 'story barks' showing aspects of mythology, spirit creatures of the rocky escarpment and, most importantly, Dreaming ancestors.

Lengthy sacred ceremonies recall the events of the Dreaming with ancestors such as Ngalyod the Rainbow Serpent, Luma-Luma the giant, and the spirit kangaroo known as Kolobar, Kalkberd or Nadulmi, as well as other names. The images of these creatures are painted on bark. The young children sit beside the master painters as they work and hear the stories; some older boys are taught the *rrark* patterns and help with the painting some time before they are told the full details of the ceremony.

The Rainbow Serpent has a significant role in all western Arnhem Land sacred ceremonies, and occurs frequently in the bark paintings. Associated with fertility and the coming of the wet season, it is a custodian of tribal law and will kill or devour offenders. The Rainbow Serpent appears in different stories in different manifestations, with a kangaroo's head, a serpent's body, buffalo horns or a fish's tail. As a serpent it tunnels underground, but it also inhabits special waterholes and lagoons. The water lily leaves on the surface are associated with its Dreaming. Numerous other spirits, both evil and benign, live in western Arnhem Land, including the mischievous Mimi.

With the increased interest of Europeans in Aboriginal paintings, many artists in remote communities are able to earn a living from sales of their

art. The best of these contemporary painters bring a new strength to Oenpelli art. The imaginative spirit images vary in individual interpretation and extend the emotional content and impact of the paintings. Frightening and forceful faces and shapes grip one with uneasy apprehension about death, the spirit world and the psychic life of the artist. Artists such as the great Gunwinggu painter Yirawala and others, including Mijau Mijau, Maralwanga, Milaybuma, Mawunjal and Njiminjuma, became well known, their work in demand by major galleries throughout the world. Yirawala, who died in 1976, was an outstanding artist with a wide range of subjects and a prodigious output. He was perhaps the finest draughtsman. His figures are agile, vital and mobile; they leap and dance around the bark. In 'Katjailen the serpent devouring the child' the coils of the powerful, flowing serpent fill the painting and surround the startled figure, who seems frozen with terror. The freshness and sureness of line in his abstract clan patterns are evident in 'Sacred body painting designs' and the small frog at the bottom of the painting has a fragile charm.

Preferring to work in series, Yirawala compiled visual representations of the main myth cycles of the Gunwinggu. These are episodic, illustrating not only the physical nature of the events portrayed featuring, among others, Luma-Luma the giant man and Kundaagi the kangaroo, but also the sacred patterns that represent each aspect of the story and are used as body designs in the dances.

Most of his work is held in the Australian National Gallery, although most museums and galleries have several examples. Picasso, shown the old man's paintings in 1971, is rumoured to have said, 'Ah, this man is an artist, I wish I could paint like that.' That does not seem an unlikely statement for the great European artist to have made when one sees a group of paintings by Yirawala.

Top 'Mimis' by Milaybuma of the Gunwinggu group, western Arnhem Land. *Courtesy Hogarth Galleries*

Bottom 'Katjailen the serpent devouring the child' by Yirawala of the Gunwinggu group. *Collection Art Gallery of South Australia*

CENTRAL ARNHEM LAND

Much early writing about bark paintings divided the work into eastern and western styles. The people of central Arnhem Land did not fit easily into either classification; although their mythology related to the east, the paintings had a separate identity and clear differences.

Central Arnhem Land encompasses both a geographical area and a group of related people. Broadly, it includes the clans and language groups whose land lies east of the Liverpool River through to Ramingining and its outstations on the mainland and Milingimbi, an island just off the coast adjacent to Ramingining. The main gatherings of central Arnhem Land artists are therefore at Maningrida, Ramingining and Milingimbi, with numerous outstations in the bush being serviced from these centres. These artists are also related to the clans of the far north-eastern tip of Arnhem Land, although the paintings are quite different.

Along the coast the landscape is lush and tropical. In the dry season people travel great distances hunting and food gathering, whereas in the wet the rivers swell and flow across the plains, forming vast swamps and making road travel impossible. Small family groups gather to join outstations that may include any number of simple dwellings from two upwards, some accommodating up to 150 people. The camps are made close to rivers, lagoons or other fresh water supplies on land that, through mythology, is owned by the resident families. No outstation is ever made on land not owned by the people who camp there.

There are prominent artists in most clans of central Arnhem Land, but work is most frequently seen from the Djinang, Liyagalawumirri, Ganalbingu, Djambarbingu and Gubarbingu. Other clans are resident in the area and their paintings, as do those of each clan, show both mythological and stylistic differences. However, the impression that one clan paints more than another is usually due to the work of several prominent and productive individuals. Another group, the Rembarrnga, whose paintings are very different in style, are included in this category, not because of kinship and mythological connections but largely because their outstations, deep into the interior of Arnhem Land, are serviced from Ramingining and occasionally Maningrida, so the work is displayed and sold as central Arnhem Land painting.

The art of Bulu Bulun and Milpurru, both Ganalbingu, is characterised by excellent draughtsmanship, curved flowing lines and close intertwining forms. The motifs create an overall curvilinear pattern on a plain background, usually of red or yellow ochre. To the eye accustomed to Western art values, there is strong decorative appeal in the best paintings by these artists because of their elegance of line and composition. Both Bulu Bulun and Milpurru paint the totemic animals and plants of their clan country, occasionally executing a more elaborate and formal painting with additional mythological information in the subject matter. As paintings reveal more ceremonial information, they tend to tighten up; the artist is more concerned with placement and decoration of animals and human figures and adds representations of ceremonial emblems. Some clans arrange the composition into halves or quarters or organise the totems, animals or figures around an emblem or waterhole.

'Niwuda, honey of the Yirritja' by Djembungu of Ramingining, central Arnhem Land. These two paintings show in abstract form the Niwuda honey cells of Yirritja wild bees. At the top the cells are sealed and full of honey, while at the bottom they are unsealed and therefore either empty or not yet full.

A group of central Arnhem Land paintings recently acquired by the Australian Museum were all on the 'bush honey' theme. In central and eastern Arnhem Land the gathering of bush honey is not only one of the delights of hunting, being one of the very few sources of natural sugar, but the finding of bush honey in the creation era is commemorated in myth and ceremony. The songs recount that 'the creation ancestors of the Yirritja moiety were travelling across Arnhem Land from east to west. One man used his sacred stick to prise off some bark from a tree and when he did so, the "sugarbag" honey came out. The finding of bush honey was commemorated in a ceremony. But a fire broke out and a quail, picking up a burning twig, flew west. As he flew, a spark fell down and ignited the tall grasses of the plains so that there was soon a raging bushfire. The bees in the paper bark trees were frightened so they flew further west to Gubarbingu country'.[6]

The paintings of the 'bush honey' series were all collected from painters around Ramingining and Milingimbi, although the bush honey design is also known in Yirrkala. Two Yirritja paintings, painted by Niwuda, are purely symbolic representations of the 'honeycomb'. Other paintings show a simple scene of the hunter and the sugarbag tree with some of his implements; in others, some sacred *rangga* appear.

Observing the group of honey paintings before they went to the museum, Ray Munyal, a senior Dhuwa artist, contrasted his own painting with that of his son, Andrew Marrgalulu, saying, 'This is my painting, and this is my son's painting. I am teaching him. My painting is the interesting painting. He is learning, painting little more interesting, putting tree, axe, hunter. I am giving him little bit more interesting.' Munyal's use of the word 'interesting' related specifically to the amount of information conveyed by the work. A young man just learning could not paint the details that an older man could; the father's paintings were therefore more 'interesting', more informative and more important.

One of the central myth cycles for the people of this area is the Wawilak story. The Wawilak are ancestors of the Dhuwa moiety and their story is enacted in ceremonies throughout eastern Arnhem Land, as well as being the subject matter for numerous bark paintings incorporating snakes, waterholes and other creatures.

The Wawilak sisters travelled over the land from east to west, giving names to birds, animals, plants and fish. When the younger woman was about to give birth, they camped beside a clear lagoon in which the Rainbow Serpent lived. After they had made a shade from stringybark, the baby was born. As the older sister went to collect paperbark in which to cradle the baby, she accidentally polluted the waterhole with her menstrual blood. The Serpent was very angry and, rising into the sky as a rainbow, he made a thunderstorm and caused lightning, rain and thunder to fall. Then he devoured the women and the newborn baby.*

---

* In western Arnhem Land, the Rainbow Serpent is often female, whereas in the central and eastern Wawilak story, it is male.

The lengthy cycle of songs and dances that tell of the Wawilak sisters recounts many side incidents and encounters with other animals in the course of the sisters' journey.

A great many central Arnhem Land paintings concern mortuary themes, the funeral ceremony in which the bones of the deceased are placed in a hollow log coffin and the spirit is sung safely to the home of the spirits of the dead, the island of Baralku. When a Dhuwa person dies, he or she is taken over the sea in a spirit canoe that travels early in the morning along the light cast by the morning star.

The light is actually a feathered string tethering the star to Baralku. An old spirit woman, Marlumbu, keeps the star in her dilly bag and if you could see inside it would appear as a glowing ball of light. Each morning the old woman opens her bag and lets the star loose into the sky, soaring like a kite. She unravels more and more string so the star can bring the morning light to the mainland. Then the old woman pulls the star home as night falls. She heaves on the feathered string as though pulling in a shark, and hides it in her bag again. As the pale morning star light appears at dawn the people are reminded of the journey their spirits must take when they die. Singing at funerals often lasts all night, culminating at dawn with the coming of the morning star.

David Malangi is a central Arnhem Land artist whose paintings deal predominantly with two themes, the Djankawu sisters (in this area synonymous with the Wawilak sisters) and the ancestral hero Gurrumirringu. When he was asked to explain his paintings, he began, 'Even you see the many pieces, and the people staying there – this is no ordinary place – this is my country. They [the people] are really from the country – they didn't make it but came from it. Our ancestors – big people – strong people, stuck to it and then we grew up and this is our story and our country. This is our traditional area and that is why we don't want mining or *balanda* [white men] fishing there.'

David Malangi is an important man who owns three tracts of land on the mainland opposite Milingimbi: Dhamala and Ngurrunyuwa on the western and eastern banks of the mouth of the Goyder River and Dhabila about sixteen kilometres along the coast from the mouth of the river. On the eastern side is the country of the ancestor Gurrumirringu and on the western side is the country of the Djankawu sisters. The two areas of country have special rocks and waterholes created by these ancestral heroes, and their stories, including the animals they encountered as well as the natural features of the landscape, are the subject of Malangi's paintings.

In 1983 he executed a series illustrating the mythology and topography of these two places.[7] He planned the series and its exhibition at the Art Gallery of New South Wales with consideration of the way in which viewers would perceive his message. The Gurrumirringu series consists of six paintings and the Wawilak series of three, with one large focal painting linking them. The focal painting, which is the largest and most detailed, shows an aerial view of the Goyder River with to the left the Gurrumirringu story shown in symbolic form, and to the right the Wawilak story. The animals of the stories are shown, together with the symbol of the rock at the mouth of the river, which is the metamorphosed

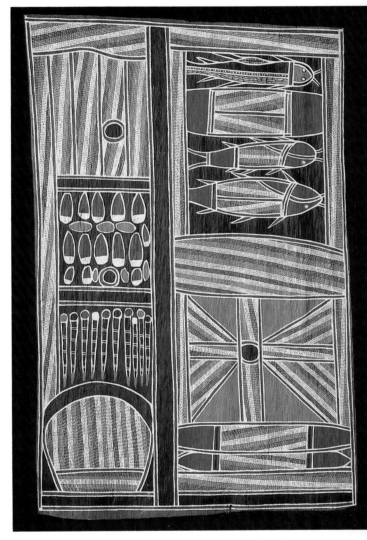

'Map of Malangi's land in the Goyder River', by David Malangi of the Liyagalawumirri group, central Arnhem Land. The painting is a major work declaring ownership of land in order to prevent mining and fishing by *balanda* or white men. The left-hand panel is composed of symbolic information about the ancestor Gurrumirringu and the right-hand panel shows the sacred story of the Djankawu sisters. Such paintings may be seen as title deeds, indicating that the artist painting the story owns the connected land under traditional law.
Collection Art Gallery of New South Wales

body of Gurrumirringu, and the abstract symbolic clan pattern denoting the Djankawu waterhole. The smaller paintings Malangi designed to hang on either side of the 'map', each telling a segment of the story. These paintings differ from the central important map. They are simple compositions freely painted, sometimes just two lizards or two catfish, denoting animals in the story.

The Gurrumirringu story has become famous; sections of Malangi's designs for it were used as Aboriginal art on Australia's $1 note. Perhaps because of Malangi's subsequent fame, he paints this design frequently, fully elaborating in a naturalistic fashion on the tree under which the hunter rested, and on the birds and plants of the bush. In some paintings he extends his ordinary range to paint kangaroos with x-ray features like those of western Arnhem Land. Malangi included one large Gurrumirringu 'story' painting in the series, together with other related 'not much story' paintings.

Among the more remote Rembarrnga, paintings are often abstract representations of the landscape of the artist's own area. Bark pieces are roughly cut and the brushwork is broad and unrefined. Occasionally the overall surface of the bark is left unpainted, with figures, trees and dotted lines forming the images. Rembarrnga artists seldom use yellow ochre, creating dramatic abstracts with deep red, black and white ochre against the natural texture of the bark, the broad white dots giving the work its fresh, distinctive and immediately recognisable style.

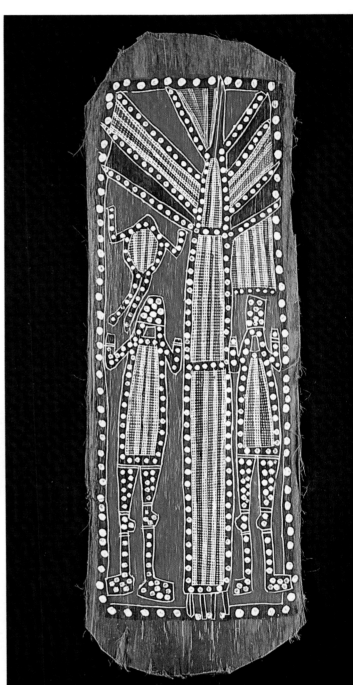

Above 'Cabbage fan palm with figures' by Djanbardi of the Rembarrnga group, central western Arnhem Land. The frog symbolises the wet season and the figures are celebrating the renewal of life with the coming of rain.

Left Mambarara working on a painting in his house at Ramingining, central Arnhem Land.

Opposite 'Magpie, geese and waterlilies at the waterhole' by Johnny Bulu Bulun of the Ganalbingu group, Maningrida, central Arnhem Land.
Collection Northern Territory Museum of Arts and Sciences

199

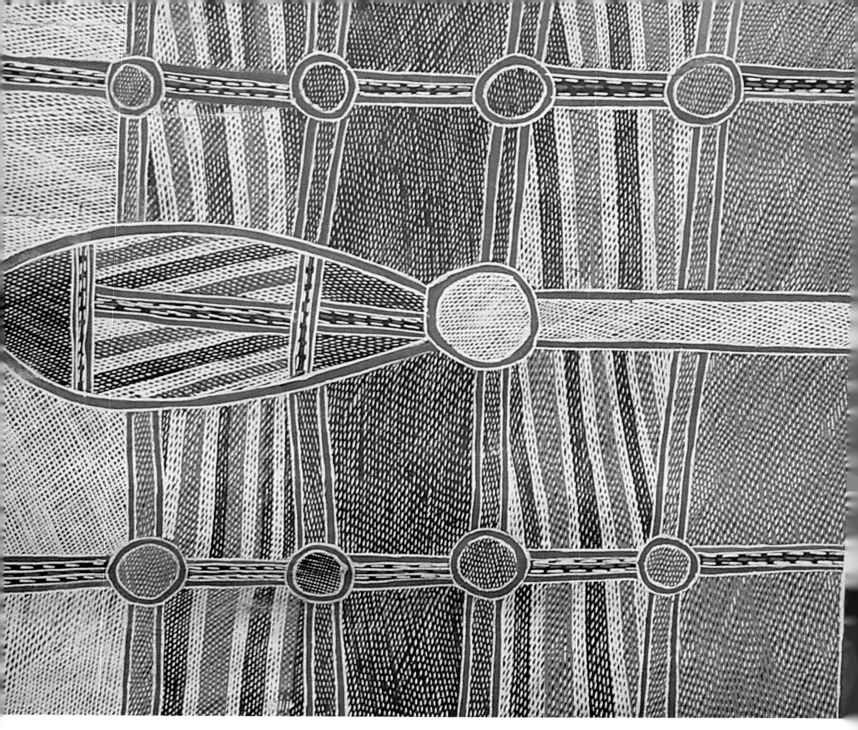

'Djankawu story' by Daypurrun of Elcho Island, eastern Arnhem Land. This symbolic painting shows the important Djankawu sites at Elcho Island and the adjacent mainland.
Collection Hogarth Galleries

EASTERN ARNHEM LAND

In eastern Arnhem Land bark painting is a flourishing activity, though there is no tradition of cave painting. Here the paintings are complex, highly involved patterns of grids and lines, diamonds and other geometric symbols used as a codified design language. Figures are superimposed on these all-important, clan-owned patterns.

In this book, the area of eastern Arnhem Land includes the whole of the north-eastern land surrounding the coastal mining town of Nhulunbuy, with Yirrkala being the main Aboriginal settlement. It includes the outstations of Yirrkala, Lake Evella on the mainland to the west and Elcho Island. (Although the clans of Milingimbi and Ramingining are related, their art has been discussed as central Arnhem Land painting.) The people of this area all refer to themselves as Yulngu, which means 'person' or 'we people' and they speak related languages which are mutually understood. The clans are divided into two moieties or halves, the Dhuwa and the Yirritja, membership of which is traced through the father to different creation ancestors, and these are depicted in the paintings. Great spirit ancestors of the Dhuwa are the Djankawu, the Wawilak sisters and the thunderman Djambuwal. The Yirritja ancestors are Barama and Laintjung. The great song cycles of the clans

tell of these ancestors and form the central focus of ceremonies for each moiety. The paintings illustrate episodes in the great sagas.

The stylistic features evident in Yirrkala paintings are clear in the older works collected by Mountford, as well as in contemporary examples. The area of the painting is frequently delineated by a rectangle placed just within the edges of the bark. This is then filled with the design. The artist may divide this area yet again or arrange the figures and patterns as one unit. He uses all the space available to him, filling gaps with cross-hatching patterns.

Representations of the great ancestors in human form are common, as are fish, birds, animals and sea creatures. Individual figures are seldom painted showing any realistic movement but appear simple and static, sometimes clumsily drawn; the pattern and subject matter are important, not refinement of line in the representational figures. One of the outstanding painters, whose work was collected by Mountford and Berndt in the 1940s, was Mawalan of the Riratjingu clan, who acted as a principal informant to the Berndts.

An immediate difference can be observed between the older Yirrkala paintings and contemporary examples. The older ones are rough in comparison and the ochre colours softer. Today painters from Yirrkala

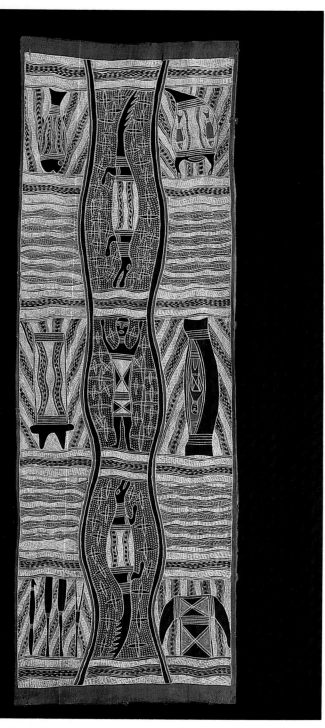

'The Milky Way' by Narritjin of the Manggalili group of Yirrkala, eastern Arnhem Land. The central panel shows the Milky Way with one fisherman and two crocodiles. Other images represent a rock cod, a hollow log coffin and an anvil-shaped thundercloud. *Collection The Australian Museum*

Opposite 'Minala the long-necked turtle' by Malinjin of the Dalwongu group, Yirrkala, eastern Arnhem Land. *Collection Northern Territory Museum of Arts and Sciences*

and its outstations frequently use intense black pigment that was not available at the time of Mountford's visit. Their works are startling in contrast to the older pieces. Cross-hatching has developed to the point of extreme detail with symbolic linear patterns filling all spaces, both around the figures and on them.

The importance of the art's mythological content has remained, although Yirrkala is undergoing radical change in response to the huge neighbouring bauxite mine and town at Nhulunbuy. Artists continue to produce the traditional patterns and to depict the stories owned by their clans. The ancient designs have altered little, though their execution, placement and composition have, with the result that the paintings now appear quite different. The designs or paintings are in Yulngu eyes independent of the surface on which they are painted. The same design appears as a bark painting, as decoration for sculpture, as a painting on the body of a dancer, the lid of a coffin or a memorial post.

The ancestors gave the designs, songs and associated ritual to the Yulngu by performing them in creation times; the shark ancestor of the Djapu clan travelled from the sea to Wulwulwuy where he became a tree that still stands. The activities of the shark not only form the subject of Djapu paintings and ceremonies, but their own homeland's housing plan is based on the shape of the shark. Each member is related to a part of the shark's body, the leader at the head and others at the tail and fins.

The main Dhalwangu clan centre is at Gangan where the ancestor of the Yirritja, Barama, first appeared. Paintings by Dhalwangu artists illustrate the river at Gangan as well as the freshwater tortoise Minala and crayfish. The diamond motif prevalent in these paintings represents the pattern made by the reeds on Minala's back as she swam.

Similarly, Manggalili clan paintings represent topographical features of Djarrakpi, their homeland centre. Such paintings may contain a lot of mythological information or comprise only one segment of the story. To the artists, the whole story is summoned to mind by even a single appropriate image.

The Riratjingu homelands centre at Yelangbara is the beach on which the Djankawu ancestors of the Dhuwa clans first landed when they came by canoe from Baralku. There were three of them, Djankawu himself, the elder sister Bildiwuwiju, who had already borne children, and the younger sister Maralaidj. They paddled to the wide beach at Yelangbara, singing, and the waves carried their canoe to the shallows, where it changed into a rock. Djankawu plunged his *mawalan* or walking stick into the sand; water appeared and a well was formed. His stick is now a she-oak tree. They heard the cry of the black cockatoo and then, glancing at the sandhills, they saw the tracks of an animal. It was a goanna and Djankawu named it *djunda*.

They left many children in the caves and then travelled on to Bilirri, Borkinya and Ganungyala. At Bilirri, Djankawu saw the sun rise over the hill, spreading its rays across the sky. (*Bilirri* means 'the spreading rays of the sun'.) Djankawu named the places he saw and all the animals they found. At Borkinya he named the wild turkey, and at Ganungyala Djankawu stayed until dawn and saw the morning star. All these places are in the country of the Riratjingu people.[8]

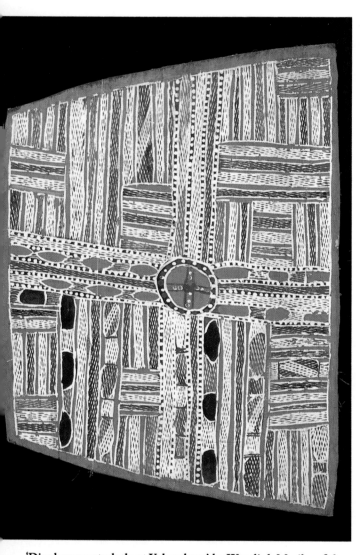

'Djankawu waterhole at Yelangbara' by Wandjuk Marika of the Riratjingu group, Yirrkala, eastern Arnhem Land. When the Djankawu arrived at Yelangbara, they plunged their digging sticks into the sand and made the fresh water flow. The central circle is the well, the black shapes are *trepang* in the sea and the clan patterns represent sand and sea.

The paintings of Wandjuk Marika, who told this story, closely follow those of his father Mawalan. However, there is some personal style in the placement of figures, shape of the heads and overall composition. Most of Wandjuk's work illustrates the Djankawu, Wawilak and Djambuwal stories. In his important one-man exhibition held in Sydney in 1983, he chose to fully demonstrate his clan's ownership of and connection to their lands at Yelangbara by painting a series that not only told the story of the Djankawu in stages but also contained detailed symbolic references to all the specific natural features of his land that the Djankawu had made: the sunrise on the water became a particular pattern of cross-hatching, the sacred canoe an abstract shape, the three large rocks, which are the metamorphosed brother and sisters, became three humped shapes. The *mawalan* (sacred digging stick) and the hills and animals that the Djankawu found on the land were also variously symbolised.

The paintings were important to the artist on many levels. They were a declaration and manifestation of his ritual leadership in Djankawu ceremonial matters. They were a revelation of the formation, meaning and associated symbolism of the features of the land at Yelangbara. They were a statement that he, with his clan, owned that land and they were a means of preserving the visual cultural knowledge in a museum for future generations, as well as teaching existing members of his family deeper levels of meaning. Lastly, by their sale to a museum, they were intended to finance Wandjuk's move with his family away from the destructive influences of Yirrkala to the seaside peace of Yelangbara, sixty kilometres away, enabling them to build houses, sink bores and begin life in the bush again.

GROOTE EYLANDT

Groote Eylandt is a large island lying off the eastern coast of the Northern Territory in the Gulf of Carpenteria. Its people are linked to the mainland people through mythology and language, although the Groote Eylandt myths place a much greater emphasis on the importance of the winds. The winds aided the islanders' canoes on their voyages to the mainland, and rituals calling up Mamariga the south-east wind, Bara the north-west wind and Demboru the north wind were performed at various totemic sites on the island.

Many of the great Australian museum and gallery collections contain examples of old Groote Eylandt paintings, but few have been seen in recent years. The paintings done today have absorbed features of the mainland art with the introduction of more detailed patterning and the inclusion of the background as part of the design. Old paintings collected by Mountford in 1948 show a markedly different and distinct Groote Eylandt style. The immediate impact is one of space and dramatic simplicity, or a few small and delicately delineated forms against a deep black or occasionally yellow background. Patterns on the figures are frequently made up of chevrons and broken lines. The division of the bark into many separate areas, common in the art of Yirrkala, is limited in Groote Eylandt to two or three simple strokes across the width of the painting, in no way interfering with the spaciousness of the design.

Human figures are not prominent in the art of Groote Eylandt, usually playing a subsidiary role to animals, birds, fish and reptiles. The most common subjects refer to the activities of mythological ancestors always represented in their animal form: for example, kestrels, mud crabs, doves and sharks. Boats, both dug-out canoes and Macassan *praus*, obviously played an important role in the island economy and are usually shown with tiny figures hauling in fish of exaggerated size. Here, as in many parts of Arnhem Land, Macassan fishermen who visited the coast in traditional sailing vessels for centuries before Europeans arrived intrigued the artists of Groote Eylandt; Macassan subjects were painted.

The Macassan sailing boats travelled to Groote Eylandt on the wet season's wind, Bara. They collected *trepang* and pearl shell, then returned to Macassar with the south-easterly monsoon wind, Mamariga. The winds give each season its particular character and are therefore major factors in the life of the people. The dry season wind, Mamariga, blows from the east or south-east from about April to September. As it gets hotter towards the end of the dry season, the north-east wind takes over, and finally about mid-November Bara begins, bringing with it thunderstorms and torrential rain.

Mythology and art emphasise the winds, symbolising their origins in totemic rites. Designs incorporate rectangular areas representing the trees or rocks that are the totemic centre of each wind.

An outstanding feature of the Groote Eylandt paintings is the rich black so often applied to the background. This intensifies the lighter red, yellow and white ochres painted over it. Black pigment is made from manganese, found extensively on the island but not on the mainland, where until recently colours were lighter unless black had been obtained through trading. The most striking feature of the Groote Eylandt paintings is the very positive attitude to the space around the figures; this space has a dynamism very sympathetic to sensibilities attuned to modern art. The animals and especially the birds have a particular elegance with their full, swelling and pattern-filled bodies contrasted with their tiny heads.

On Chasm Island, off the coast of Groote Eylandt, cave paintings are found, some of the few in the north-east. The cave paintings of Groote Eylandt show more emphasis on human features and must be considerably older than the bark paintings. These paintings were some of the first Aboriginal art works ever seen by Europeans, for they were sketched by Westall from Matthew Flinders' ship as he charted the coastline of the Gulf of Carpentaria in 1803.

The cave paintings and more recent bark paintings of Groote Eylandt share many similarities in subject matter, including a series of fishing scenes showing disproportionately large fish being caught by a line. The simple silhouettes of animals and men in the cave paintings are less intricate in detail than in the bark paintings.

In 1963 a manganese mine was established on Groote Eylandt and this development, together with the growth of an associated township, has led to a decrease in the number of artists actively involved in bark painting. The delicate, spacious early style has gone, but Groote Eylandt art remains distinctive.

'Fishing scene' by Nangapiana, acquired on the American-Australian Scientific Expedition in 1948. Three fishermen are harpooning a green turtle and a dugong from a dugout canoe. *Collection Art Gallery of South Australia*

THE IMPORTANCE OF VARIATIONS IN STYLE

The style of bark paintings can be affected by individual variations from within Aboriginal society, by the exigencies of the market and by the artist's perceptions of what the buyer wants. Notwithstanding, bark painting as a commercial activity has become fully integrated into Aboriginal social and ceremonial life. It is the main means of imparting mythological information and the meaning and relationship of the clan to special features of their land. Paintings have been used in land rights court cases, standing as title deeds, and they are also seen as property that can be used as a form of exchange.

In this context, only some individual variations in paintings are permitted. In most of the areas discussed, an artist learns and follows his father's designs, occasionally his mother's and his maternal grandmother's. This system is determined by the complex kinship rules of Aboriginal society, and mistakes or 'stealing' of another clan's designs are serious offences.

An artist who learns the designs from his father must retain the important appropriate clan symbols and patterns exactly. However, in superimposed figures and animal shapes and in the overall composition of the painting, each artist tends to bring his own personal style into play. Thus bark paintings do not remain exactly the same from generation to generation. In eastern Arnhem Land one man may paint the ancestor figures with rounded heads, another with triangular heads. The eyes, mouths and limbs of animals may vary, but the patterns on their bodies and in the background will be the same.

In western Arnhem Land, individual variations in bark painting are also seen. In the areas around the Alligator and Liverpool Rivers, strong imagery is used to convey the menace and ferocity of spirit creatures and the power of ancestral heroes. In the distant past, the Rainbow Serpent sometimes metamorphosed from snake to kangaroo to crocodile. Today, paintings can show the Serpent with features of some or all of these creatures; an antler-like headdress, for example, and a barbed snake tail. Similarly, the lightning spirit is shown with a multitude of facial expressions and physical attributes. Each artist gives his interpretation.

Cautionary tales told to the artist in childhood and verbal descriptions of the physical features of spirit creatures can inflame his imagination and still influence his own version of his subject matter. There appears to be more scope for the depiction of fearsome imagined spirits in the west than in the east, though, of course, individual artistic variations occur in all painting areas. Another means by which traditional bark paintings change is through dreams. Dreams play a significant role in the religious and imaginative life of Aboriginals and can be the means whereby a new design element is introduced into an artist's work.

There is no doubt that the quantity and upsurge in bark paintings in their present form has emerged through the interaction of Aboriginal society and outside influences; firstly anthropologists, followed by missionaries, government administrators and more recently by art historians and art galleries. Painting is now a major economic activity and the demands and criteria of the buyers have been integrated into the work. At centres where there is an adjacent market in the form of a European town (for example, Nhulunbuy in north-east Arnhem Land), small bark paintings are produced to provide a souvenir trade for the workers and visitors to the mine. The arts centre at Yirrkala, the Aboriginal community, only eleven kilometres away, sells up to sixty per cent of the work locally and some artists sell direct to the people in the town. Major and important ceremonial paintings are also painted alongside this art, supplying a growing demand for fine paintings in the wider art market. In one sense, it is hard to separate the two styles of painting; the smaller souvenir paintings may actually be segments or episodes of the larger ones. They will then have mythological importance and may be well painted. On the other hand, despite the mythological relevance, they are sometimes simply 'rough' paintings, quickly executed on inadequately prepared bark, with either flaking paint or too much fixative, resulting in a hard, glossy and unappealing surface.

It is obvious that both the disposition and motivation of the artist affect the work. A well known middle-aged painter was in Sydney and observed several of the paintings on display in a gallery. These were, to European eyes, rough, crude paintings with little aesthetic appeal; they were priced accordingly. Interested to know the master painter's reaction, the author asked him his opinion of the works, which were both from his own cultural area. The first depicted a single large black image of a fish on a simple cross-hatched background. The artist commented, 'This one's a bit rough. I think he need the money so he could go to Nhulunbuy for drink. It comes from Yirrkala, not the homeland centre. Some lines are missing, something is left out.'

The second painting showed a black crocodile against an irregular diamond pattern. His comments were, 'I know the crocodile who owns that story. This man is very old and has passed away – his hand shaking badly never do good painting. These supposed to be little diamonds. He's left out things. He has left out the black, the ashes of the fire. If the young people want to know the right way to paint [this story], they have to go to another old man.'

When asked to value the works, the commentator predictably placed a higher value on the old man's crocodile, out of deference not only to his age but also to his ritual standing in the community, despite his worry that the painting was not a good educative tool.

One interesting feature of the development of marketing bark paintings has been the emergence of artists whose paintings are perceived to have more individual style and to be more attractive and desirable than others by the European collector. Whereas in his traditional society the artist is not a separate figure, today some who have been able to earn their living and support the family well on the proceeds of their paintings are now seen by their community as artists. Being a recognised artist carries with it some status. However, unless the artist is an important man in ritual matters, having achieved a high level of knowledge of design, songs and ceremony, this increase in status is limited to temporal things. Clan ceremonial leaders continue to exhibit complete authority over their designs, songs, rituals and use of their lands and designs on a coffin or burial post are inspected to ensure their accuracy.

Papunya Painting

Traditionally, every adult man and woman in the desert regions is an artist. Men use ancient abstract symbols to create ground designs in feathers, pulverised plants, ochre and blood, and these same materials create designs on their bodies in ceremonies. Circles, lines and dots are also used to carry through the same symbolic language to three-dimensional ceremonial sculptures and other traditional items such as shields, weapons and carrying dishes. Women use abstract designs in their own parallel expressive arts and paint their bodies for women's ceremonies.

The symbols are a form of visual language in which the ancestral renewal of life is celebrated and its continuance ensured. The arts all express — indeed, establish — the relationship of the people to their ancestors and to their tribal lands through stories of ancestral travels across the landscape. Various aspects of the journeys that must be remembered by future generations are included.

Perhaps the most important subject of western desert ceremonial art is the Tingari cycle. The Tingari were a group of men who lived in the Dreaming and who travelled across the land, making many features of the landscape. The exact nature of the Tingari men and details of their feats remain shrouded in total secrecy. Accompanied on their journey by Tingari women and by young men undergoing various stages of initiation, the Tingari men established all the rituals of initiation for the desert people, as well as creating geographical features of the landscape and defining relationships between men and women, customs and social behaviour. Tingari ceremonies consist of hundreds of song verses which are sung and chanted well into the night.

The Tingari cycle, with its related body decoration, ground drawings and ceremonial performance, is part of the contemporary initiation training of young men. During their teenage years, youths are separated from the rest of the community and spend time with their senior male relatives, undergoing training and manhood tests, one of which is to successfully spear a kangaroo. The youths are instructed in their own Dreaming; they are taken to ancestral paths and tracks. They learn the religious significance of all the natural features of their country, as well as practical food lore and the skills of discovering water. The finding of soaks is directly connected to knowledge of the places at which the ancestors stopped and found water.

This training period is commonly called 'high school' in English. The use of this phrase was coined as an attempt to put the status of the traditional education process clearly, so that Europeans would understand the importance of such education to desert Aboriginals. The term also relates to the age group of young men undergoing the ceremonies — the same group that would otherwise be ready for high school in Alice Springs. Having speared a kangaroo, the novice is ready to be shown his inherited Dreaming designs in the form of secret ground patterns, body decorations and emblems.

Opposite **Detail of a painting by Charles Egarli of a wallaby Dreaming story.**

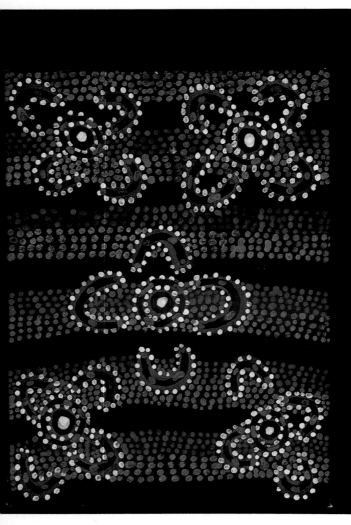

Painting by Emily Andy Napaltjarri of a women's story. Women are painting more frequently, extending their colour range from earth colours to brighter hues.

The ground drawings, which are almost sculptures, as they are raised, low relief patterns composed of hundreds of small pieces of plant or feather down, no doubt have extremely ancient origins. Many designs recorded in early reports contain spirals and circles that are still salient features. These and bird tracks can be found in similar formations in ancient rock engravings and paintings thousands of years old. The ground designs depend for their power and effectiveness not only on the pattern but on the substances used and circumstances of manufacture. It is from these dotted combinations of line and colour that a whole school of new paintings, executed on canvas, has developed. Desert belief and ceremonial practice are very much parts of a living religion and therefore living religious art. When these concepts are transferred to canvas, the men who paint in acrylics for a commercially oriented art market still hold the ground designs and ancient mythological sites in their minds as they paint circles and dot the background with delicate foliage patterns.

Women's art and ceremony in the dry arid interior run parallel to that of the men. There are 'women's Dreamings', stories of women ancestors who travelled across the desert gathering food, often pursued by men. Various sites are exclusively women's places where men avoid going, and these centres are sometimes associated with fertility and 'baby essence'. At some places, as legends and songs tell, the men caught the women and, according to the women's euphemistic accounts, 'sat down with them'; these sites are marked with special rock formations or caves.

Women spend a great deal of time in company with other women, discussing the minute daily affairs of camp life, discussing women's ceremony (variously termed *yawulya* or *awulya* in the Walbiri language) and going on extensive hunting trips. The hunting trips are eagerly planned. Available vehicles are crammed with people, each woman bringing a billy can for tea, an axe for witchetty grubs and a crowbar with a splayed, flattened end for digging out lizards or rabbits. The women's Dreaming stories abound with descriptive information of the same hunting trips taken by the ancestral women in the creation time, including the food they gathered — wild raisins, bush yams, seeds from grasses, wild tomatoes and many others. The ceremonies, consisting of dances with bodies and breasts painted with designs symbolic of the landscape stories, are held among the same groups of related women, who also hunt together. The chanting of song cycles accompanies and instructs the dancers in their movements, telling of the ancestral travels, hunting, looking for food and digging.

Dancing is loose and rhythmic, with the women in a line taking short jumps and slightly dragging their feet. Along the soft sand, the rows of separated feet produce a ridged pattern in the sand; this is an important aspect of the dance, being evidence of ancestral beings' tracks, and therefore a visual record of the ancestral journeys.

Painted designs on the women's bodies are only one aspect of the whole ceremonial performance, but they are made with patience and loving care, each woman proudly displaying her own designs on her breasts and shoulders. At a recent women's ceremony at Kintore, a remote community in the western desert, over twenty women gathered beneath the shade of a tree to begin singing their own ceremonial songs in preparation for a men's ceremony which was to be held not far away. Kinsmen and their families had assembled over weeks and were camped together awaiting the trucks which had been on the 'muster', the term used to denote the gathering of the young men for manhood ceremonies. Each evening at about five p.m., the women gathered, and, painting their bodies, sang and danced until dusk. They indicated that they were 'singing those women to here', re-enacting the ancient events that led to the arrival of two ancestral women to the place where the people were camped, the Kintore ranges. Kintore itself is a very sacred place to the Pintubi people and the men's ceremony that followed carried the women's beginnings to fruition. The women were integral to the whole preparation and anticipation, although they would not attend the 'business', or 'office' as it is known. The women who sing and paint their bodies at these ceremonies are generally mothers of several children or older senior women, knowledgeable in ceremony with power and prestige.

Women's body painting emphasises the breasts, which are full and hang low. The skin is first smoothed and oiled with goanna fat or (more commonly) margarine, and then one woman applies designs to another with her finger, tracing the ochre lines slowly and carefully to give curved lines of even width and colour intensity. In fading light, the designs stand out clearly. A row of twenty seated women with their torsos painted and contiguous curving lines dipping and following the deep contours of each breast creates a human tableau of irregular scallops in white and brown.

Detail of the beginning of a dingo story painting by William Sandy, a Pitjantjatjara artist resident at Papunya.

A group of men prepare to make a ground design at Warumpi near Papunya, Northern Territory. The plant in the foreground (*Helichrysum apiculatum*) is used as the raw material for making the design.

GROUND CONSTRUCTIONS

Traditional desert designs made on the ground for ceremonies have been termed sand mosaics, ground paintings or sand paintings. In reality, they are closer to sculpture or performance art. Neither paint nor brushes are used, and dance and song are vital parts of the performance.

To make three-dimensional patterns, a relatively flat area of ground is cleared of small shrubs, grasses and all debris. Before a design is constructed, the area is covered with a thick sludge of pulverised termite mound and allowed to dry. This provides an even, flat and hard surface that will not throw up dust and dislodge the design.

For important and sacred ceremonies the substances used to make the patterns include bird down, native kapok, red ochre, white clay and blood. Within the last five years, some ground constructions have been made outside their ritual contexts to demonstrate to Europeans the ancient religious symbols and their construction. One Walbiri man, a member of a group making such a work in the Musée d'Art Moderne in Paris was quoted in the catalogue as saying, 'We present you with a glimpse of the way we venerate the sacred heroes who have given us our identity, so that Europeans can have some understanding of what we are.'[1]

The ancient ground constructions are most elaborate. Some of the design elements in themselves are not considered dangerous, but the situation in which they are exposed can release the forces and power of ancestral beings and harm the uninitiated. The dancers and the objects used in a ceremony become infused with the power of the ancestral beings. During the ceremony the dancers obliterate the ground design and the decorations on their bodies are destroyed so that the designs are never seen in secular situations.

The artists who create the ground paintings are all mature men, who have gone through extensive rituals so that they are knowledgeable and competent in depicting the designs, singing the songs and dancing correctly at the relevant sites.

Five Walbiri men resident at Warumpi, an outstation of Papunya, agreed to construct a simple version of a sand design especially for publication in this book. They wished to demonstrate their immense feeling about such designs, their relationship to the land and to life and death and by extension to reveal that other similar designs on canvases and carrying dishes were all part of the same Dreaming. For a non-ceremonial demonstration such as this, no feathers or human blood were used, and powdered white clay was replaced with plain flour – the artists were seeking to reveal the design and its construction, rather than releasing power inherent in the more meaningful substances. The basic material used was a very small flowering herbaceous plant. For the design, the entire plant is pulverised; stems, leaves and small yellow flowers are gathered, bunched up and chopped finely with an axe. Many such plants are needed for a large ground design.

Chopping the plant used in the design is itself a skill; the plant is fed to the axe deftly and quickly, each blow cutting the stems cleanly into very small pieces. The plant fibre is then divided into two heaps, each to be coloured separately, one deep red, the other white. For the red, called *wanjari*, a lump of deep red ochre is ground onto a flat stone, forming red ochre powder. Taking some fat or lard into his hands, the artist holds the plant stuff and rubs it into the red ochre on the stone. The resultant mass is deep red material, similar to fairly dry papier-mache pulp. The fat aids in binding the ochre to the plants and allows the material to be manipulated with the fingers into small or large dollops. The second half of the chopped plant stuff is coloured in a similar way, with kitchen flour replacing the red ochre and being substituted for the white clay used on ceremonial occasions. The white coloured pulp is termed *turrijirri*.

The design chosen was a series of concentric circles, one element of a much more elaborate composition. Paddy Carroll, who, with Two Bob Tjungurrayi, was owner of the design, combined with two other men, Dinny Nolan and Elgin Djambijimba the *kutungulu*, to make the ground drawing. Each design marks an important place, the centre of the power for a particular Dreaming; these sites have owners as well as *kutungulu* who ensure that the owners carry out their duties correctly. All four men participated as well as a fifth, a younger related man, Don Tjungurrayi, who assisted.

The men were silent and respectful as they sat around the flattened earth. Slowly, working from two sides simultaneously, they made a small circle of tightly packed dots of plant pulp, making a ridge about 2.5 centimetres high. Then an outer circle of the second colour was added, the pattern being first traced on the ground with a wet paintbrush. Circle after circle went down, dot after dot, slowly, meticulously, reverently. One man began a small song and then left off just to gaze at the design, his mind going to the Dreaming and the first time he saw the pattern.

'This is really dear one, bush tucker, we call 'im *yalka*. Little round one, like onion. Bush onion place all in this one, we call 'im *yunga*, bush onion place. Might be different story, 'nother story, still they do 'im same. When we camp in high school in the bush only men know, pretty tickly. Young men in high school can't see this one till they get kangaroo.'

When the design was complete and photographs taken, it was carefully covered with sheets of corrugated iron and bushes. Other trusted Europeans in Papunya were invited to look at the painting as well as some men from other areas. One who approached, a Pintubi artist noted for his works on canvas, was reticent, but as he drew nearer he was invited to share the experience with the ground artists, and, kneeling, he placed his hand in the centre of the circle.

The experience of this ground design enhanced and expanded all our perceptions about the canvas paintings. Although the design was specifically made for publication* its motives could not be separated from its deep religious meaning, and its manufacture was clearly a religious act and a pleasure for all participants.

A windbreak is made of bushes, the ground is cleaned and termite mound is spread across the surface to give a hard, flat base for the construction. The design proceeds slowly, circle after circle.

---

* The five men who made the ground drawing pictures in this book requested that they be published to show the deeper arts of the desert men beside those of Aboriginals in other parts of the country. However, they remained reticent about any revelation of the design to Aboriginal women. They requested that if this book is purchased and kept in communities amongst their desert relatives — Pitjantjatjara, Walbiri, Pintubi, Aranda or Loritja, in houses frequented by Aboriginal women — that helpful owners seal these pages to avoid any worry for the women.

1 Applying the pellets of plant pulp to the ground.
2 Chopping the stems, leaves and flowers.
3 The plant is rubbed into a mixture with animal fat and red ochre.
4 The artists' materials ready for use, coloured red with ochre and white with kitchen flour.
5 Yalka bush onion design. Ground construction by Paddy Carroll, Two Bob Tjungurrayi, Dinny Nolan, Elgin Djambijimba and Don Tjungurrayi, at Papunya in 1983.

Opposite The concentric circular construction is one element of a larger ground design. The pattern symbolically represents a bush onion and is the site of bush onion Dreaming

CONTEMPORARY WORKS ON CANVAS: PAPUNYA-TULA PAINTINGS

Ground constructions or mosaics are the most elaborate Pintubi-Walbiri art forms, and it is from these that the modern paintings draw their inspiration. The dramatic contemporary development of an art industry centred at Papunya and based on the ancient ground paintings is most extraordinary.

The movement began in the early 1970s, stimulated by Geoff Bardon, a teacher. Bardon was attempting to paint a mural on the school wall, trying to achieve some semblance of 'Aboriginality' by using geometric shapes and symbols such as circles and zigzags. Intrigued, some of the older men came closer, and upon encouragement, took over the task, completing a traditional design over the whole wall. Other murals followed and the interest and fervour of the men to paint their Dreamings grew until up to twenty artists were using available scraps of masonite and board, and grinding ochres or obtaining paint from Bardon, producing many paintings in completely traditional symbols. Bardon was told later[2] that one old man considered himself responsible for 'giving' the initial Dreaming — the honey ant story — to the school mural. Papunya settlement is built close to a low ridge of the MacDonnell Ranges, the site of the honey ant Dreaming. In giving his authorisation, old Tom Onion Tjapangati allowed others to follow.

Bardon showed the paintings to the Australian public in the form of exhibitions, which, although immediately appreciated by European gallery audiences, caused some Aboriginal concern and a reassessment by the artists. The use of some symbols and the realistic portrayal of particular sacred objects were subsequently omitted from the paintings after the artists had held lengthy meetings. In the enthusiasm for the new medium and pride in the recognition and appreciation of what was most dear to them, their Dreaming stories, the painters had inadvertently let too much out and they drew back, seeking a compromise.

The paintings that have flowed since those early years have not suffered in any way. Federal grants secured the services of an adviser to take Bardon's place when he left, and several people have held this position, acting as agent, organiser and intermediary between these artists, their co-operative company Papunya-Tula, galleries and the public.

At present about sixty-five artists are painting wonderful works on canvas in geographical locations hundreds of kilometres apart, although most are at Kintore, a settlement 300 kilometres due west of Papunya in the Kintore Ranges, not far from the Western Australian border. To some extent some stylistic differences are evident between the paintings of some of the language groups, particularly the Pintubi and Anmatjira, with the paintings of other groups developing features of each.

Pintubi tribespeople were the last to adapt to a settled existence. The remaining groups of nomadic Pintubi, thought to be starving in the desert, were brought in to Papunya in the late 1950s and early 1960s,[3] and they are occasionally termed 'bush' Pintubi by other Aboriginal groups, indicating their relative lack of contact and adjustment to European values and ways. Pintubi territory extends west of Papunya and throughout vast areas of Western Australian desert.

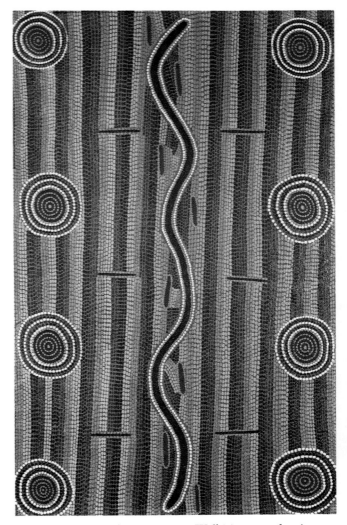

Painting by Two Bob Tjungurrayi, Walbiri group, showing an important site at Central Mt Wedge.

Opposite **Don Tjungurrayi painting at Papunya. First he paints the important sites, the two circles. Then, keeping these in mind, he begins filling in the painting, telling the journey of the ancestors as they went from one site to another.**

Painting by Charles Tjaruru Tjungurrayi of the Pintubi.

The Pintubi are proud, determined and intensely religious people. Pintubi paintings are principally geometric, two-dimensional representations of sacred Dreaming sites and ancestral journeys. Circles, U shapes, tracks and linear journey markings frequently combine in symmetrical, relatively simple paintings, using a limited colour range.

The Anmatjira are related to the Aranda, whose territory extends south to Alice Springs. Many Aranda and Anmatjira have had lengthier contact with Europeans on cattle stations, and it is amongst the Aranda of Hermannsburg that the famous school of realistic watercolour landscapes grew up around Albert Namatjira in the 1950s and 1960s.

Anmatjira paintings are complex compositions of dots with some symbolic geometric Dreaming references as well as tracks. The dots, in different colour blocks, represent vegetation in the landscape as it changes from place to place and from season to season. Moving through the Australian desert during the flowering or seeding season is a visually exciting experience as wide patches of spinifex grass give way to low grey-green bush foliage, or to mulga trees, wattles and daisies. The vegetation itself grows in dots and patches of colour, like the paintings. The artists are providing not only a topographical map of ceremonial sites and hence mountain ranges, waterholes and other geological formations, but the Anmatjira in particular are also showing the important vegetation changes — the places where bush fruit can be gathered or where grass seeds give flour for bread or damper. The brushwork is freer and, at times, a three-dimensional optical effect clearly sets the Anmatjira paintings apart.

Clifford Possum Tjapaltjari is an exceptional Anmatjira painter, whose work has now won several art prizes, and has been featured in Australian contributions to international contemporary art symposia.

Despite stylistic variations, the central theme of all paintings, as of ground designs and ceremonies, is the events of the Dreaming. Each painting is about a place, frequently the birthplace of the artist or of his Dreaming ancestors. Each painting represents not only the site but the event that took place there in the Dreaming. Sites may be specific rocks, waterholes, special trees, mountains and many others. The creation ancestors, which can be honey ants, bush onions, wild kangaroos, sweet potatoes or budgerigars, are thought to be at rest at these places, but their power and force become one with the dancers during ceremonies. For example, the flying ant is an ancestor of the Anmatjira people; he was immense and had a long beard and wizened face. Occasionally he rested, and paintings of this story concern the sites at which he did so. Concentric circles not only represent the site but also the earth mound homes of the flying ant — wavy lines symbolise the travels as well as the journeys underground. Flying ants are an important source of food to desert people; they are gathered in hundreds in the wooden carrying dishes and their wings are singed off in the fire.

Another painting may depict the travels of the witchetty grub ancestors beneath the ground. The painting could be interpreted as showing the emergence of the witchetty grub from the ground or through the hollow tree, and its metamorphosis into a moth. At a deeper level it may symbolise the journey of a boy to manhood by means of his initiation ceremony.

Opposite A water dreaming story painting attributed to Old Mick Jagamara of the Ngalia group, 1975.

Over page Water Dreaming painting done in 1981 by Dick Pantimatju Tjupurrula of the Loritja group of Kalipinya. The central pattern of wavy lines shows water, with the symbol of a water man ancestral figure at both ends. Between these lines, the space represents sand dunes. Bird tracks show the birds feeding after rain. On either side are two versions of a story about an old man wallaby and the kangaroos at a site named Tjikarri. The circle with curved lines represents the whiskers of the kangaroo. A kangaroo killed for food has been painted against the foliage of bush tucker, including *wangi*, a type of flower, and pink areas representing claypans.

Women's Dreaming painting by Daisy Leura Nakamarra of the Loritja group, showing food gathering activities.

It is not possible for outsiders or Europeans to fully comprehend the elaborate and extended multilevel meaning of the central Australian ground designs from which the paintings are derived. Certainly no women are permitted, and only a few European men have passed through the secret stages of initiation.

Each man may only produce the paintings connected with sites that he owns himself, although in recent years a number of paintings have appeared in the contemporary stream that have been executed under unusual circumstances. An artist who does not himself paint on canvas can ask another painter to paint his own Dreaming site. For the artists, as for the public, the paintings may work on several levels. They not only tell the story in symbolic form, but the artists use them to recall the legends to their own minds as they paint. It is common for an artist to sing as he paints and for another artist to sit beside him and to trace the patterns on the canvas with his own fingers, singing along.

Like Arnhem Land art, the paintings are maps of the land, prescribing the extent of the territory owned by the artists and connected to the Dreaming being painted. In a new way they are beginning to be individual artistic expressions. Some artists are developing reputations for being more extravagant and flamboyant in their work. They are extending the bounds of tradition, slightly bending it to their own wills, incorporating contemporary themes or striking non-traditional colours.

Another most important feature is the personal nature of the symbols. One artist cannot be sure that he is interpreting another man's painting accurately. Although the symbols are limited and familiar to each man, each artist uses them subjectively so that only he himself could give a full interpretation of the many levels of meaning that his painting has for him.[4]

Right Painting by Mick Tjapaljari of a bush tucker story, circa 1972, one of the first Pintubi paintings to be done in acrylics. *Photograph Geoff Bardon*

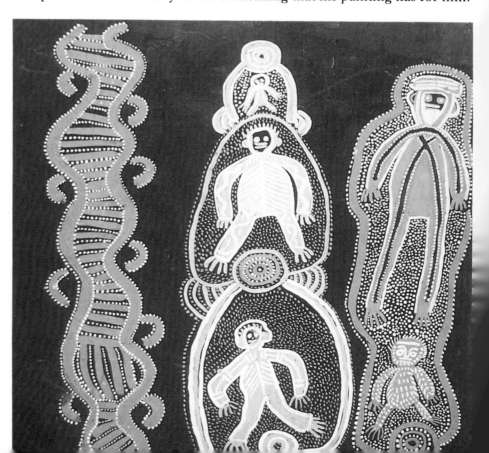

WOMEN ARTISTS

The Papunya-Tula canvas paintings were exclusively done by men until very recently. Gradually, as canvases grew larger for important commissions, the wives of some artists helped paint the dotted backgrounds and so acquired skill with paint and brushes. Women have now begun small paintings of their own, which, in size and simplicity of statement, are very similar to the first men's paintings on small boards produced in the early 1970s. Women paint 'women's stories', generally about special sites, depicting women seated around a campfire in the traditional U shape, and with their digging sticks and *coolamon* or wooden carrying dish nearby. Women as well as men own the important Dreaming sites, and the Papunya honey ant Dreaming story of Papunya itself is one of the first Dreamings to be given expression. Some women such as Entalura Nangala, wife of Don Tjungurrayi, and Daisy Leura are pleased to paint in order to earn more income for the family, and do so at the request and with the support of their husbands. Other women paint as the only alternative to dole cheques, ('sit down money'), or pension money; besides, in an otherwise quite relaxed life they feel a need to express themselves artistically. Occasionally a husband who has been a successful painter has turned to drink to alleviate stress in Alice Springs and the wife is now painting out of economic necessity.

So far women have not painted Dreaming stories featuring male ancestors, though men, perceiving the beginning of new interest in women's paintings, are increasing their production of 'women's Dreamings'. The men are indicating to the external world that, although the women may assist in economic matters and paint their own pictures, the men wish to retain their place and authority in the Papunya-Tula Company.

The canvas paintings from the Papunya school have been more easily accepted into the mainstream of Australian contemporary art than the bark paintings of the north. Arnhem Land paintings commonly employ figurative designs; this and the use of natural tree bark as a painting surface have kept them in the philosophical mould of artefact rather than art in the minds of contemporary European artists and curators. The Papunya acrylics on canvas are more easily accessible to the Western art tradition of abstractionism. The treatment of landscape subjects, acrylic paint and canvas surface are all familiar, allowing the Papunya painters to be accepted into contemporary art circles as painters rather than 'primitive' artists.

The sale of Papunya-Tula paintings has now become a major economic support to the artists in the difficult process of adjusting to European values and their need to acquire European goods such as cars and radios in increasing quantities. The paintings have been widely exhibited and individual artists are now receiving large public commissions in recognition of the beauty and importance of their work in Australian contemporary art.

Top Painting by Lottie Nangala of Loritja women at a rockhole just east of Papunya. The black ovoid shapes are *coolamons* for carrying bush tucker and the irregular black shapes are *piti*, deep *coolamons* for carrying water.

Bottom Luritja artist Entalura Nangala explains her painting of a women's Dreaming site. U shapes are seated women; the ovals represent their *coolamons* and the central circle is the sacred site.

223

Carved Weapons and Utensils

Elegant, inventive weapons and utensils hold a central place in Aboriginal material arts, not only because of their excellent design, balance and appropriate use of materials, but also because they demonstrate Aboriginal artists' apparent love and appreciation of the qualities of decoration itself. Artists invariably go to great lengths to select a branch or root of a tree in which the shape and grain are appropriate for the form of the implement to be made. Many excellent weapons and utensils are still made in traditional communities. The Aboriginal carver has always chosen his wood carefully, considering the function of the weapon. Heavy hardwoods were used to make narrow shields needed to deflect attack from a club or boomerang, whereas broader, flat shields were required for defence against spears, and these could be made of lighter timber. All over Australia, the surfaces of most shields, clubs, and spear throwers were decorated; in the south with very fine engravings and in the north with complex painted surfaces. Even in areas where craftsmen eschewed decoration on weapons, they were invariably concerned with the beauty, quality and grain of the wood.

Aboriginal carvers have always enjoyed making things to be used, sitting peacefully with others and undertaking work that gave them great satisfaction. In the design of weapons and domestic items, some of the earliest examples of the inventiveness unique to Australia can be found. Both the returning boomerang of the south-east and the leaf-shaped spear thrower of the central desert area explore concepts of multiple use and simplicity of design, which have intrigued all who have come in contact with them. Though the boomerang has long enjoyed fame, not only as a symbol of Aboriginal arts but also of all things distinctively Australian, the leaf-shaped spear thrower is relatively unknown.

In the design and manufacture of weapons, tools and other utensils, primary consideration was given to their effectiveness and portability. Each item had to be carried, often for long distances, and therefore if one piece could perform several tasks it saved the burden of too many possessions. Although simple, the weapons and implements were so ingeniously designed that a few light, transportable tools equipped nomadic people with the means of obtaining all their daily requirements. The boomerang, for example, although primarily a hunting and fighting weapon, was also used for making fire, stoking the coals when cooking and for scraping and smoothing other tools. Boomerangs were also used in traditional games. The design of the leaf-shaped spear thrower was such that it could be used as a chisel, knife or engraver, a receptacle for mixing ochres and a fire-making saw, as well as a spear launcher. Women bore the brunt of the load and were also often required to carry their babies on their backs, on their shoulders, or on their hips.

Opposite The hardwood spear throwers from south-eastern Australia were finely engraved with geometric patterns. The example on the left is one of the first attempts to add realistic images associated with European presence. *Collection Museum of Victoria*

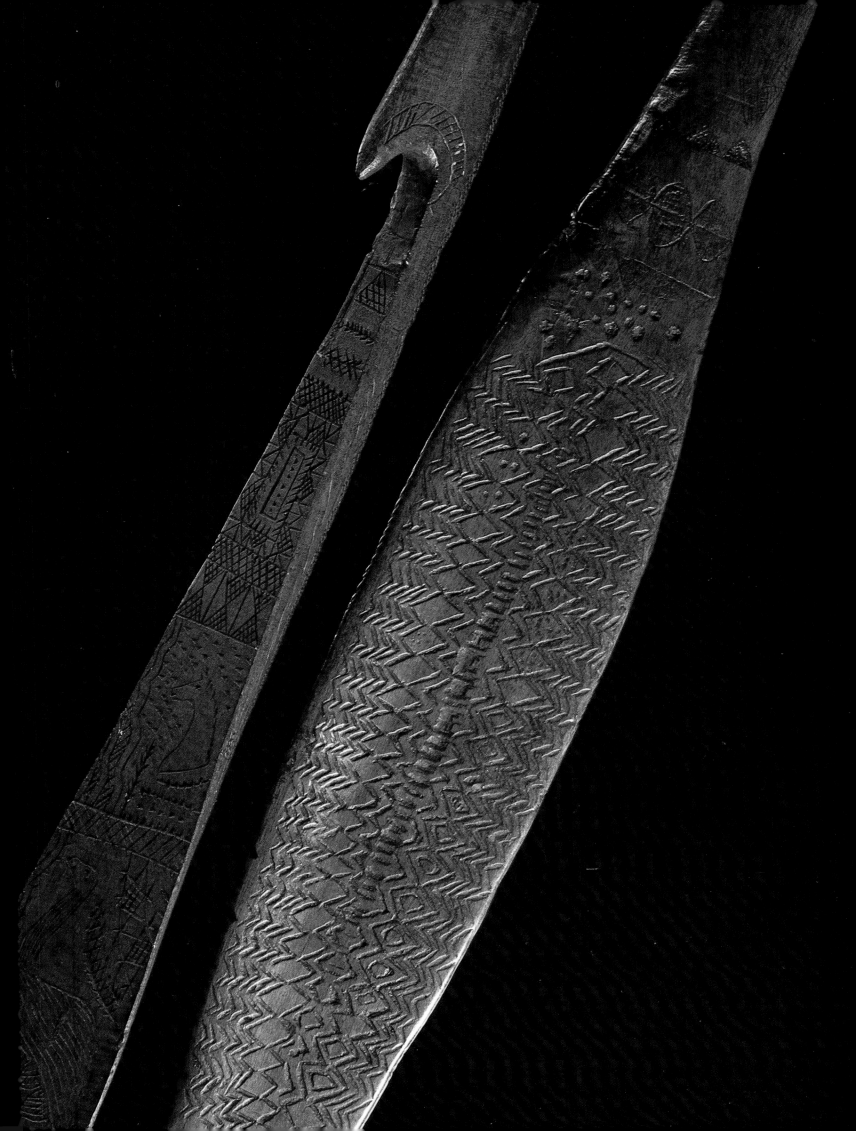

Despite this need for practicality, weapons were never simply tools, apart from stone flakes used as knives. People had a strong sense of personal identity related to their membership of tribal groups and those groups' ownership of land. As discussed in other chapters, every person was related to ancestral beings who gave physical form to their land; ceremonies recalled this to mind and summoned the ancestral heroes to continue their influence over the cycle of life. All over the country, the decoration of weapons and domestic objects provided an additional forum for the display of clan designs and illustrated the ownership of land. This intention is clear not only in painted designs of the northern Arnhem Land areas, but also in the complex geometric engraved patterns on weapons made in south-eastern Australia. Even the carrying dishes of the centre, now patterned with designs formed by impressions made with red-hot wire, are decorated with journeys of ancestral characters and special places in the landscape. It is clear that even in the everyday, so-called 'secular' arts, there are frequently mythological and ancestral allusions in the decoration, bearing out the frequent statements by artists that they are 'showing their Dreaming', *tjukurpa* or spirit.

Above South-eastern Australian spear throwers from the Gundagai region of New South Wales, acquired from homesteads circa 1890 to 1900. *Collection The Australian Museum*

Opposite Wood carving skills are highly developed and still maintained in central Australia. Don Tjungurrayi is pictured carving with a traditional adze. A metal blade has been substituted for the original stone cutting edge.

227

From left Bulbous-headed club from Lachlan River area, New South Wales; hooked boomerang-like club from western New South Wales; *lil-lil* from Lake Narran, New South Wales; incised *yachi* club from the Murray River area; club termed *langeel* from the Paroo River, New South Wales.
Collection The Australian Museum

SOUTH-EAST COASTAL AND RIVER AREAS

In the well-watered areas of Victoria and New South Wales there was great variation in weapons and utensils, with many unusually shaped clubs and throwing sticks as well as boomerangs. Each was developed to fill a particular need for acquiring food, fighting or maintaining and making other utensils.

The Aboriginal communities of the south-east bore the early brunt of European invasion and gradual usurpation of land for pastoral use by the new colonists. Whole tribes were decimated very quickly, not only by violence resulting from forcible land occupation but also by the spread of European diseases, particularly smallpox. An Aboriginal song composed in the early nineteenth century likens the burn of infectious smallpox to the spikes of a porcupine. Sung mournfully, imitating a dying person, the song (as recounted in 1881 by James Dawson[1]) is one of the few recorded verbal laments of the agony that must have been part of Aboriginal existence as people watched their own families dying within a generation. Composed somewhere in the Sydney area, the song could be heard in many different Aboriginal languages.

Porcupine spikes
Burn like heat of fire
Someone pinching me
When I am up high
With affection like a sister.
Grinning, grinning, grinning,
Teeth mine.

The diaries of early colonists frequently comment on the appearance, customs and activities of the Aboriginals who lived on the edges of towns and who retained their camps close to country properties. The nineteenth-century fascination with the 'childlike' but faithful qualities of the people was coupled with a desire to collect examples of the unusual weapons and implements with which they had 'eked out their existence' in what seemed to the newcomers an inhospitable and forbidding land. Clubs, spears and shields drew the attention of the men; few European women spent much time among Aboriginal people.

The weapons that remain in museum collections are now the only evidence available of the decorative arts and skills of the south-east people. It is unfortunate that only the objects themselves have been preserved; none of the meanings of the designs. Although the patterns all had particular symbolic meanings to the artist, these were never elucidated. Like territorial maps, the patterns all related to tribal country and might have had much more detailed significance.

Records of Victorian pieces include descriptions of several types of club. Clubs were used in single combat, in fighting, both between women and men, in tribal warfare and in hunting wild game where they were used to kill the prey after it had been caught in specially constructed nets. The simplest club was the *nulla nulla*. To make these, a young tree was pulled up and simply fashioned into a club, the root forming the knob. The end was usually sharpened and the implement could therefore be used as a sharp missile or for digging up roots. More elaborate forms of clubs included the *kud-jee-run* of the Yarra River, the *kul-kul* of the Gippsland people and the *lil-lil* used in Victoria and throughout New South Wales. Clubs which are found along the Murray River and called by the people of this area *moonoe* or *mannup* are similar in form to the *kud-jee-run*, but much more sharply pointed around the flange at the hitting end. The pointed end of the *kud-jee-run* is exceptionally sharp and is sometimes thrown to enter the body of the enemy. These clubs are similar to others termed *erambo* in New South Wales.

Forms of the club or waddy vary with every tribal group; even men of the same tribe use clubs that are made and decorated differently. According to R. Brough-Smyth[2] the upper parts of some are pear-shaped. Others may be like two cones placed base to base and so made as to present a cutting edge. A husband's chastisement of a wife who was thought to be unfaithful was usually carried out with a *kud-jee-run*. Another remarkable waddy is the *kul-kul*, once used by the people of Gippsland. Its shape is similar to a wooden sword but it is thicker and heavier. These weapons were decorated or bound with string at the handle end.

The *lil-lil*, also called a throwing stick, is one of the most unusual weapons. It was used either as a club in close combat or thrown at the enemy from a distance, like a boomerang. The shape of the *lil-lil* was such that it could hook around a shield and strike the enemy in the face. The edge of the *lil-lil*, shaped like a hatchet or axe, is very sharply ground and may be beautifully decorated with fine engraving. Another form of club had a head similar in shape to a pineapple and comparable to some found in the Pacific islands and New Guinea. It was carefully carved of hardwood, the sunken parts commonly painted with white clay and the protuberances with red clay.

Many different boomerangs were made. Of six examples illustrated by R. Brough-Smyth[3] as the weapons used in Victoria in the late nineteenth century, only one is of the returning variety, and this is known as the *wonguin*. Others were variously shaped and could be used either as missiles or in close combat, like swords.

Spears were of soft and hard timber and could be barbed, using embedded pieces of flint or stone, or with the barbs elaborately carved along one or both sides of the spearhead. Special spears were used for every purpose. There were spears for kangaroos, for fish and even for eels. Along the lower Murray River reed spears were used. They had barbs attached with the sinews from kangaroo tails, similar to those made in central Australia by the Pitjantjatjara today.

Throughout the south-east spears were generally launched with the aid of a spear thrower, called a *womerah* or *woomera*. Many different spear throwers were made, some carved from a single piece of timber with flattened shafts. Others were made by attaching pegs with the aid of kangaroo sinew. These pegs were occasionally made from the teeth of kangaroos or other game. Many of the spear throwers are elaborately decorated and some designs are the artists' first attempts to record the coming of the British colonists. Examples of spear throwers on which simple figures can be seen, as well as guns or ships signifying aspects of an alien culture, are to be found in the major collections of the southern Australian states.

Top Double pineapple-headed club collected from the Warrego district, New South Wales.
Centre Club from the Murray and Darling River areas. A pointed stick has been inserted into the club head.
Bottom Hexagonal-handled club with deeply rounded grooves in the head, western New South Wales.
Collection The Australian Museum

There are two principal types of shield: narrow hardwood shields for warding off blows from clubs generally used in single combat and broad shields to use against spears. Hardwood shields provide us with the widest range of decorative examples of the south-eastern wood engraving skills. Examples in collections and illustrated in early ethnographic works show the tendency of the artist to fully decorate the outer surface of these shields with fine patterns, frequently of parallel zigzags, diamonds and other linear non-symmetrical designs. Occasionally the shields are decorated along the full length with a series of concentric diamonds, or they may be separated into bands, again with predominantly diamond or zigzag decorations. When compared with the carved trees, or dendroglyphs, of the south-eastern region the stylistic similarities are apparent and it is quite clear that these shields represented, as did the trees, the totemic affiliations and land patterns of the owners. The handle of the hardwood shield is integral to the body and the underside is seldom decorated. The space allowed for holding by the hand is very narrow and combatants often wrapped a piece of possum skin around the hand before inserting the fingers through the handle. The broad shield was seldom used in single combat, being more frequently employed during tribal warfare in which spears would be hurled at opposing groups. Used skilfully, these shields could protect all parts of the body from spears.

Shields are made from the outer bark of the gum tree, and, in parts of north-western New South Wales there are still scars on old trees where the bark was removed for these shields last century. The bark was stripped from the tree and roughly shaped with the aid of an axe into the general form. Then a mound of earth was made about seven centimetres long and about the breadth of the piece of bark. Hot ashes were placed on the mound and the bark was then laid on top, covered with heavy stone and weighted. The green bark slowly took on the curve of the mound and this gave the wide shield its gentle, curved shape. On most broad shields the handles were attached separately; a piece of wood was formed into a handle when green and thrust into holes made to receive the ends. When dried, this could not be extracted easily, and formed a firm handle.

Like the narrow hardwood shields, these weapons were elaborately engraved and decorated. An observer along the Darling River in New South Wales described the technique of decorating the early weapons in that area[4] which could well apply to any of the south-eastern weapons. The rough shape of a boomerang was carved on the spot after the wood was removed from the tree. This was either taken to camp or to any desired spot, where it was finished while green and full of sap. The craftsman squatted over the piece of half-formed wood on the ground, holding it between his thigh and one foot, and an adze-flaked chisel held in both hands gradually reduced the wood to the shape required. This technique is still widely used in the desert to form spear throwers, boomerangs, dancing boards and other wooden weapons and implements. The fine finishing work was once done with a stone scraper and adze, but today in central Australia it is accomplished with a rasp or with other modern tools. Detailed designs were finely engraved on old weapons with the use of a stone made from black basalt, with an edge finely chipped to a point, or with an incisor tooth mounted on a wooden

Top, from left Nail-studded club from Dubbo, New South Wales; wooden pineapple-headed club from the north coast of New South Wales; painted club; *erambo*-type club.

Bottom from left Nail-studded club, collected 1892; knobbed, bulbous, conical-shaped club from the Moree district, New South Wales; flat-sided, conical club from the Moree district, New South Wales; nail-studded club with incised decoration from the Wagga Wagga district, New South Wales, collected 1865; decorated club from the Culgoa River, Queensland.

Opposite Nail-studded club from Dubbo, New South Wales.

All pieces in the Collection of The Australian Museum

231

handle. Both these tools were bound with string and gum, held firmly and the end struck with the palm of the hand to etch fine lines of equal thickness. To obtain the desired sheen and finish of weapons and utensils, the pieces were hardened in ashes on the fire and greased. Ochred pigment was rubbed into the incised design.

Weapons throughout the south-east were not consistent. Along the Richmond and Tweed River areas of northern New South Wales where a rainforest economy prevailed, the *womerah*, for example, was unknown. Although there was advanced technology in this area comprising elaborate hooks, nets, traps and basket work, there were neither multi-pronged, tipped spears nor spear throwers. It has been suggested that the *womerah* was simply not needed where the rainforest could provide a multitude of foods. It was invariably used for hunting large marsupials, particularly the kangaroo, and they did not inhabit the rainforest. Wooden implements used in the Richmond and Tweed areas included simple spears, shields, boomerangs and throwing sticks as well as women's digging sticks and fighting clubs. The women in all areas were exceptionally skilled at fighting with clubs. Not only were the men renowned for feats of strength and for hunting and fighting prowess, but the women were looked upon as exceptional fighters and some individuals were particularly feared.

Finely decorated broad shields, New South Wales. The examples above and centre are from Gundagai and the Darling River. The handles are attached separately and the surfaces are engraved and decorated with ochre. The other example is from western New South Wales or Queensland.
All pieces in the Collection of The Australian Museum

One fine utensil, ingeniously carved out of a single piece of wood, was the dish made by women to carry water from one place to another. In many places oval bark dishes with curved interiors were used to carry water or food, but a particularly interesting bowl or pot was made from the elbow or root of a tree, and this was used to store food and water. The gnarled protuberances commonly found on eucalyptus trees were deftly hollowed out with the aid of stone tools to form examples of wood craftsmanship which can be marvelled at centuries later.

Among the Kaurna of the Adelaide plains two types of shield were made. The first was called *mulubakka*. This was made from the inner layer of the bark of a gum tree, usually the hard red gum. The second shield, termed *wocaltee*, was made from bark. Shields were painted with a mixture of animal fat, red ochre and white clay and were frequently carved. Some were blackened over the fire and then decorated with cuts and incisions that were then filled in with ochre. The Kaurna shields are strikingly simple in their bright decorations, but few examples remain in collections. The following is an early description of the use of such shields and the agility with which the people all over Australia used their weapons in combat and warfare.

> *The shield is the only defensive weapon they possess and the manner in which it is handled is particularly striking. When they quiver their limbs, shake their spears, clatter their shields and raise them above their heads accompanied with shouts, the effect is wild. The shield is grasped in the left hand and the spear in the right. In the attitude of defence it is held slantingly across the breast ready to move in any direction required. Add to this a fierce face, bone through the nose, and feathers, etc., on the head, a naked body ornamented with white and red dots or stripes and then the beau idéal of a savage is pictured. In this mode of warfare a disregard for life is very observable, but very few are killed, on account of the extraordinary agility they possess in evading the spears. It is nothing uncommon for a native to jump on one side to escape a spear, at the same time stoop to another, and the next minute jerk his body to avoid a third, and this is done with perfect composure and with all imaginable sang-froid.[5]*

Native grass trees were frequently used for spears in the Adelaide area. The shaft was formed from the grass tree stem and was between seven and thirteen centimetres long. Into this was fixed a well polished and hardened piece of mallee wood about 180 centimetres long. A kangaroo tooth was fastened to the *womerah* with string made from kangaroo tail sinew and packed with gum resin.

The *wirra* (the Kaurna word for *nulla nulla*) was formed in this area from the trunk and root of small bushes. The root formed a knob and was hardened by fire and streaked with patterns. The weapon was used for fighting and hunting, and the Aboriginal hunter was extremely adroit. He would walk or stand with his arms elevated, holding the club in one hand with the knob resting on his shoulder and his eyes intent on the prey. The club was thrown from this stationary position with unerring aim. It was one of the principal weapons in procuring food, either knocking down birds or killing game, and its force on impact often broke limbs.

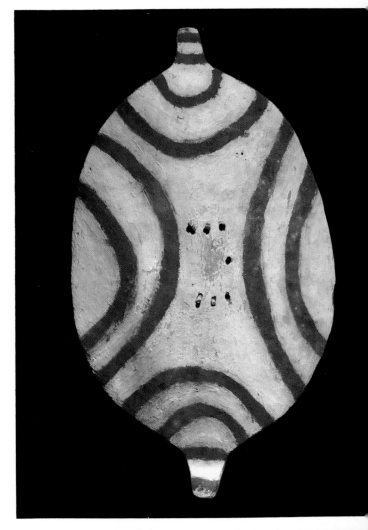

Top A rare bark shield made by Koolmatrie of the Kaurna from Point McLeay, South Australia, in 1914. The simple design is painted with animal fat, white clay and red ochre.
Collection the South Australian Museum

Bottom Water carrying vessel carved from the gnarled protuberance of a eucalyptus tree. *Collection The Australian Museum*

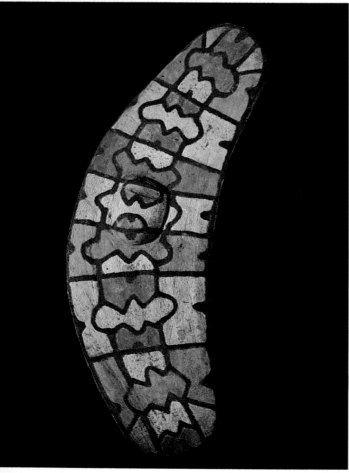

Shields made from flanged buttress tree roots, unique to the Tully-Cardwell rainforest area of north Queensland.
Collection The Australian Museum

Opposite Fire sticks from Aurukun, Queensland, called *thumpup*. The fire sticks are kept in a bamboo and wax container decorated with red abrus seeds.

QUEENSLAND

In Queensland, shields were made from light, soft wood, including corkwood. They were both carved and painted and each main encampment used separate characteristic patterns on the surfaces. Examples in the Queensland Museum collections are all decorated with designs including fine parallel fluting, half diamond patterns and polychrome painting in red, white and black.

It seems that the shields were not used in the Cape York Peninsula and the need for defence against clubs or spears was fulfilled by the use of the broad-bladed spear thrower. Shields that were common south of the Mitchell River were slightly convex on their outer surfaces with simple decorations including blackened bands and white spaces or central blackened panels. Around the Tully River and the rainforest areas of north Queensland, a particularly distinctive shield was made from the flanged buttress root of the pican tree. It was cut from the tree by making a curved incision in the flange above and below and the shape of the shield was then chipped out. The shields were therefore more often kidney-shaped than exactly oval. A handle was attached to the back of the shield by piercing the wood with hot cinders and the shield's surface was smoothed using pumice stone, excess wood being scraped off. A variety of patterns were used but no meaning or interpretation has been given for these.

Nulla nullas or clubs were common throughout Queensland although few examples of women's digging sticks were ever collected. In the Tully River area and along the north-eastern coast of Australia, the decorative pineapple club was found.

In the Rockhampton district, *nulla nullas* were made from wattle and there were six or seven varieties. These could be heavy or light, small or large, depending on use. Heavy *nulla nullas* were used for hand-to-hand combat and light ones were thrown from a distance. Excellent examples show fine fluting that could be done with a stone chisel. In later years weapons were collected in which the craftsman's ingenuity was used to great effect by utilising cast-off materials of European settlers. Weapons were improved by the addition of horseshoe nails stuck into the ends of the *nulla nullas* in imitation of the pineapple ridges. Queensland *nulla nullas* include single-pointed, knob-headed examples, as well as pineapple-headed, three-pronged, flattened spatulate and big-headed types.

One of the most interesting weapons made in Australia in past times was the sword from the lower Tully region. A two-handed sword was once known in the Rockhampton district and was used to strike with either the convex or concave edge. Swords were from ten to twelve centimetres in length, although this varied. Single-handed swords were found in the Cardwell and Bloomfield districts and on the lower Tully River. To make these, slabs of wood were taken from the tree and split down the centre, then adzed into shape. A handle was formed at one end, bound with hand-spun string and covered with beeswax. The edge of the sword, usually the convex edge, was finally sharpened.

A range of boomerangs was found in Queensland although they were not known in Cape York. An interesting variation was the bent or moon-shaped spear thrower used to spear fish or birds at close quarters. It was comparatively short and made of light timber.

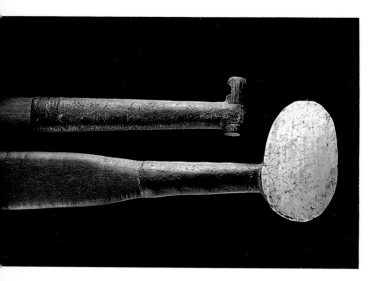

Top Cape York *womerahs* are made in various lengths to suit the throwing arm.

Centre Detail of the shell handle and wooden peg of a Cape York *womerah*.

Bottom Spear fishing along the Archer River, Cape York.

Unique spear throwers up to a metre long are still made in the Aurukun area of Cape York, just as they have been for centuries. These *womerahs* are made from wattle, scrub wattle or ironwood trees. The heart of the tree is removed and the sap scraped away with a mud shell. The wood is then warmed in the fire and straightened. If this proves difficult, sugar-bag wax is spread onto the warm wood which melts and makes it easier to bend. The notch in which the spear must be fitted is bound to one end. This is termed *thul kaa*. The *thul kaa* is bound to the spear thrower by pandanus twine or sinew. Heated gum from ironwood roots is spread over the binding to form a smooth finish. The handle of the *womerah* is formed from two pieces of bailer shell. The size of the hand piece is marked out onto the shell to fit the palm of the hand accurately, and the shell is carefully tapped off to the marked area, which is then smoothed with a stone. The pieces of shell are called *thul pinch*, and these are stuck together and attached to the *womerah* with sugar bag wax. The wood is finished off by rubbing down with fish or goanna fat.

One of the most interesting craft items still made in Aurukun is the fire stick, or *thum-pup*. Fire sticks are made from the *yukpoop* tree and after being collected they are warmed over the fire and skinned. When two sticks have been cut to the same length they are straightened against the knee and left to bleach in the sun. Sugarbag wax is rolled and squeezed in the hand and then left to dry until all the honey has been removed in the sun and the wax is smooth. Two small bamboo sticks are then tied together with string and covered with wax, which is moulded into a large ball on top. Red abrus or giddie seeds are pushed into the wax to form colourful decorations. Then the stem of the Cooktown orchid is placed in ashes from the fire. The top layer or skin of the orchid lifts and is easily peeled. The underskin may then be removed, scraped and dried. It is then wound around the bamboo, making a watertight top to protect the head of the fire stick. Fire sticks are kept in the bamboo container and fire is made in the traditional way by twirling one on top of and at right angles to the other to give friction. Fire sticks are now sold as traditional craft items and are generally tested before use.

With several other senior men at Aurukun, Jackson Woolah makes traditional spears from *ockan* or *timpin* wood (red wattle or lance wood). Lighter spears to catch birds are made from bamboo. The wood is warmed in the fire, scraped, straightened and dried. Kerosene tree leaves are used to smooth the wood and a shell may be scraped along the surface. Stingray barbs are particularly important and are used in several different spears as single barbs, multiple barbs or a series of barbs inserted down one or both sides of the spearhead. The barbs are inserted into the spearhead, bound with string and covered with gum and the whole head is then inserted into the handle. Wooden pronged spears are made from wattle or ironwood. A sliver of bone from a wallaby or brolga leg is bound to the top of each wooden prong with bush string, then covered with gum from the ironwood tree. Red gum from the date palm tree is rubbed into the prongs to give them a shiny finish. The handle is split in order to insert the head, and this is bound on with bush string which has been spun on the thigh. Warm gum is then rolled on to a *kayaman*, a wooden pallet used for smoothing a mixture of gum and wax when making spears and *womerahs*, and the string is coated. Perspiration from the forehead is mixed with gum on the *kayaman* and then smoothed onto the spear to give it power and efficacy. A black finish can be obtained by mixing animal blood, charcoal and water and this is frequently rubbed along the entire spear shaft. Such spears are used for hunting, whereas for fighting, spears are painted with white ochre, yellow clay and charcoal.

THE DESERT AREAS

Most people of the arid central desert regions of South Australia, central Australia and Western Australia continue to fashion the basic tool kit of weapons that have been made and used in these areas for many thousands of years. Spears, spear throwers, boomerangs, shields, clubs, chisels and digging sticks form the basic requirements of any family group, individual objects that were multi-functional.

The most extraordinary weapon still made in Central Australia is the spear thrower, called *miru* by the Pitjantjatjara. The *miru* is one of the world's most ancient hunting weapons; it is thought to have existed in the upper Palaeolithic cultures of Europe and more recently was used by the Aztec Indians of South America. The desert Australians are therefore one of the last peoples in the world to have continuously used this implement since its invention thousands of years ago.

The Pitjantjatjara spear thrower can also be used as an adzing tool, a receptacle and a fire-making saw. Its concave blade was probably developed because of the need for velocity and distance in spearing the large, scarce kangaroos and emus in the desert regions. In nearly a century of observation the Pitjantjatjara leaf-shaped spear thrower has altered very little, though the use of steel axes and tomahawks in place of stone hand tools has widened the range of usable mulga trees and quickened the manufacturing process.

The ritual of spearing a kangaroo has always been fundamentally important in training young men in the desert areas. Once speared, the kangaroo had to be prepared in a special way and the spear thrower was most important in the gutting of the animal at the point of killing. Older men today take great pride in attempting to spear the kangaroo but, if this fails on the first attempt, they quickly resort to a rifle. In the old days, spear throwers were smeared with kangaroo blood; today blood has been replaced by red ochre.

Walter Pukutuwara, an experienced Pitjantjatjara craftsman and assistant craft adviser in the Amata Arts and Crafts Centre, recently demonstrated in detail the making of a modern spear thrower. From a Toyota car in which he was travelling, he sighted a suitable mulga tree about fifty metres away, leaped down and made shaped cuts at the top and bottom of a selected section.

After cutting the flitch of timber, Walter Pukutuwara used a tomahawk for the initial shaping. When the flitch was removed, it already had an arched back similar to the appearance of the spear thrower in its final form. Using a metal adzing tool, the interior of the blade was chipped out and the form refined and smoothed. Sinew which had been gathered from the leg of a kangaroo and chewed to make it pliable was used to bend

Pitjantjatjara women from Amata make carrying dishes from the roots of the central Australian river red gums. The dishes, or *piti*, vary in shape and size depending on their use for winnowing, digging or for carrying loads. The *piti* are decorated with designs burned into the surface which record the travels of ancestral beings.

a wooden spear peg to the blade. These two pieces were carefully bound together and as the sinew dried, it tightened. A ball of gum made from spinifex was softened over the fire and moulded around the spear thrower handle. The spear thrower was then finished with the insertion of a small piece of quartz to act as a cutting edge.

Desert people have a 'mental template' of the form they seek and they see this as they pass various trees. The idea of the object's form is always in the mind of the maker and, as people walk or drive through the countryside, they bear in mind the objects they wish to make. Gould[6] described an incident when he was out in the desert with some people. One woman, Katapi, said '*Ngayulu langkuru nyangu*' ('I saw a spear thrower'). Gould thought she said she had found a ready-made spear thrower in the bush, but in fact, while hunting, she had seen a tree with a form perfect for making a very fine spear thrower. Gould and Katapi's husband later collected the flitch of timber.

Other weapons still made with care, skill and great pride by Pitjantjatjara craftsmen include spears, or *kulata*. These are made from the tecoma tree, though the heads are of mulga wood. Boomerangs primarily used for hunting are also made from mulga wood. The convex surfaces may be smooth or incised with fluted linear designs.

The women's utensils include that fundamental and most important implement the digging stick. These unobtrusive and simple-looking objects perform a multitude of functions and are extremely important personal possessions for each woman. One end is pointed, the other blunted. The points are kept sharp, and before the relatively recent metal digging sticks, now widely used and consisting of crowbars with flattened and pointed ends, they were the main tools used for digging for lizards and roots in the desert, as well as for fighting.

The women's essential carrying dishes are called *piti*. These are made entirely by women and they vary in shape and size depending on function. Roots of the river red gum are dug and hollowed out. Larger bowls are used as receptacles and are carried on the women's heads, occasionally with a circular head ring made of rolled bark and bound with hand-spun hair string. Smaller bowls may be used for winnowing seed, to make flour for damper or for winnowing spinifex resin to make gum. Yet another type of *piti* may be used for digging out the burrows of lizards or goannas. The inner surface of these dishes is smooth, while the outer surface may be crenulated and left as the natural timber, or smoothed and decorated with burnt designs using hot wire. The practice of decorating these *piti* has arisen in the last thirty years. Designs invariably relate to the women's own version of their landscape and how it was created and peopled by their ancestors. A series of connecting curved lines imitates the pattern made in the ground by the women when they dance during their *inma*. Two of the legends which are frequently illustrated are the story of the Seven Sisters and the story of Piltadi, or the two sisters.

Ceremonies and accounts of the ground journeys of the seven sisters and one man (Orion and the Pleiades) extend from the Warburton Ranges in Western Australia through the Rawlinson, Petermann, Mann and Musgrave Ranges and through to Glen Helen Gorge. Important related art sites include Cave Hill (Walinga) and Ayers Rock paintings.

Sinew is extracted from a kangaroo leg, bound around the spear thrower and it contracts when dry.

Opposite Walter Pukutuwara of the Pitjantjatjara making a spear thrower at the Amata Crafts tent, Uluru or Ayers Rock. His leaf-shaped spear thrower or *miru* is shown in detail below.

Detail of the decoration of a Western Australian desert shield collected just before the turn of the century.
Collection Museum of Victoria

The man who pursued and repeatedly had intercourse with the women is known as Jula and Nirunja, the women being referred to as Kunka Punkara or Kunka Kangkalpa. At various places the women dug holes and extracted the wet sand, putting it over their hot bodies to cool themselves These places are now water soaks known to all the people.

The story of Piltadi tells of two sisters who left their camp in search of edible lizards and goannas which burrow underground. Unbeknown to them, they were being followed by two snake men. In following their false tracks, the sisters dug up a large tract of earth, opening up burrows that never yielded any substantial game. Finally the women came to a large hole in the earth. They became excited, thinking they had found the entrance to the burrow of some enormous animal. They began digging again, following and opening up two underground burrows that led to the foot of mountain ranges just west of Amata. Here, however, instead of

242

finding the game they had hoped for, they found the two snake men waiting for them. The sisters managed to wound one of the snake men and run away, but their escape was temporary as the two snake men finally caught up with them and swallowed them. The country at which these events took place and the ceremony in which the story is told is known as Piltadi.

The Pitjantjatjara people's skill with carving has, in recent years, been extended to the making of animals found in the desert. These are generally representations of all types of local birds, lizards, echidna and even cats. Decorated with extracts of ceremonial designs or the natural markings of the animals, they vary in size but demonstrate a great deal of skill as well as humour. Women make these animals as a social activity and sit in groups laughing and joking as they shape the animals from the irregular roots of the river red gum. Occasionally an oddly proportioned animal will arouse hoots of laughter as women imitate the prancing lizard, goanna or echidna.

The Pitjantjatjara shields of the Mann, Musgrave and Tomlinson Ranges are similar to those found across to the west. Used primarily for defence from spears, they are broad, with large handles. Decorative fluted patterns made with finely pointed chisels relate to the ancestral dreaming paths. The Pitjantjatjara-speaking people of the more westerly regions around Wingellina in Western Australia create the most elaborately decorated adzes, spear throwers and shields, employing fine zigzag patterns, diagonal lines and the interlocking key design can still be found on some exceptional pieces. This design is thought to have been passed from the Kimberley region of Western Australia, where it originated on shell pendants known as *longka-longka*. These shells were traded through Pitjantjatjara country with other wooden items such as 'hairpins' — carved oblong wooden decorations worn in a man's chignon. The finely engraved geometric patterns found on present-day desert weapons are the closest in style of all Aboriginal art forms to the detailed zigzag and other symbols on Aboriginal weapons of the south-eastern coast.

NORTH AUSTRALIA

The use of traditional weapons has largely given way to metal tools and rifles for shooting game. However, fishing spears are still used and many craftsmen, when encouraged, will fashion a traditional spear, net or implement. In Arnhem Land, boomerangs are unknown as weapons for fighting or hunting, but large decorated pairs were traded from the centre and used as clapsticks in ceremonies.

Coastal Arnhem Land has witnessed enormous changes in geography, climate and vegetation over the ages in which man has been present in the region. The tools used, spears, *womerahs* and boomerangs, have also changed according to requirements, food supply and changes in human population. These have been recorded in the older rock paintings of human and spirit hunting figures of the Kakadu National Park region. In coastal Arnhem Land, patterns painted on spear throwers are the same as those painted on the chest, on bark paintings and other cultural items. The designs are clan patterns signifying aspects of the artist's Dreaming and connecting him to his tribal lands.

Spear thrower and adze from the western Pitjantjatjara communities. The designs are identical to those made last century.

Sculpture

Before the arrival of European settlers in Australia, all Aboriginal three-dimensional sculptures were ephemeral, designed through inspiration from the Dreaming or *tjukurpa* and translated into reality for a brief moment of ceremony. Unlike many African nations, for example, Australia had no tradition of venerating ancestors through carved wooden or moulded images. Ritual objects in Australia were either designed to influence the spiritual powers by allowing their life force to enter the temporal world during dance and ritual, or to encourage the spirits of the dead to leave the temporal world and pass into the landscape whence they came.

For the purpose of bringing the life force of ancestral beings into ceremonies, fibre representations of snakes, birds and animals were made, both in symbolic shapes and realistic representations. After use in ceremonial dances and rituals, these were then destroyed or discarded. To encourage the departure of the spirit to the ancestral home of the spirit, Tiwi mortuary practices included making sculpted wooden grave poles and, in Arnhem Land, hollow bark and wood bone containers were painted with special designs. These also were left to disintegrate over time; no attempt was made to restore or to repaint them.

Some facets of Aboriginal creative life were, however, designed to last. Ancient stone formations found in many arid zones were thought to be the work of spirits themselves and at the time of European contact were only repaired by living people. Sacred stone discs or carved and decorated *tjuringa* were also thought by desert peoples to be the core of power of a particular ancestor and were kept hidden for generations, produced only for secret men's ceremonies. The ancient carvings on trees that marked burial and initiation sites in New South Wales and south-eastern Queensland lasted for the life of the tree.

The patterns and constructions made on the ground for ceremonies in central Australia discussed in the chapter on Papunya painting, as well as low moulded and mounded earth constructions made in the south-east for *bora* initiation ceremonies, could also accurately be termed sculptures, but, like other forms of Aboriginal sacred arts, these were not shown publicly at the time of their creation, and they may not be seen publicly now. The *bora* mounds have largely disappeared, with only a few overgrown hillocks now protected from destruction.

The complex dancing headdresses and constructions carried on the shoulders in Western Australia, central Australia and South Australia should also by rights be included in the spectrum of Aboriginal sculpture, and these are also considered sacred and private objects. In Cape York wooden sculptures were made to represent animals and fish in dances commemorating mythological events. These and unique elaborate dancing masks set apart the sculptural arts of the Aboriginals of Cape York, linking the visual arts strongly with those of the Torres Straits and Papua New Guinea.

Opposite Carved and painted ironwood figures by Declan Apuatimi, Bathurst Island.

When Tiwi figures are carved, ochre patterns are painted on the surface. Talented younger members of the family frequently assist elderly artists who have failing eyesight.

TIWI SCULPTURE

The spectacular carved poles unique to the Tiwi of Bathurst and Melville Islands are made for the *pukumani* ritual and placed around the grave during protracted ceremonies for the dead. The word *pukumani*, translated broadly, means 'taboo' or 'dangerous', and it is applied to the relatives of the dead person. They must not handle food or fulfil certain tasks. The name of the deceased is termed *pukumani* and must not be spoken, sometimes for several years, depending on the dead person's importance. The brilliant Tiwi sculptures and dramatic rituals originated with the earliest legends of the Tiwi, recounting how death came into the world due to the misdemeanours of Bima, the wife of Purukapali, in creation times. Purukapali instituted the first *pukumani* ceremony in which men and women intricately paint their bodies, wear elaborate armbands, head ornaments and body decorations, and dance for days. Between three and fourteen poles are erected around the grave site and these are carefully carved and painted.

Pukumani ceremonies are multi-faceted. At the time of death the body is placed in a grave about a metre deep and covered with sand and paper bark. The posts are erected several months or even a full year later and at this time extensive dancing and singing take place. The close relatives of the dead must commission the posts to be made, as well as carved and decorated ceremonial spearheads. This can be quite a complex economic transaction.

Individuals are still known for their exceptional skill in carving and decorating the very hard ironwood used in making these artefacts. Once the posts were made with stone tools, but metal hand axes, hammers and chisels have replaced these since early this century. In a fascinating personal account of time spent among the Tiwi in the 1920s, Hart[1] described two old men ('cronies' as he called them), Tu'untalumi and Timalarua. One was a singer, dreamer, dancer and canoe maker, the other a quiet, resolute man who spent all his leisure time singlemindedly making ceremonial spears and grave posts. The Tiwi admired both men, one for his canoes, the other for his posts. They saw no difference between the canoe and the posts as skilfully made objects or between them as artefact or art. However, Timalarua's posts were greatly admired. Hart says the Tiwi described them in detail for him, tracing the designs in the air as they looked at them, clearly impressed with his decoration.

These days *pukumani* posts are made for ceremonies and for sale. The economics of their production have changed only slightly; now the clients are European art buyers more often than bereaved relatives, but there is a group of artists who earn their living through the sale of their art and carving and who are therefore virtually professional artists. However, in the process of commissioning and payment, the system generally follows traditional Tiwi lines.

The posts described at the turn of the century[2] were painted by several individuals simultaneously and the designs consisted of vertical bands running in wavy lines down the posts, with other oval designs arranged in rows lengthways. All the camp watched the progress of the decorations and the preparation was clearly a social event. On some posts a rectangular space was hollowed out, leaving thin perpendicular supports for the upper part; others were finished on top with two prongs or with a rounded cap. More recently, the painted designs on the surface of the poles have become detailed horizontal bands of pattern and the finishes on the top include barbed spearheads, birds and human figures. The designs on the poles are identical to those that each man paints on his face during *pukumani* ceremonies and that are repeated on other ritual items, including spears, bark armbands and bark containers. They are invariably broad, bold abstract designs using strong red, yellow, white and black ochre, often against a white or black background. The huge, heavy painted spears are made only for display and use on ceremonial occasions; they were never used as functional objects for hunting or warfare. The cutting and painting of these took a great deal more time than a grave post, and all men at an important *pukumani* funeral would carry at least half a dozen as a symbol of status.

The Tiwi practice of carving birds and human figures stems from the *pukumani* carving tradition, though it is a relatively new development. A man called Katu first carved a human figure on top of a *pukumani* post in about 1945. When he was asked why he had carved this post, he answered that he had seen such carvings on a visit to Darwin.[3] Katu carved another post for presentation to Queen Elizabeth II in 1954, and since that time the carving of mythological characters, birds and animals from the environment has been a central part of Tiwi craft. The main myth illustrated in these carvings in the round is that of Purukapali, Tapara and Bima. A complete set depicting the entire myth, including a fine piece of Bima holding the dead child in her arms on a paper bark cradle, is in the collection of the Darwin Museum.

Elaborate poles consisting entirely of tiered figures up to four or five metres high, are also commissioned by major institutions. Many of the human figures are dressed as though for ceremony, complete with pubic cover made of bark, cockatoo feather headdresses, armbands and body painting decorations. The practice of carving the extremely hard ironwood on Bathurst and Melville Islands was traditionally only carried out by men; even the paintings were the province of the men only. Today this has changed and many younger women are learning to paint the decorations from older men, usually their fathers. One young woman was observed painting traditional designs on a carved owl, seated close to her old father who was almost blind.

Tiered figures and birds illustrating characters from the Purukapali myth.
Collection Northern Territory Museum of Arts and Sciences

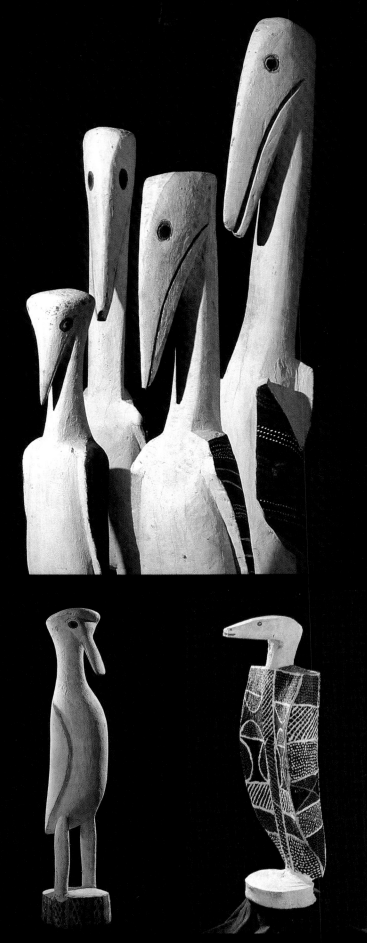

Tiwi ironwood carvings.

Above Carving of an ancestral being by a Tiwi artist from Milikapiti, Melville Island. The treatment of the body resembles both funeral decorations and Macassan clothing.

Opposite Bima, wife of Purukapali, holding her dead child in a paper bark cradle. The painted designs are the same as those worn on the face and body for modern ceremonies.
Both pieces above Collection Northern Territory Museum of Arts and Sciences

Top Carving of a group of pelicans that began the dances at the first Tiwi *pukumani* funeral ceremony.

Bottom left Undecorated white painted carving of a spoonbill ibis by a Tiwi artist from Milikapiti.
Both pieces above Collection Northern Territory Museum of Arts and Sciences

Bottom right Painted ironwood bird by Victor Adam. *Hogarth Galleries*

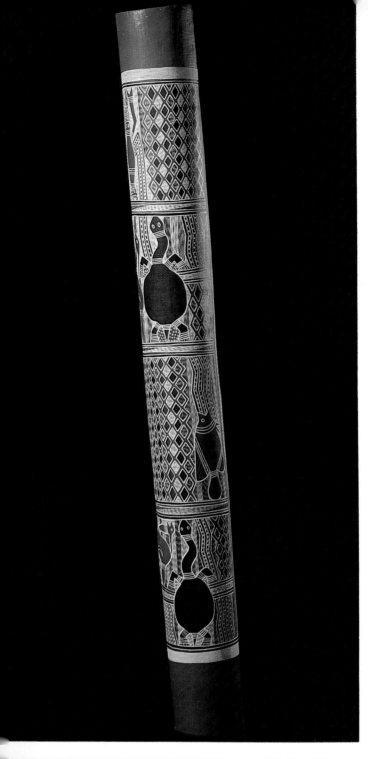

MORTUARY SCULPTURE IN ARNHEM LAND

Elsewhere in Arnhem Land, particularly in the eastern part, Aboriginal people, or Yulngu, were taught by their ancestral heroes to place the bones of the deceased in hollow logs. At the initial funeral these days, close relatives sing his spirit to its resting place and paint the clan designs on his chest or coffin. The songs instruct the spirit where it must go when it leaves the body.

Most Aboriginal communities greatly fear the desire of the spirit to stay around the living after death, particularly close relatives. Relatives beat themselves and cut their faces and heads to show their grief, as well as painting an intricate abstract design representing the dead man's clan country either on his body or his coffin so the ancestors can see to which totem the man belonged and carry the spirit straight there.

Mortuary rituals extend over a long time and assist the spirit to find its final resting place in the land of the dead. Once the spirit has found its home, it will therefore not return to harm the living relatives. Recently on a small island off the coast of Arnhem Land, a young child was lost when some women and their children were on a camping expedition. Although Darwin police found that a crocodile had probably taken the child, the relatives were quite convinced that her deceased grandmother had seen her wandering in the bush and taken her away. Spirits of the dead will always attempt to bother the living unless they are placated and put to rest in peace.

For the past fifty years or so, the Tiwi and many people of Arnhem Land have been Christian and therefore the burial ceremonies frequently combine both Christian and traditional practices. Bodies are generally buried, whereas, in the past, they might have been placed on a tree platform. The bone coffins, or *lorrgon*, can be made of wood or bark. They are hollow, but in some areas they are finished with two prongs at the top, imitating the barbs of the swordfish.

Among the Yulngu, grave or memorial posts are still erected at the place of burial. In the past, several months after death and burial, the body was exhumed and the bones were cleaned, covered in red ochre and placed in a circular bark container. The bark container was decorated with sacred clan designs, as the body had been. Further west the bones, when exhumed or taken from the tree platform, were placed in hollow logs which were simple branches of trees, previously hollowed out by termites. These were elaborately decorated as well. Both bark coffins and *lorrgon* are decorated with the totemic design of the deceased. According to Warner[4] the hollow bark coffins were simply preparatory receptacles to be used before the bones are placed in the final hollow log coffin at the end of the mortuary ceremony.

The clans of central Arnhem Land are divided into two halves or moieties, Yirritja and Dhuwa. At mortuary ceremonies the songs, decorations and procedures follow the traditions of each division. If the bones belong to a Dhuwa, red parrot feathers are fastened around the edge. After the bones have been placed inside the cylinder, the two ends are stuffed with grass or paper bark. Some hollow logs are carved and have two holes near the upper rim; these symbolise the eyes of the deceased so he can see his way to the land of the dead. Hollow log coffins

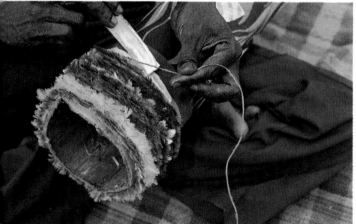

Top Decorated bone coffin from Yirrkala, eastern Arnhem Land. The same clan designs are painted on bodies, bark and bone coffins. *Collection Hogarth Galleries*

Bottom At Maningrida, a hollow log coffin is painted and red rainbow lorikeet feathers are glued to the rim with bush string.

Tiwi grave site. Traditional *pukumani* poles and a cross symbolise the fusion of cultures. *Photograph Margaret West*

that have the swordfish prongs symbolise the way in which the swordfish swallows the dead person as the bones are placed through the mouth of the coffin. The mouth of the swordfish is then sealed with grass and paper bark. Abstract clan designs, or occasionally representational images of funeral ceremonies including drawings of relatives and kin with clapping sticks, are painted as part of the designs.

The hollow log coffins are placed upright in the camp with the bones inside and left to decay naturally, the bones scattering and disintegrating. Occasionally the coffins may be sent back to the clan country to be erected in the bush where rain, winds and bushfires ensure that the spirit of the deceased will return to its source.

ANCESTORS AND ANIMALS

Painted and carved representations of totemic animals and ancestral figures were created throughout north-eastern Arnhem Land for use in particular ceremonial cycles. Today along the coast of Arnhem Land — at Yirrkala, Elcho Island, Milingimbi, Ramingining and to a lesser extent at Maningrida — soft wood carvings of birds, animals and fish, as well as ancestral heroes, are made by many artists. The shapes are carved from a single piece of wood and broad colour areas are then painted onto the surface of the carving, using natural ochres mixed with commercial fixative. The surface designs are engraved into the wood through the painted surface with a sharp knife, exposing the pale wood beneath and contrasting with the painted patterns. The carvings are all highly decorative, intricately designed and exceptionally light.

The surface patterns all relate to clan designs or other aspects of the myths in which the carved figures occur. The origin of carved human figures in eastern Arnhem Land seems to lie with the visits of Macassan fishermen. As reported by Mountford,[5] who visited the area in 1948, Mawalan recounted that his father Djuakan was taught by the old Macassan fisherman Bopalindi how to carve a human head on top of a burial post. The art was passed from Djuakan to his son and he in turn passed it on to others. According to Mountford, at first the Dhuwa moiety were the only group to carve such posts and the Yirritja people commissioned them to carve the mortuary posts for their graves. Mountford commented that in just over two generations Aboriginals had taken the simple post figure of foreign origin and were at the time of his visit carving full-length human figures in wood.

Ancestral and animal figures from eastern Arnhem Land.
Left Straw-necked ibis by Johnny Mayarra from Ramingining.
Top left Djambuwal the thunder man, a wooden sculpture by Mawalan, Yirrkala, 1948. *Collection Art Gallery of South Australia*
Top right Guldana the spirit by Mungurrawuy, Yirrkala, circa 1976. *Photograph Uwe Steinward*
Opposite Ancestral spirit with dilly bag by Lartjanga, Yirrkala. *Hogarth Galleries*

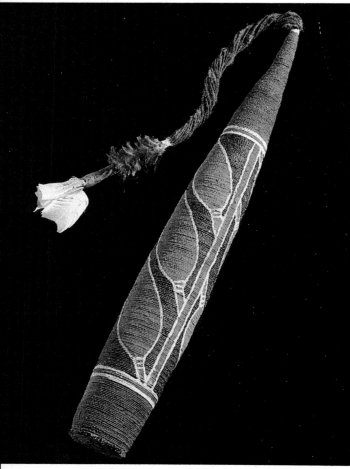

Top Group of Mimi spirit sculptures by Guningbal of Maningrida.

Bottom Paper bark emblem representing a yam. The bark is rolled, then bound with bush string. The painted design represents the yam vine above ground. *Hogarth Galleries*

Opposite Poles from the Marradjiri ceremony used as ritual payment to families hosting the ceremony. The poles are of wood bound with string, painted and decorated with feather bands and strings. Maningrida area.

The first carving in the round to be collected from Yirrkala by a visitor was made by Mawalan in 1938. At the time, the Reverend F. W. Chaseling was a missionary in the small village and in one of his sermons he had expressed grief at the loss that the nation had suffered by the death of King George V. The sermon and the missionary's feelings so impressed Mawalan that he carved a mortuary post similar to the traditional memorial grave posts for the dead king. The piece was sent to the Australian Museum and consisted of a hardwood post with a long face and an elongated beard. The pole was simply decorated with ceremonial string.

Only a few years later, during World War II, an Air Force camp was established near Yirrkala and many Aboriginals were employed there. These people learned to use pocket knives, tomahawks, wooden rasps and files, and with these they made many wooden sculptures. The Berndts[6] worked at Yirrkala shortly after this and they mentioned that although the artists used knives they were still also using spear points to carve.

At present, softwood carvings include a great variety of birds and ancestral figures. The figures are generally major characters from the great clan ancestral heroes. Like the Tiwi, who are carving replicas of the main mythological heroes, Purukapali, Tapara and Bima, the clans of eastern Arnhem Land are using the repertoire of their own traditional stories to carve exceptionally skilful images in the round.

CEREMONIAL EMBLEMS AND SPIRIT IMAGES

Natural materials such as bark, string, feathers and other fibre were utilised in a wide variety of ways throughout Arnhem Land to make ceremonial sculptures in the forms of symbolic animal, plant and bird images or abstract totems representing sacred objects or food emblems, such as yams. None of these have found their way into the commercial art markets and they are not made as part of the arts and craft industry in the north. They form an essential part of most important ceremonies. Termed *rangga*, paper bark emblems are made throughout Arnhem Land and many of the finest examples exhibit great beauty and elegance of form. They are shaped from folded or rolled strips of paper bark which are then tightly bound with hand-spun bush string. Realistic heads of birds or animals may be added, carved out of small pieces of wood and painted before being fixed into place. The tightly wound string is then painted with ochre decorations and feather strings may also be added as decorative elements.

In western Arnhem Land, the intense imaginative quality that gives form to weird bush spirits on bark paintings also reveals itself in other three-dimensional carvings. One artist, Guningbal from Maningrida, has specialised in painting and carving the Mimi spirits that live in the dark crevices of the rocky western Arnhem Land sandstone escarpment. Guningbal's Mimi are instantly recognisable as angular spotted figures with round heads and large, staring eyes.

Among the Yulngu of eastern Arnhem Land, the spirits of the deceased which are still wandering about the bush are called *mokoy*, and these form subjects for sculptures as well as paintings.

CARVED TREES OF THE SOUTH-EAST

Carved trees, or dendroglyphs, have been recorded in Queensland, the Northern Territory and south-eastern Australia, although most of the trees are found in the territories that once belonged to the Kamilaroi and Wiradhuri people in New South Wales. Most of the trees have been carved in vertical sections using metal tools, suggesting that those that still exist were carved after 1800.

Decorations on carved trees were made to mark burial sites or initiation ceremonial grounds. Each design has a mythological significance and is owned by a clan or local group. These are the largest carvings of any Aboriginal group in Australia. Most of the designs are geometrical, including curvilinear patterns, spirals, scrolls and diamonds. Representational figures also occur, including goannas, snakes, turtles and fish. It would appear that initiation trees are distinct in that only the outer bark of the tree was carved, whereas burial memorials were designed to last much longer and the designs were cut deeply into the undersurface.

Many of these trees can be found in remote parts of New South Wales, tucked away in the storerooms of local museums, and several magnificent examples are in the collection of the Australian Museum. One tree, five metres in height, has a design of concentric diamonds cut all around the trunk from top to bottom. As the old trees grow *in situ*, the bark tends to cover the ancient designs and in the process of restoring some trees, conservators are attempting to strip back the outer bark to reveal the designs once again. Contemporary Aboriginal people of New South Wales have a great pride in their heritage and are seeking to classify such sites as important cultural resources and sacred areas of their people.

The designs on the carved trees are very similar to the patterns used on decorated weapons and some elements are similar to patterns from the Kimberley area. (Very few stylistic similarities are found to the work of the people of the central desert areas.) Of nearly 3000 trees surveyed in 1982,[7] most of the tree carvings were characterised by non-figurative motifs and continuous lines enclosed in a space. Such carvings were widely distributed throughout inland New South Wales. Other carvings belonged to two smaller groups. One centres on the New South Wales north coast, bounded by the Great Dividing Range in the west and the Manning River in the south. These carvings were characterised by enclosed spaces with interior infills and the repetition of one or two motifs over a large area of the tree trunk. They were carved into the bark only. The second group comprised only a few trees in central New South Wales that had animal motifs. The bark had been removed within the outline of the figures, exposing the wood. There are very few examples on which to base the hypothesis that there were styles of dendroglyphs in New South Wales, but the evidence points to the fact that cultural boundaries defined technique and motif.

Although there might once have been thousands of carved trees in New South Wales, there are now only a few hundred.

Dendroglyph near Nyngan, New South Wales.

Opposite Dendroglyph near Gin Gin, New South Wales.

Return to the Land

Throughout tribal Australia there has been a strong resurgence of traditional life and ceremony. Families have left government settlements and missions where their parents had lived since they were born and have established small self-reliant communities in areas from 40 to 400 kilometres from the nearest main settlement. This has happened in the central and western desert regions and throughout the 'top end' of the Northern Territory including Arnhem Land; a few have also begun in Cape York.

As art is an integral part of Aboriginal life, the effect this has had on Aboriginal artists' creative output has been profound. The proximity of Dreaming sites has strengthened ceremonial activity. Associated dance and body decorations, ritual designs and sculptures have become not only more plentiful but also more carefully and elegantly executed, reflecting the joy of the artists in their homelands.

The significance of this move is only clear when one considers the history of the interaction between the Aboriginal and European cultures in Australia.

Since the Dreaming, each Aboriginal clan group has owned or held in trust a series of Dreaming sites at which particular ancestors appeared, formed the landscape and produced children who became the human ancestors of the people. Periodically, at sacred sites on this land, the people re-enacted, in chant, mime and dance, the actions of their Dreaming ancestors. The older men initiated young men; the women danced their own celebration of fertility and childbirth and the regeneration of all life. Each group continued the traditions of body painting, making weapons for survival, sculpting the ground for ceremony and painting images of the spirit ancestors and spirits of special places on rock and on bark.

The performance of these ceremonies was the core of the people's religious life. The ceremonies were essential, otherwise the annual cycle of life, the periodic reproduction of species, indeed the whole functioning of the cosmos, would not continue in the manner ordained by the ancestors. If a person were deprived of his homeland or if special sites on that land were destroyed, he would lose all connection with his ancestors and be left in a void.

With the expansion of European settlement in the late eighteenth century and throughout the nineteenth century, an increasing number of people were encouraged to leave their homelands or were forced from them. As the concepts of Dreaming sites and sacred lore were alien and incomprehensible to the invaders, tribal lands were occupied without regard to traditional owners. When objections were raised, the results were often violent massacres.

Opposite Goanna meat provides a delicious source of food on desert hunting trips.

The spread of imported diseases took an even greater toll. In the south-eastern areas of the continent, this dispossession was rapid and, for many tribes, final. In these areas ritual and ceremonial life ceased early this century and traditional art forms disappeared. By 1900 the Aboriginal population has been reduced from 300,000 to 50,000. In the more remote central desert, Arnhem Land plateau and coastal plains, in Cape York and in the Kimberleys, Aboriginal people continued to live their traditional lives, relatively ignored by Europeans in general.

It was believed the Aboriginals were a dying race and in an effort to 'smooth the pillow' of the doomed people, missions and government stations were established and reserves of land set aside for them. The government position of Protector of Aborigines was established and an era of welfare and protectionism began. From 1900 to 1960, with the coming of the missions and settlements, the traditional economic foundations of Aboriginal society changed. Access to basic rations was offered, together with small amounts of medical care, education and housing. The population began to increase again. Fewer children died under the age of five, women survived childbirth, and the elderly, who might otherwise have found survival hard, were nourished from local European rations. But in return for the benefits offered, the people on the settlements were expected to make profound adjustments to meet the objectives of the missionaries and settlement managers. The missions aimed at spiritual conversion and, consciously or unconsciously, a complete change in their 'charges'' basic pattern and values of life.

The settlement officers put into practice government policies of protectionism followed by assimilation. They saw their role as offering benefits, particularly those of education and social adaptation, which would assist Aboriginals to assimilate fully into the wider society. But these large communities had brought together groups of people who spoke different languages, often peoples who, only ten years previously, had been enemies. The psychological stress was great and talk of withdrawal from missions and settlements was commonplace, but, due to long-standing inertia and dependence on the supplies, it was seldom put into practice. Grievances concerned growing gaps between age groups, the erosion of traditional patterns of authority, the aimlessness and drinking problems in the young men and the general and all-pervasive disruption to the social organisation. There was more and more evidence that prospectors and tourists were trespassing on the land where sacred sites lay unprotected.

Bauxite mining that began at Gove (Nhulunbuy) in the early 1970s, only a short distance from the Yirrkala mission, became a catalyst. Despite a legal battle, the mine developed into a huge project with a large associated township. Almost simultaneously, in an attempt to protect their own land and sacred sites, Aboriginal people throughout tribal Australia began to move away from the missions and settlements to establish small remote communities known as centres, homelands or outstations. Government support has increased for these Aboriginal moves towards self-management. Legislation now provides for 'land rights' or freehold title to traditional lands in the Northern Territory covering up to twenty-five per cent of the total area, with other states following. The dispossession of Aboriginal land is the injustice about which Aboriginals feel most strongly and the security of land for the future, or compensation for its loss, became the central issue for the 1970s and, so far, into the 1980s as other states begin to rectify the omissions of the past.

In the remote communities of the deserts and Arnhem Land, small and large groups have gathered close to water supplies and away from the social dislocation they felt at the government settlements. Australia is, in a sense, being repopulated. Tribal groups are keeping ceremonies alive and are living close to the earth and sacred landscape, while beginning to educate their children in bicultural and bilingual programmes.

Tribal men and women have retained full knowledge of the sacred areas in the land, together with extensive ceremonial cycles that commemorate their formation by the ancestral heroes. In these places, ritual life is not disrupted by competing priorities of work or other influences, and in the desert areas particularly, where people have moved vast distances, ceremonies associated with previously inaccessible sacred sites are being renewed. All facets of traditional religious arts flourish.

The survival of these small centres is dependent, to some extent, on their self-sufficiency. Cash is necessary to purchase a range of goods; cars and petrol, utensils for cooking and hunting, building materials, clothing and luxuries such as radios. In large centres, television and even video recorders are now part of Aboriginal society and are seen as desirable. Although hunting is an important source of food, dependence on the regular visits of the supply truck is also a fact of life.

In the early 1970s, one government administrator said:

The most difficult problems of such communities from the point of view of government are those of reconciling self-determination for the Aboriginals with help to enable them to obtain access to essential stores and services upon which they have come to depend, without imposing on them excessive economic dependence. It would serve little long-term purpose if we free Aboriginals from the bonds of bureaucratic paternalism and, at the same time, make them wholly dependent upon financial subvention from the community. Apart from the ever-present risk of white 'backlash', dependence is insidious, in the long run impossible to disguise, and, in due course, destructive. As we are now trying to do in social affairs, the objective must be to make the economic conditions of Aboriginals reflect their own aspirations, efforts and capacities. [1]

Aboriginal people have subsequently taken up that challenge and have decisively followed a program of self-determination and self-management in which the sale of art plays a significant role. In a large centre such as Maningrida on the Liverpool River in Arnhem Land, the outstations have their own council, with representatives from each small community. This council meets to discuss the specific management and support of more remote places without distracting attention from the business of managing the larger community. White advisers, if needed, are now employed by the Aboriginal councils and are responsible to them. While accepting goods such as television sets and services that, to the outside eye, are alien to a romantic concept of a 'traditional' lifestyle, the outstations are ensuring their continued viability by taking from the dominant culture only what is useful, attractive or entertaining, while maintaining their religion and its practices in ceremony and art.

The fortnightly visit to Manmoyi outstation south of Maningrida. When outstations are cut off in the wet season, they are serviced by plane. The artists sell their paintings and weaving and buy essential foods.

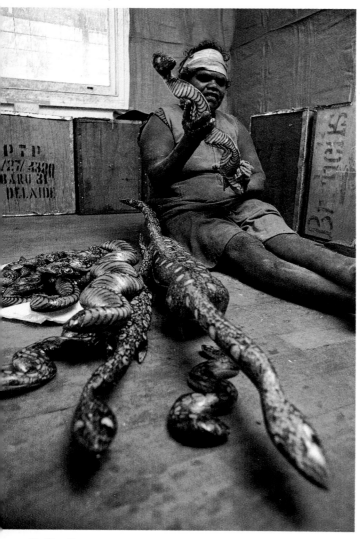

Nellie Patterson polishes her carved animals at the craft collection centre at Amata, South Australia. Community craft centres market art pieces to galleries, museums and private collectors.

The increase in production of traditional arts and crafts on the outstations and homelands centres is not only a direct response to life in the bush, an adequate supply of good materials, and a renewal of ceremonial contact with the power of the spirit ancestors; it has also become a most essential factor in the cash economy. Depending on location, hunting and gathering can supply up to sixty per cent of the food requirements, but cannot supply cash. This must be obtained by the sale of art and from social security benefits. Cash enables food to be bought from servicing trucks and light aircraft. Over 150 outstations and homelands have now been established throughout tribal Australia and most of these produce some form of art for sale.

The continuation of traditional arts in remote communities also has an enormous effect on their pride and self-reliance. In many ways, art is the most important way in which tribal people communicate with the wider society. When their great works of painting, sculpting, carving or weaving are appreciated, shown in galleries and bought for high prices, the artists feel that there is a simultaneous appreciation of their world view, their great Dreaming designs, their songs and ceremonies. In recent years the beauty and strength of Aboriginal art in all its forms have been recognised in international arenas. Aboriginal artists, musicians and dancers now form part of every Australian contingent participating in international cultural festivals.

Many researchers have asked whether the sale of traditional religious art necessarily leads to its downgrading and eventual destruction. But, as already mentioned, in all their art forms Aboriginal communities do not see that they are selling the designs themselves; they are merely transposing them into forms that are portable for Europeans and receiving some payment for sharing the designs. Extensive legislation is under discussion to protect Aboriginal copyright just as the artists see it as protected through their own moral laws.

Generally, traditional Aboriginal art is sold from centrally based communities. The satellite outstations produce most of the work but it is collected and fed through larger depots such as Maningrida, Ramingining and Yirrkala in Arnhem Land, and Papunya and Amata in central Australia. Most of the Aboriginal councils have formed artists' companies or co-operatives, which employ local craft advisers by means of government subsidy. These advisers have many duties, including assistance with collection of paints, ochres, barks or canvases, timber for sculpture, resin, and even hunting kangaroos to obtain the sinews for making weapons. They act as both buyers and sellers of the art, travelling through extremely inhospitable areas during the wet season, carrying bark paintings in trucks over creeks or flying in small aircraft to collect the works. The logistics of providing a continuous service for the artists are such that the prices that the art must eventually fetch in southern cities are substantial. The vast distances between Australian capital cities and the remote outstations where Aboriginal families now live mean that freight bills, on top of the community arts and crafts costs, are high. The craft's advisers also negotiate prices and deal directly with galleries and the government-subsidised network of arts and craft outlets.

The result of the upsurge and increase in quality in traditional Aboriginal arts has been their acceptance and adoption as part of the contemporary mainstream of Australian art. Critics are now unanimously reporting on Aboriginal art exhibitions; this was unheard of in Australia ten years ago, when only major exhibitions, sponsored by the principal state art galleries, rated mention. Not only does the new acceptance of Aboriginal art increase the status of Aboriginal communities in the eyes of Australian society in general, it also, as mentioned, considerably assists communities in gaining economic self-sufficiency. Very good individual artists are able to earn large incomes from the sale of their paintings. Exhibitions now tend to be organised in an attempt to recognise individual artists rather than clans and to show the meaning of the works as well as their visual appeal. In that process, older artists are now achieving some recognition. Their work may not be as technically proficient or perfect as that of younger artists, because of age and poor eyesight, but on the other hand their ceremonial knowledge is recognised and their illustrations of the meaning of the landscape to them through ceremonial series have been received with interest in the wider community.

Younger artists whose paintings are innovative and yet traditional have also achieved recognition in their own right. Some are able to maintain their own crafts centres and are successful businessmen. In a few instances, and these are quite spectacular success stories, one-man shows have assisted artists to set up their own homeland centres.

There is a continuum in Aboriginal art that stretches directly from the first and most ancient scratches on rock deep in the Koonalda cave under the Nullarbor Plain through to modern works on canvas done by desert masters. Lines and symbols have remained the same for thousands of years and, even in modern works by young artists, this essential view of life has been retained. There is a new and very strong sense of pride in being Aboriginal among Australians of Aboriginal descent, and in most parts of the country, a cultural revival is taking place. Many younger Aboriginals who might not have grown up within traditional religious principles are seeking to retain or regain what they once had. Aboriginal art is not a relic of a primitive culture usurped by an invading race; rather, it is a living tradition held with great pride and love in the minds of all Aboriginals and which should be respected and appreciated by all others. It should be allowed to take its place as the expression of one of the important philosophies of the world.

Aboriginal religion has permitted its followers to live on the Australian continent following its principles for the longest span of any culture now surviving in the world. Although it is an ancient culture, so old as to be almost beyond our imagination, the very nature of the practice of Aboriginal art, its role at the centre of life itself and its multifaceted nature, incorporating as it does all aspects of performance, painting, constructions, body painting, song, dance and ceremony, as well as painted and sculptured images, allows these ancient arts to slip easily into any modern definition of great art and to be truly considered as treasures of Australia.

APPENDIX
The Antiquity of Aboriginal Art

Dramatic advances have been made in the archaeological investigation of Australia's prehistory over the last quarter of a century. During that time discoveries have extended the time mankind has occupied the continent from just several thousand years to 40,000 years, with some adventurous theorists postulating that people might have been in Australia for 120,000 years.[1] Large areas of Australia await investigation, and a great deal of work is needed to give a more comprehensive data sequence for Aboriginal culture and art. The excitement of discovery still hangs over this work, which is vitally important to Aboriginals themselves as well as to the wider community in general.

Many vast galleries of rock engravings and paintings have been discovered, but few have been excavated and dated. Much of the sequencing of sites and the antiquity of the art is therefore based on inference and, in a number of significant sites, on the presence of associated deposits of ochre. These sites have provided the basic framework now generally accepted for Aboriginal rock art.

It is probable that, because ochre is used in all facets of contemporary Aboriginal life, it also assumed an important role in antiquity. Almost every excavation of sites older than 10,000 B.P. (before the present) has uncovered quantities of ochre pigment in pellets or as a stain. Pieces of ochre were obviously used as crayons, as some fragments have smooth edges. Large quantities of ochre have always been used in ceremonies and accounts exist of supplies being gathered from certain quarries for this purpose, and being traded throughout the country. Nearly all of these quarries hold mythological significance to the owners; a particular one in the Lake Eyre region was visited by up to 70 Dieri tribesmen who annually travelled 500 kilometres from central Australia to the Flinders Ranges to gather the ochre and to carry it home for ceremonies. These same people travelled across the Simpson Desert, where they exchanged ochre for the leaves of the *pituri* bush (*Duboisia topwoodii*)[2] a form of native tobacco that is chewed, producing a mild narcotic effect.

The earliest evidence of human occupation of Australia has been found in the Willandra Lakes region of south-western New South Wales. This extraordinary area has been declared a World Heritage site because it is significant not only for the cultural heritage of Aboriginal Australians, but for the world. The area is a distinct geological entity. In the Ice Age, when temperatures were lower and the precipitation from the eastern mountains greater, Lake Mungo, which then covered 135 square kilometres, was a chain of freshwater lakes along the Willandra Creek. The site was discovered in 1967 by Australian National University geomorphologist Dr Jim Bowler.[3] As often happens in archaeology, Dr Bowler was investigating something else entirely when he came across bone protruding from a wind-eroded bank. These fragments turned out to be part of a human burial site, one of three found at the lake. Over the past 20,000 years or so, the entire drainage system has virtually fossilised the evidence of landform and environmental conditions during the last Ice Age on a scale unequalled elsewhere. Archaeological evidence at Mungo and at other nearby lake sites subsequently dated human occupation to well beyond 35,000 years – at the time the earliest fully established date for human presence in Australia.

This site was also important in showing more about Aboriginal aesthetic and ritual practices. The bones of a male corpse dated to about 32,000 B.P. and the adjacent grave were stained red, indicating that they had been coated with ochre from pigments unobtainable locally. This showed that ochre had a special significance for the people of those times and that it had been carried for long distances to be used in ceremonies. The presence of ochre and the fact that bodies were buried rather than simply abandoned indicates that the people believed in an after-life, and that there was probably ritual associated with burials. The presence of ochre indicates an aesthetic sense, the need to decorate the grave and perhaps the body.

However, the evidence of ochre does not necessarily indicate that a form of art was practised. The ochre should therefore be seen as having associations that are ritualistic rather than being artistic.

The real significance of Lake Mungo is that the dates it established indicate that human occupation of Australia began even earlier. It is postulated that the movement of population across the continent began in the far north; it would have taken many millennia to spread a small original population from there to Lake Mungo, New South Wales. The Lake Mungo dates of about 35,000 years are therefore in no sense final.

Galleries of rock art abound throughout the Australian continent, and engravings are by far the most widespread form of art activity. Ranging from single images to groups of hundreds on wide expanses of rock, they are the oldest art works. The designs in rock art include simple geometric markings, animal tracks, representations of fish and game nets, a multitude of birds and animals and a wide range of figures with recognisable human features such as bodies, arms and legs; these often have other elements, such as headdresses or supernatural or superhuman features, denoting ancestral hero status. Many have exaggerated heads, arms or genital organs. Aboriginal people probably practised all the art forms of a multifaceted society in ancient times much as they do today, though evidence to support this, apart from general descriptions in the song cycles, has been lost. Only rock art is left to give a visual explanation of the creative forces at work in ancient Aboriginal society.

Some rock engravings that diverge from other examples have given rise to novel and, in retrospect, somewhat amusing suggestions about their origin. In 1909, Lawrence Hargrave claimed that a pattern series on Woollahra Point, Port Jackson, was made by Peruvian slaves who were part of the crew of a Spanish ship commanded by Lope de Vega that became separated from a fleet led by Medana that was visiting the Solomon Islands. These men sighted the Australian continent in 1595. The claim was countered by another settler, Captain

Watson, who claimed that the engravings were the work of convicts. Yet others have attributed them to Indonesians, citing Hindu symbolism as proof.[4]

In other parts of the country, notably the Kimberleys, the style of Wandjina rock paintings has been responsible for the suggestion that Indonesians visited the area and influenced the art. Along Cape York and the eastern coast, many have suggested that successive sea visits by Papuans or New Guineans influenced the material culture.

From small fragments of ochre found in many archaeological deposits, it is clear that the use of paint was widespread. A grinding dish found in the Alligator Rivers area and dated to 19,000 B.P. had traces of ochre on its surface. Old stone implements were obviously decorated and, as designs now appear on bodies and wooden implements, it is highly probable that ochre has been ground and used in this way since the first people came to Australia.

In any large rock art gallery, particularly painting sites, the full range of the artists' work can be seen. Sometimes well painted figures occur beside simple and roughly made markings; at other sites, successive layers of paintings form a sequence through time. In painting galleries such as those found in Cape York, the Kakadu National Park and the Kimberley region, ancient red paintings show clear differences of style and subject matter compared to later paintings in the same galleries. These shelters convey an enormous amount of visual information about the previous landowners and artists. Animals depicted, styles of ceremonial regalia, weapons and other features can give important pointers to historians, as well as giving pleasure to those interested in the overall impact of the paintings. Rock engravings have spanned almost the full period of Aboriginal occupation of Australia, ranging from an actual date of up to 20,000 years (at Koonalda cave, South Australia) to examples executed this century and showing European boats and other aspects of the invading white culture.

Cave paintings may well date back to a time similar to that of the engravings. However, they disintegrate rapidly, so few may be very old. Many of the important paintings were retouched by the artists or the caretakers of the sites, but now that this has ceased, many magnificent galleries are at the mercy of chemical and physical weathering, vandalism, and insect and animal damage. The most recent known cave paintings were done between 1958 and 1965.

The oldest and most significant art site discovered so far is in Koonalda cave, beneath the Nullarbor Plain in South Australia.[5] The cave runs off a deep sink in the desert in a very isolated area close to the Western Australian border and only twenty-two kilometres inland from the sea. The caves were first examined by speleologists in 1904 but the art at the site was not even reported, let alone brought to the attention of archaeologists as having any significance.

The fact that the caves were once occupied by humans was first noted in 1957 by Dr Alexander Gallus, whose name was given to the site. Gallus excavated the cave in 1960. He dug a pit in the floor of the main chamber, resulting in the discovery of flint tailings that clearly indicated the role of the caves as a flint mine for making stone tools. Gallus also noted the existence of the art at the site and specialists subsequently investigated it, establishing its importance in the art history of the world. Ancient people had made a series of marks on the limestone walls up to 20,000 years ago. These marks have tremendous significance; they are the oldest art discovered in Australia and they predate much of the Palaeolithic art of Europe.

In the harder limestone sections, the marks consist of deeply engraved V-shaped lines in random groups with no apparent pattern. The lines are predominantly vertical with some indiscriminate crisscrosses. The only exception is one section on which a recognisable pattern can be seen, a grid of approximately 1.3 square metres in area. In another part, two concentric circles are faintly discernible. In other areas of the cave, which were where the stone walls were once soft, there are recognisable patterns made by running the four fingers of the hand down the wall.

The caves had been used for ritual purposes as well as for the mining of flint. However, though there was an abundance of flint in the main chamber in the front section of the cave, art areas were on narrow ledges above water, which made access difficult. They were very deep in the recesses of the cave and in complete darkness; people would have had to carry light into the cave in order to gather the flint and to make the marks on the wall. They would have achieved this by using torches and it is this practice which has furnished us with the evidence of antiquity. Fortunately, the artists must have dropped their brush torches on rocks as they climbed over the rubble of rock in the cave. Examining the carbon produced by the extinguished torches on the floor of the cave has enabled archaeologists to date the engravings to 20,000 years ago.

More recent Aboriginal inhabitants of the area avoided the sink and the caves, believing them to be the home of Ganba, a malevolent serpent. Reports of this belief go back into the nineteenth century, and the legend was mentioned in the writings of Daisy Bates.

Other excavations of particularly interesting rock engravings include the Cape York discovery of the early man shelter. A frieze of pecked designs of possibly human and kangaroo tracks continues 1.5 metres below the floor level of this shelter. Associated carbon dates indicate an age in excess of 13,000 years B.P.

At Ingaladdi in the Northern Territory, a section of rock showing abraded grooves was found and dated to 6800-4920 years B.P. This site includes deeply incised linear grooves and bird tracks on rock fragments. It is interesting to note that at Delamere, only eighty kilometres away, identical grooves have been found and were observed being rubbed at a ceremony only fifty years ago.[6] Thus abraded grooves are not necessarily a measure of age in themselves.

At Mt Cameron West, Tasmania, remarkable engravings have

been discovered similar to the rock engravings that occur throughout the arid region from South Australia to the Northern Territory, from the Pilbara region of Western Australia across to New South Wales and Queensland. Some argue that these are linked in style and technique, being done by people with a common culture who lived across the whole of Australia, including Tasmania, before Bass Strait was flooded 12,000 years ago.[7]

In the Hawkesbury region surrounding Sydney a few rock engravings of European ships have been found. These indicate that, although the tribes of the area were decimated very early in the history of European invasion, some survivors recorded seeing such ships coming up the Hawkesbury River as settlement flowed along the river from Sydney to Windsor.

Dating Rock Art

Rock art in Australia can be dated by inference and also by absolute methods such as radiocarbon analysis. Dates of a relative or imprecise nature are inferred from an examination of subject content of the art or by reference to other potential associations. For example, the inclusion of a European sailing ship in a painting will indicate that it could not have been made before European ships were in the vicinity. Thus a relative date may be inferred from the time that such ships were common. More precision is gained if the type of boat has some special characteristics. In Arnhem Land rock art and in paintings on Groote Eylandt, lugger-type boats appear; such types of vessel were common at the turn of the twentieth century.

Arguments and new discoveries rearrange the sequence, or assumed sequence, of past events in Australian art history. Archaeologists can infer dates by associating the art with other substances and objects found in the digs, such as stone tools and ochre. For example, it is known that stone tool technology changed over the centuries and that certain types were used for a period before being entirely replaced by others. Backed blades gave way to contemporary stone technology about 750 years ago. In the Southern Alps, an investigation of art sites showed that the art was exclusively associated with a stone technology that post-dated backed blades;[8] thus it could not be older than 750 years.

Dates provided by ochre deposits are extremely widespread. Western Arnhem Land has yielded the earliest of these dates for rock paintings. Ochre found in deposits dated at 22,000 years B.P. has been used to infer a date for paintings in the Alligator River region. A site on Deaf Adder Creek, Northern Territory, has been dated by the same means to about 19,000 years B.P.[9] Similarly, Kenniff cave in southern Queensland has been dated to 19,000 years B.P. Although the paintings could not be associated with particular layers of deposit, ochre was found down to the 19,000-year-old level. It is assumed that the ochre was used in the paintings of the rock faces.

In many areas, painting galleries and rock engravings have no role as part of the living sculpture of current inhabitants, and are frequently ascribed to 'spirit' artists. When the painted figures at Port Bradshaw in the Kimberley region of north-west Australia were recorded in the nineteenth century, their discoverer, Bradshaw, was unable to find any living Aboriginal who could give the meaning of the paintings. They were said to have been painted by the spirit ancestors. Similarly, the Mimi paintings in western Arnhem Land are said by the Gunwinggu people to have been the work of the spirits. Clearly these paintings were created by people living in these areas before the present occupants.

Within one vast rock art gallery, differing styles of painting and engravings can be placed in sequence by studying the superimposition of succeeding styles. In many painting galleries and engraving sites, successive generations of artists have used styles particular to their own culture. As these cultures succeeded one another in time, the paintings and engravings overlapped and as the superimposed layers are untangled, the sequence of styles and therefore cultures can be determined. The rock painting galleries at Obiri Rock in western Arnhem Land are some of the most spectacular multilayered galleries in the world. Faded red stick figures known as Mimi are the earliest paintings and simple monochrome figures and animals of a different style have been superimposed over these. Over both of these appear polychrome, x-ray-style paintings.

In many engraving sites, great age can be inferred if the surface on which the engravings occur has changed. Over a very long time, the surface might have cracked or even fallen into pieces. Part of the engraving may remain in its original place; other parts might have fallen onto the ground or been subsequently covered by debris. In other places, rock ledges have split along faults and have fallen away, leaving the engraving site in an inaccessible position. While specific dates cannot be determined where rock surfaces have split or fractured and fallen onto the ground, the fracturing of rock faces by natural weathering takes a very long time indeed.

In many areas, paintings and engravings have been covered with a fine layer of silica. It has been argued that the process of developing this silica patina takes thousands of years.

In the past, some have made attempts to indicate great antiquity for a small number of sites by citing references to extinct animals in the art. These arguments have been advanced at Carnarvon in central Queensland, in the Hawkesbury area of New South Wales, in the Kakadu National Park and at Panaramitee in South Australia. At Panaramitee a giant crocodile is engraved on the rock surface. There are also a large turtle and the tracks of a large bird. These images have been identified as extinct animals from the Pleistocene era.[10]

Since the 1950s, the development of dating techniques by technological means has been staggeringly rapid. All the techniques are complicated, requiring expensive laboratory facilities and the results are sufficiently reliable to be termed absolute. The most useful absolute dating technique to be introduced into Australia is radiocarbon dating, commonly known as C-14, a method developed by Nobel laureate Willard

F. Libby. It is recognised that all organic matter has a certain amount of radioactive carbon – C-14 – in it and that in living matter the amount is constant. Any loss of C-14 is made up by ingesting or photosynthesising more from the environment, so there is a balance between the environment and all organic matter in it. When the organism dies the process is stopped; no more C-14 is taken in from the environment. At the same time, C-14 is lost from the dead organism at a uniform rate. By measuring the amount of radiation emitted as a result of the disintegration of C-14, the date of the organism's death can be determined. A recently dead organism emits a higher level of radiation than does an organism long deceased.[11]

Because the rate of C-14 decay in the deceased organism is variable, and because of some other factors, no single year date is reliable in scientific terms. Consequently, a statistically calculated number of years on either side of a median date forms part of the date expression. All the dates are expressed in years before present, or B.P. Thus the date of a midden site at Garrki in the Northern Territory is expressed as 1305 ± 306 B.P. and dates from the Devon Downs site associated with paintings are 4250 ± 140 B.P.

The most common materials for carbon dating are charcoal, wood, shell and bone found during excavation. In the case of a rock shelter that has been occupied over many centuries, this dating method is most useful. Over the years family groups have camped at the shelter, made stone tools and other utensils, hunted, cooked and eaten their food. They have also made paintings on the walls of the shelter. After many centuries, the litter of stone tools, discarded meals and remains of campfires, as well as the dust of ages, may be many metres thick. When excavated, each layer is removed very carefully and recorded. In some of these layers organic debris, particularly charcoal, might have survived. That charcoal is then processed and subjected to C-14 dating. Each layer with datable material then represents a period point in the past. The oldest date for the deposits represents the oldest likely date for the art.

At some levels of the deposits, ochre lumps or rocks used for mixing colours might have been found. These layers indicate a possible date when painting is likely to have taken place. Thus, while the dates of the deposits are described as absolute, those for the paintings can only be called relative.

Dating methods have given new life and interest to the study of prehistoric art in Australia. Dating has significantly modified many theories concerning Aboriginal rock art, producing an increasingly reliable and useful basis for study and development.

It is clear that artists were busy in both Australia and Europe at about the same time. The grooves on the walls of Koonalda cave show some similarities to the hand grooves at the site of Altamira in Spain dated at 30,000 years ago. These are believed to be the earliest art forms produced by Upper Palaeolithic man. Perhaps the most directly comparable feature of the rock paintings on both continents is the stencilling of the hands. Stencilling is a simple and very direct technique. Pigment is chewed until it forms a thin paste in the mouth and sips of water dilute it to a thin paint. The item to be stencilled – hand or boomerang, axe or other utensil – is placed against the rock surface. The paint is then sprayed from the mouth onto the rock, over the object. When the object is removed, it leaves a silhouette stencilled on the rock surface.

Throughout Australia, many and varied everyday objects have been recorded in this way. The technique has been used since very early times and it is still in use today in Arnhem Land and north-west Western Australia where recent examples are known.

Some of the caves at Gargas in the French Pyrenees contain as many as 150 examples of stencilled hands, many showing amputated fingers.

In Australia until very recently it was common to amputate the fingers in a number of rites. Sometimes the finger of a woman was amputated if her husband died or when she married. In other places, men had their fingers amputated for different reasons. Paintings of hands with amputated fingers in different positions, with fingers apart or together, or sometimes with the index and little fingers stretched and separated from the two middle fingers of the hand, suggest different symbolic purposes. Occasionally, hand stencils appear with one finger curled over, forming the personal signature of an artist. The presence of numerous hands stencilled in galleries from Victoria through New South Wales, Queensland, across Arnhem Land, throughout central Australia and into Western Australia, in fact throughout the entire continent, strongly links the creative forces that motivated the peoples of Australia and Europe so many centuries ago.

In general it is tempting to compare the art of Altamira in Spain, the paintings of Lascaux in France, even that of the Bushmen in Africa, with Australian prehistoric art. However, in Australian art, fine anatomical detail and perspective are lacking compared to the Lascaux art, although the Mimi and Bradshaw figures are similar in depicting musculature and movement. The Australian galleries achieve enormous visual impact because of the impressive layers of paintings. Moreover, rock painting has remained a living art until the last decade or so, and the sites are vital parts of a living religion.

NOTES

Aboriginal Art, Culture and Landscape

1 Josephine Flood, *Archaeology of the Dreamtime*, Collins, Sydney, 1983.
2 R. Edwards and L. Maynard, 'Prehistoric art in Koonalda cave' in *Proceedings of the Royal Geographical Society of Australia*, South Australian branch (vol. 68, 1967), Adelaide, 1968, page 11. See also J. Peter White and J. F. O'Connell, *A Prehistory of Australia, New Guinea and Sahul*, Academic Press, Sydney, 1982, page 62.
3 For example, Kenniff cave (19,000 years before the present or B.P.) and sites in the Northern Territory (up to 22,000 years B.P.).
4 J. B. Birdsell in 'Some population problems involving Pleistocene man', *Cold Spring Harbor Symposia on Quantitative Biology*, vol. 22, 1957, pages 47-69. The figure of 300,000 was originally proposed by A. R. Radcliffe Browne in 1930; see 'Former numbers and distribution of the Australian Aborigines' in the *Official Year Book of the Commonwealth of Australia*, 23:686-96.
5 For other arguments against Birdsell, see Sandra Bowdler, *Sunda and Sahul*, Academic Press, London, 1977, pages 205ff. See also J. Peter White and James F. O'Connell, *A Prehistory of Australia, New Guinea and Sahul*, Academic Press, Sydney, 1982, pages 49-56.
6 Carol Cooper (ed.), *Aboriginal Australia* (exhibition catalogue), Australian Gallery Directors' Council, Sydney, 1981.
7 R. H. Matthews, 'Ethnological notes on the Aboriginal Tribes of New South Wales and Victoria', P. W. White, 1905.
8 Sharon Sullivan, 'Aborigines of the Uplands of New South Wales' in *The Aborigines of New South Wales*, New South Wales National Parks and Wildlife Service, vol. 2, no. 5.
9 G. K. Dunbar, 'Notes on the Ngemba tribe of the central Darling River, western New South Wales', *Mankind*, vol. 3, no. 5, December, 1943.
10 Jennifer Isaacs, *Australian Dreaming*, Lansdowne Press, Sydney, 1980, page 83.
11 Walter E. Roth, *North Queensland Ethnography Bulletin*, no. 13; *Records of the Australian Museum*, vol. 7, no. 4, August 1909, page 205. Roth reported that the shields were made from *Ficus chretioides*. The shield is called *pi-kan* by the people.
12 Walter E. Roth, *North Queensland Ethnography Bulletin*, no. 13; *Records of the Australian Museum*, vol. 7, no. 4, August 1909, page 210. Locally known in the Tully-Cardwell area as *barkur*, made from *Myrtus exaltata* and another unidentified tree, swords in this area were single-handed weapons. In the Rockhampton area, from Yamba to Broadsound, a two-handled version was made, an example of which was collected by Roth in 1898.
13 For a discussion of the development of a stylistic sequence for Australian Aboriginal rock art see F. D. McCarthy, *Australian Aboriginal Rock Art*, Australian Museum, Sydney, 1979. Also L. Maynard, 'Archaeology of Australian Aboriginal art' in S. M. Mead, I. Brymer and S. Marich, *Exploring the Visual Art of Oceania: Australia, Melanesia, Micronesia, Polynesia*, University of Hawaii Press, Honolulu, 1979. The most recent sequencing theory about the Arnhem Land area has been written by George Chaloupka, 'Kakadu rock art: its cultural, historic and prehistoric significance' in Gillespie, D., *The Rock Art Sites of Kakadu National Park: Some Preliminary Research Findings for Their Conservation and Management*, Australian National Parks and Wildlife Service, serial publication 10, 1983, pages 1-33.
14 For a discussion of the *trepang* trade, see C. E. Macknight, *The Voyage to Marege*, Melbourne University Press, Melbourne, 1976.
15 See the chapter on bark painting for some of these stories. Also Helen Groger-Wurm, *Australian Aboriginal Bark Paintings and their Mythological Interpretation, Vol. 1: Eastern Arnhem Land*, Australian Institute of Aboriginal Studies, Canberra, 1983.
16 See C. P. Mountford, *The Tiwi: Their Art, Myth and Symbolism*, Phoenix House, London, 1958, for a discussion of the Purukapali legend.
17 Albert Barunga in Jennifer Isaacs, *Australian Dreaming*, Lansdowne Press, Sydney, 1980, page 70.
18 Sam Woolagoodja. *ibid*., page 71.

The Body as Living Art

1 Walter E. Roth, *North Queensland Ethnography Bulletin*, no. 14, vol. viii, *Records of the Australian Museum*, no. 1, November 1910.
2 *Ibid*.
3 Written on Cook's second voyage and quoted in H. Ling Roth, *The Aborigines of Tasmania*, 1899.
4 G. W. Walker, *The Life and Labours of G. W. Walker*, London, 1862.
5 Jennifer Isaacs, *Australian Dreaming*, Lansdowne Press, Sydney, 1980, page 20.
6 Nancy Munn, *Walbiri Iconography*, Cornell University Press, New York, 1973.
7 Carl Lumholz, *Among Cannibals*, John Murray, London, 1889.
8 James Dawson, *Australian Aborigines*, George Robinson, Melbourne, 1881, pages 82-3.
9 H. Ling Roth, *The Aborigines of Tasmania*, 1899, page 129.
10 E. Baldwin Spencer and F. J. Gillen, *The Northern Tribes of Central Australia*, Macmillan, London, 1904.
11 See note 6 above.
12 C. P. Mountford, *The Tiwi, Their Art, Myth and Ceremony*, Phoenix House, London, 1958.
13 P. P. King, *Survey of the Intertropical Coasts of Australia: Vol. 1*, 1837, page 114.
14 J. Mulvaney, 'Origins' in *Aboriginal Australia* (exhibition catalogue), Australian Gallery Directors' Council, Sydney, 1981, pages 22 and 23.
15 G. K. Dunbar, 'Notes on the Ngemba tribe of the central Darling River, western New South Wales' in *Mankind*, vol. 3, no. 5, December 1943, page 142.
16 B. Ellis and C. Houston, *Aboriginal Inhabitants of the Adelaide Plains; Aboriginal and Historic Relics*, S.A. Museum, Adelaide, 1976.
17 All examples cited are included in the *Guide to Australian Ethnographical Collection*, published by the Museum of Victoria.
18 James Dawson, *Australian Aborigines*, George Robertson, Melbourne 1881, page 81.
19 Walter E. Roth, *Ethnological Studies Among the North-West and Central Queensland Aborigines*, Brisbane, 1897.
20 Carol Cooper (ed.), *Aboriginal Australia* (exhibition catalogue), Australian Gallery Directors' Council, Sydney, 1981.
21 F. S. Colliver and F. P. Woolston, 'Aboriginals in the Brisbane area' in *Brisbane Retrospect*, Library Board of Brisbane, Brisbane, 1978.
22 E. Baldwin Spencer and F. J. Gillen, *The Native Tribes of Central Australia*, Macmillan, London, 1899; *The Northern Tribes of Central Australia*, Macmillan, London, 1904; and *The Northern Territory of Australia*, Macmillan, London, 1914.
23 D. S. Davidson, 'The interlocking key design in Aboriginal Australian decorative art' in *Mankind*, vol. 4, no. 3, September 1949.
24 *Guide to Australian Ethnographical Collection*, Museum of Victoria, page 53.

Fibre Craft

1 Jennifer Isaacs, *Australian Dreaming*, Lansdowne Press, Sydney, 1980; see chapter 10.
2 R. Brough-Smyth, *Aborigines of Victoria: Vol. 1*, London, 1878, page 344.
3 P. Brokensha, *The Pitjantjatjara and their Crafts*, Aboriginal Arts Board, Sydney.
4 One such bag and its contents were collected by Donald Thomson in the 1930s and are now part of the Thomson collection in the Museum of Victoria.
5 Alan L. West, *Australian Aboriginal Cordage and Single Element Fabric Structures*, unpublished MA thesis, La Trobe University, 1980.
6 R. Brough-Smyth, *Aborigines of Victoria; Vol. 1*, London, 1878, pages 343 and 344.

Rock Engraving

1 F. D. McCarthy, *Australian Aboriginal Rock Art*, Australian Museum, Sydney, 1979. The theory McCarthy put forward is consistent throughout this book's four editions (i.e., 1958, 1962, 1967 and 1979).
2 L. Maynard, 'The archaeology of Australian Aboriginal art', symposium on the art of Oceania, McMaster University, 1974. Also published in S. M. Mead, I. Brymer and S. Martich, *Exploring the Visual Art of Oceania: Australia, Melanesia, Micronesia, Polynesia*, University of Hawaii Press, Honolulu, 1979.
3 R. Edwards, 'Prehistoric rock engravings at Thomas Reservoir, Cleland Hills, western central Australia', *Records of the South Australian Museum*, vol. 15, no. 4, November 1968, pages 647-70.
4 *The Voyage of Governor Phillip to Botany Bay*, third edition, John Stockdale, London, 1790, pages 126 and 127.
5 F. D. McCarthy, 'Proposal for an Aboriginal rock engraving centre in New South Wales', 1983, submitted to various government authorities for the Bicentennial.
6 Quoted in Jennifer Isaacs, *Australian Dreaming*, Lansdowne Press, Sydney, 1980, page 11.
7 E. A. Worms, 'Prehistoric petroglyphs of the upper Yule River' in *North-Western Australia Anthropos*, vol. 49, 1954.
8 P. Trezise, *Rock Art of South-East Cape York*, Australian Institute of Aboriginal Studies, Canberra, 1971.

Rock Painting

1 R. Edwards, *The Art of the Alligator Rivers Region*, Australian Government Printing Service, Canberra, 1974, page 77.
2 A party of visiting art specialists was shown these paintings by Bobby Ngainmira in 1980.
3 E. Baldwin Spencer, *Native Tribes of the Northern Territory*, Macmillan, London, 1914.
4 R. M. and C. H. Berndt, *Sexual Behaviour in Western Arnhem Land*, Viking Fund Publications in Anthropology, no. 16, New York, 1951.
5 E. J. Brandl, *Australian Aboriginal Paintings in Western and Central Arnhem Land*, Australian Institute of Aboriginal Studies, Canberra, 1973.
6 F. D. McCarthy, *Australian Aboriginal Rock Art*, Australian Museum, Sydney, 1979, page 46.
7 E. J. Brandl, *Australian Aboriginal Paintings in Western and Central Arnhem Land*, Australian Institute of Aboriginal Studies, Canberra, 1973, page 106.
8 L. Maynard, 'The archaeology of Australian Aboriginal art', symposium on the art of Oceania, McMaster University, 1974.
9 Ian Crawford, *The Art of the Wandjina*, Oxford University Press, Oxford, 1968.
10 F. D. McCarthy, *Rock Art of the Cobar Pediplain*, Australian Institute of Aboriginal Studies, Canberra, 1976, page 74.
11 P. J. Trezise, *Rock Art of South-Eastern Cape York*, Australian Institute of Aboriginal Studies, Canberra, 1971, page 10.
12 Sir George Grey, *Expeditions of Discovery; Vol. 1*, London, 1841.
13 G. Chaloupka, 'Kakadu rock art: its cultural, historic and prehistoric significance', in D. Gillespie, *The Rock Art Sites of Kakadu National Park: Some Preliminary Research Findings for Their Conservation and Management*, Australian National Parks and Wildlife Service, 1983.
14 G. Chaloupka, *ibid*.
15 R. Edwards, *The Art of the Alligator Rivers Region*, Australian Government Printing Service, Canberra, 1974, page 77.

Bark Painting

1 A. P. Elkin and R. M. and C. H. Berndt, *Art in Arnhem Land*, Cheshire, Melbourne, 1950.
2 Quoted in Phillip Adams, *The Unspeakable Adams*, Nelson, Melbourne, 1977.
3 N. Williams, 'Aboriginal art at Yirrkala: the introduction and development of marketing' in N. Graburn, *Ethnic and Tourist Arts*, University of California Press, Berkeley, 1976.
4 C. P. Mountford, *The Tiwi: Their Art, Myth and Symbolism*, Phoenix House, London, 1958.
5 Jennifer Isaacs, *Oenpelli Paintings on Bark* (exhibition catalogue), Australian Gallery Directors' Council and Aboriginal Arts Board, Sydney, 1977.
6 The bush honey myth is discussed in detail in H. Groger-Wurm's *Australian Bark Paintings and Their Mythological Interpretation, Vol. 1: Eastern Arnhem Land*, Australian Institute of Aboriginal Studies, Canberra, 1973, pages 51-7.
7 Collected by John Mundine and purchased by the Art Gallery of New South Wales, they were exhibited there in the *Australian Perspecta* exhibition of May-June 1983.
8 Jennifer Isaacs, *Australian Dreaming*, Lansdowne Press, Sydney, 1980, page 75. The story was told by Wandjuk Marika, whose paintings were collected by Mountford and Berndt (1948-50) and later by Scougall and Tuckson.

Papunya Painting

1 From the catalogue programme of the Paris Festvale d'Automne, January 1983.
2 Geoff Bardon, *Aboriginal Art of the Western Desert*, Rigby, Adelaide, 1979.
3 Pam Nathan and Dick Leichleitner Japanangka, *Settle Down Country*, Kibble Books, Victoria, 1983.
4 A. Crocker, *Mr Sandman, Bring Me a Dream*, Aboriginal Artists' Agency, Sydney, 1981.

Carved Weapons and Utensils

1 James Dawson, *Australian Aborigines*, George Robertson, Melbourne, 1881, page 80.
2 R. Brough-Smyth, *The Aborigines of Victoria, Vol. I*, George Robertson, Melbourne, 1878.
3 *Ibid.*, page 1.
4 G. K. Dunbar, 'Notes on the Ngemba tribe of central Darling River, western New South Wales', *Mankind*, vol. 3, no. 5, December, 1943, and vol. 3, no. 6, July, 1944.
5 J. Hawker, *Early Experiences in South Australia*, Adelaide, 1899: South Australian Library (facsimile edition) 1975. Hawker wrote of an incident he witnessed shortly after his arrival in 1838.
6 R. Gould, *Yiwara*, Collins, Sydney, 1967, page 84.

Sculpture

1 C. W. M. Hart and A. R. Pilling, *The Tiwi of North Australia*, Holt, Reinhart and Winston, New York, 1960.
2 E. Baldwin Spencer, *The Native Tribes of the Northern Territory of Australia*, Macmillan, London, 1914.
3 C. W. M. Hart and A. R. Pilling, *The Tiwi of North Australia*, Holt, Reinhart and Winston, New York, 1960, page 113.
4 W. L. Warner, *A Black Civilization: A Social Study of an Australian Tribe*, Harper, New York, 1937.
5 C. P. Mountford, *Records of the American-Australian Scientific Expedition to Arnhem Land. Vol. 1: Art, Myth and Symbolism*, Melbourne University Press, Melbourne, 1956.
6 A. P. Elkin and R. M. and C. H. Berndt, *Art in Arnhem Land*, Cheshire, Melbourne, 1950.

7 David Bell, *Aboriginal Carved Trees of South-Eastern Australia: A Research Report*, National Parks and Wildlife Service, New South Wales, January 1982.

Return to the Land

1 Dr. H. C. Coombs, address to ANZAAS conference, Perth, 1973.

Appendix: The Antiquity of Aboriginal Art

1 J. Peter White and James F. O'Connell, *A Prehistory of Australia, New Guinea and Sahul*, Academic Press, Sydney, 1982, page 31. See also Josephine Flood, *Archaeology of the Dreamtime*, Collins, Sydney, 1983.
2 Other native tobaccos are *Nicotina gossie* and *Nicotina excelsior*.
3 J. M. Bowler, 'Recent developments in reconstructing late quaternary environments in Australia' in R. L. Kirk and A. G. Thorne, *The Origin of the Australians*, Australian Institute of Aboriginal Studies, Canberra, 1976, pages 55ff.
4 F. D. McCarthy, *Australian Aboriginal Rock Art*, Australian Museum, Sydney, 1979, page 37.
5 For a discussion on Koonalda cave, see L. Maynard and R. Edwards, 'Prehistoric art in Koonalda cave', proceedings v. 68 of the Royal Geographical Society of Australasia, South Australian branch, 1967.
6 W. Arndt, 'The interpretation of the Delamere lightning paintings and rock engravings', *Oceania*, vol. 32, no. 3, 1962.
7 Mt Cameron West is discussed in J. Peter White and James F. O'Connell, *A Prehistory of Australia, New Guinea and Sahul*, Academic Press, Sydney, 1982; F. D. McCarthy, *Australian Aboriginal Rock Art*, Australian Museum, Sydney, 1979; and in the section on Tasmania in *The Heritage of Australia*. See also R. Edwards, *Australian Aboriginal Art*, Australian Institute of Aboriginal Studies, Canberra, 1979, page 142.
8 Josephine Flood, *The Moth Hunters*, Australian Institute of Aboriginal Studies, Canberra, 1980.
9 R. Edwards, *The Art of the Alligator Rivers Region*, Alligator Rivers Region Environmental Fact Finding Study, 1974, page 102.
10 C. P. Mountford and R. Edwards, 'Aboriginal rock engravings of extinct creatures in South Australia', *Man*, 1962, pages 97-9.
11 J. W. Michels, *Dating Methods in Archaeology*, Seminar Press, New York, 1973.

BIBLIOGRAPHY

ADAM, L., *Primitive Art*, Penguin, London, 1954
—— *The Bark Paintings of Groote Eylandt in the Melbourne University Collection*, Museum für Volkerkunde, Basel, 1951
ALLEN, J., and JONES, R. (ed.), *Sunda and Sahul: Prehistoric Studies in South East Asia, Melanesia and Australia*, Academic Press, Sydney, 1977
ARNDT, W., 'The interpretation of the Delamere lightning paintings and rock engravings', *Oceania*, vol. 32, no. 3, 1962
BARDON, GEOFF, *Aboriginal Art of the Western Desert*, Rigby, Adelaide, 1979
BASEDOW, HERBERT, *The Australian Aboriginal*, F. W. Preeve & Sons, Adelaide, 1925
—— 'Notes on natives of Bathurst Island', *Royal Anthropological Institute Journal*, vol. 43, January 1913
BELL, DAVID, *Aboriginal Carved Trees of South-Eastern Australia: A Research Report*, National Parks and Wildlife Service, Canberra, January 1982
BENNETT, K., *List of Australian Weapons, Implements, etc., from the Darling and Lachlan Rivers in the Australian Museum*, Government Printer, 1897
BERNDT, R. M. and C. H., *Sexual Behaviour in Western Arnhem Land*, Viking Fund Publications in Anthropology, no. 16, New York, 1951
—— *The First Australians*, Ure Smith, Sydney, 1967
—— *Aboriginal Australian Art: A Visual Perspective*, Methuen, Sydney, 1982
—— *The World of the First Australians*, Ure Smith, Sydney, 1964
—— 'Secular figures of north-eastern Arnhem Land', *American Anthropologist*, vol. 51, no. 2, 1949
BERNDT, R. M., *Kunapipi*, Cheshire, Melbourne, 1951
—— *Djanggawul*, Routledge and Kegan Paul, London, 1952
BERNDT, R. M., (ed.), *Australian Aboriginal Art*, Ure Smith, Sydney, 1964
BERNDT, R. M. and PHILLIPS, E. S. (ed.), *The Australian Aboriginal Heritage*, Australian Society for Education Through the Arts with Ure Smith, Sydney, 1973
BEVERIDGE, P., *Aborigines of Victoria*, M. C. Hutchinson, Melbourne, 1889
BIRDSELL, J. B., 'Some population problems involving Pleistocene man', *Cold Spring Harbor Symposia on Quantitative Biology*, vol. 22, 1957
BLACK, LINDSAY, 'Notes on material culture of Aborigines of Darling River', *Mankind*, vol. 4, no. 3, September 1949
BLAINEY, G., *Triumph of the Nomads: A History of Ancient Australia*, Sun Books, Melbourne, 1975
BRAIN, R., *The Decorated Body*, Hutchinson, London, 1979
BRANDL, E. J., *Australian Aboriginal Paintings in Western and Central Arnhem Land*, Australian Institute of Aboriginal Studies, Canberra, 1973
BRAYSHAW, H., 'Aboriginal stone arrangements at Kempsey' in McBryde, I., *Records of Time Past*, Australian Institute of Aboriginal Studies, Canberra, 1978
BRIGHAM, W., *Mat and Basket Weaving of the Ancient Hawaiians*, 1906
BROKENSHA, P., *The Pitjantjatjara and Their Crafts*, Aboriginal Arts Board of the Australia Council, Sydney, 1975
BROUGH-SMYTH, R., *Aborigines of Victoria: Vol. 1*, George Robertson, Melbourne, 1878
CHALOUPKA, G., 'Kakadu rock art: its cultural, historic and prehistoric significance', in Gillespie, D., *The Rock Art Sites of Kakadu National Park: Some Preliminary Research Findings for Their Conservation and Management*, Australian National Parks and Wildlife Service, Canberra, 1983
—— 'Aspects of the chronology and schematization at two sites on the Arnhem Land plateau', in Ucko, P. J., *Form in Indigenous Art*, Australian Institute of Aboriginal Studies, Canberra, 1977
CHASELING, W., *Yulengor, Nomads of Arnhem Land*, 1957

COLLIVER, F. S. and WOOLSTON, F. P., 'Aboriginals in the Brisbane area' in *Brisbane Retrospect*, Library Board of Brisbane, Brisbane, 1978
COOMBS, DR. H. C., Address to ANZAAS conference, Perth, 1973
COOPER, CAROL (ed.), *Aboriginal Australia* (exhibition catalogue) Australian Gallery Directors' Council, Sydney, 1981
COTTON, B. C. (ed.), *Aboriginal Man in South and Central Australia*, South Australian Government Printer, Adelaide, 1966
CRAWFORD, I. M., *The Art of the Wandjina*, Oxford University Press, Melbourne, 1968
—— 'The engravings of Depuch Island', Western Australian Museum special publication, vol. 2
—— 'The relationship of Bradshaw and Wandjina art in north-west Kimberley' in Ucko, P. J. (ed.), *Form in Indigenous Art*, Australian Institute of Aboriginal Studies, Canberra, 1977
CROCKER, A., *Mr Sandman, Bring Me a Dream*, Aboriginal Artists' Agency, Sydney, 1981
DAVIDSON, D. S., 'Interlocking key design in Aboriginal Australian decorative art', *Mankind*, vol. 4, no. 3, September 1949
—— 'Australian netting and basketry techniques', *Polynesian Society Journal*, vol. 2, no. 4, December 1933
DAWSON, JAMES, *Australian Aborigines*, facsimile edition (1881), Australian Institute of Aboriginal Studies, Canberra, 1981
DUNBAR, G. K., 'Notes on the Ngemba tribe of central Darling River, western New South Wales', *Mankind*, vol. 3, no. 5, December 1943 and vol. 3, no. 6, July 1944
EDWARDS, R., 'Prehistoric rock engravings at Thomas Reservoir, Cleland Hills, western Central Australia', *Records of the South Australian Museum*, vol. 15, no. 4, November 1968
—— *Aboriginal Art in Australia*, Aboriginal Arts Board of the Australia Council, Sydney, 1978
—— *Australian Aboriginal Art*, Australian Institute of Aboriginal Studies, Canberra, 1979
—— *Australian Aboriginal Art: the Art of the Alligator Rivers Region, Northern Territory*, Australian Institute of Aboriginal Studies, Canberra, 1974, 1979
EDWARDS, R. (ed.), *The Preservation of Australia's Aboriginal Heritage*, Australian Institute of Aboriginal Studies, Canberra, 1975
ELKIN, A. P., *The Australian Aborigines*, Angus and Robertson, Sydney, 1974
ELKIN, A. P. and BERNDT, R. M. and C. H., *Art in Arnhem Land*, Cheshire, Melbourne, 1950
ELLIS, B. and HOUSTON, C., *Aboriginal Inhabitants of the Adelaide Plains*, Aboriginal Relics and Administration, South Australian Museum, 1976
ENRIGHT, W., 'Dilly bag from north coast of New South Wales', *Mankind*, vol. 21, December 1932
FLOOD, JOSEPHINE, *Archaeology of the Dreamtime*, Collins, Sydney, 1983
—— *The Moth Hunters*, Australian Institute of Aboriginal Studies, Canberra, 1980
GOULD, RICHARD A., *Yiwara*, Collins, Sydney, 1969
GREY, SIR GEORGE, *Expeditions of Discovery: Vol. 1*, London, 1841
GROGER-WURM, H., *Australian Aboriginal Bark Paintings and Their Mythological Interpretations: Vol. 1*, Australian Institute of Aboriginal Studies, Canberra, 1973
HADDON, A. C., *The Races of Man and Their Distribution*, Cambridge University Press, Cambridge, 1924
HARNEY, W. E., *The Significance of Ayers Rock for Aborigines*, Northern Territory Reserves Board, Darwin, 1970
HART, C. and PILLING, A., *The Tiwi of North Australia*, Holt, Reinhart and Winston, New York, 1960
HAWKER, J., *Early Experiences in South Australia*, facsimile edition (1899), South Australian Library, Adelaide, 1975

HOLMES, SANDRA LE BRUN, *Yirawala: Artist and Man*, Jacaranda Press, Brisbane, 1972

HORTON, HELEN, *Around Mt Isa*, University of Queensland Press, Brisbane, 1970

HOWITT, A. W., *The Native Tribes of South-East Australia*, Macmillan, London, 1904

—— 'Native tribes of south-east Australia', *Journal of the Royal Anthropological Institute*, London, 1907

ISAACS, J., *Australian Dreaming: 40,000 Years of Aboriginal History*, Lansdowne Press, Sydney, 1980

KUPKA, K., *Dawn of Art*, Angus and Robertson, Sydney, 1965

KING, P. P., *Survey of the Intertropical Coasts of Australia: Vol. 1*, London 1837

KIRK, R. L. and THORNE, A. G., *The Origin of the Australians*, Australian Institute of Aboriginal Studies, Canberra, 1976

LING ROTH, H., *The Aborigines of Tasmania*, 1899, facsimile edition, Fullers' Bookshop, Hobart

LANARD, HENRY, 'Aboriginal net making', *Mankind*, February 1950

LANE, K. H., 'Carved trees and initiation ceremonies on the Nambucca River' in McBryde, I., *Records of Time Past*, Australian Institute of Aboriginal Studies, Canberra, 1978

LEVITT, DULCIE, *Plants and People: Aboriginal Uses of Plants on Groote Eylandt*, Australian Institute of Aboriginal Studies, Canberra, 1981

LUMHOLZ, CARL, *Among Cannibals*, John Murray, London, 1889

MACKNIGHT, C., *The Voyage to Marege*, Melbourne University Press, Melbourne, 1976

MASSOLA, ALDO, *The Aborigines of South-Eastern Australia as They Were*, Heinemann, Melbourne, 1971

—— *Journey to Aboriginal Victoria*, Rigby, Adelaide, 1969

—— 'These relics tell tales', *Walkabout*, May 1963

MATHEWS, JANET, *Totem and Taboo*, Collins, Sydney, 1978

MATTHEWS, R. H., *Ethnological Notes on the Aboriginal Tribes of New South Wales and Victoria*, 1905

MAYNARD, L., 'Archaeology of Australian Aboriginal art' in Mead, S. M., Brymer, I. and Martich, S., *Exploring the Visual Art of Oceania: Australia, Melanesia, Micronesia, Polynesia*, University of Hawaii Press, Honolulu, 1979

—— 'Archaeology of Australian Aboriginal art', art of Oceania symposium, McMaster University, 1974

MAYNARD, L. and EDWARDS, R., 'Prehistoric art in Koonalda cave', proceedings v. 68 of Royal Geographical Society of Australasia, South Australian branch, 1967

MCBRYDE, I., *Records of Time Past*, Australian Institute of Aboriginal Studies, Canberra, 1978

MCCARTHY, F. D., *Australian Aboriginal Decorative Art*, Australian Museum, Sydney, 1958

—— *Rock Art of the Cobar Pediplain in Central Western New South Wales*, Australian Institute of Aboriginal Studies, Canberra, 1976

—— *Australian Aboriginal Rock Art*, Australian Museum, Sydney, 1979

—— 'Australian Aboriginal basket makers', *Walkabout*, no. 23, September, 1957

—— 'Arnhem Land baskets', *Australian Museum Magazine*, September, 1955

MCCOURT, THOMAS, *Aboriginal Artefacts*, Rigby, Adelaide, 1975

MEAD, S. M., BRYMER, I. and MARTICH, S., *Exploring the Visual Art of Oceania: Australia, Melanesia, Micronesia, Polynesia*, University of Hawaii Press, Honolulu, 1979

MESTON, A. L., 'Aboriginal rock carvings on the north-west coast of Tasmania', proceedings 12-14 of Royal Society of Tasmania, 1931

MICHELS, J. W., *Dating Methods in Archaeology*, Seminar Press, New York, 1973

MORPHY, H., 'Schematisation to conventionalisation: a possible trend in Yirrkala bark paintings', in P. J. Ucko (ed.), *Form in Indigenous Art*, Australian Institute of Aboriginal Studies, Canberra, 1977

—— 'Manggalili art', Faculty of arts, Australian National University, Canberra, 1978

MOUNTFORD, C. P. and EDWARDS, R., 'Aboriginal rock engravings of extinct creatures of South Australia', *Man*, 1962

MOUNTFORD, C. P., 'String figures of the Adnyamatara tribe', *Mankind*, vol. 4, no. 5, September 1950

—— 'American-Australian Scientific Expedition to Arnhem Land', *Vol. 1: Art, Myth and Symbolism of Arnhem Land*, Melbourne University Press, Melbourne, 1956

—— *The Tiwi: Their Art, Myth and Ceremony*, Phoenix House, London, 1958

—— *Ayers Rock, Its People, Their Beliefs and Their Art*, Angus and Robertson, Sydney, 1965

MOUNTFORD, C. P. and EDWARDS, R., 'Rock engravings of Panaramitee Station, north-eastern South Australia', proceedings 86:131-46 of the Royal Society of South Australia, 1963

MULVANEY, D. J. *'Origins' in Aboriginal Australia*, exhibition catalogue, Australian Gallery Directors' Council, Sydney, 1981

—— *The Prehistory of Australia*, London, Thames & Hudson, 1969 (revised edition Pelican Books, 1975)

MUNN, NANCY D., *Walbiri Iconography*, Cornell University Press, New York, 1973

NATHAN, PAM and LEICHLEITNER JAPANANGKA, DICK, *Settle Down Country*, Kibble Books, Victoria, 1983

NATIONAL MUSEUM OF VICTORIA, *Australian Aboriginal Art*, Government Printer, Melbourne, 1929

NUNN, ROBIN and WEST, ALAN, *Notes for a Work Shop*, Melbourne, National Museum of Victoria, 1979

PARTINGTON, JAMES EDGE, *Album of Weapons, Tools, Ornaments*, facsimile edition, London, 1969

ROBINSON, R., *The Feathered Serpent*, Edwards and Shaw, Sydney, 1906

ROTH, W. E., 'String and other forms of strand; basketry, woven bag and net work', *North Queensland Ethnography Bulletin*, Home Secretary's Department, Brisbane, no. 1, January 1901; no. 4, March 1902, no. 5, January 1903

—— *North Queensland Ethnography Bulletin no. 13, Records of the Australian Museum*, August 1909, vol. 7, no. 4

—— *North Queensland Ethnography Bulletin, no. 14, Records of the Australian Museum*, 1910, vol. 8, no. 1

SPENCER, W. B. and GILLEN, F. J., *The Northern Tribes of Central Australia*, Macmillan, London, 1904

—— *The Native Tribes of Central Australia*, Macmillan, London, 1899

SPENCER, W. B., *The Native Tribes of the Northern Territory of Australia*, Macmillan, London, 1914

STANBURY, P. and MYERS, P., 'Proposal for an Aboriginal rock engraving centre in New South Wales', 1983

SULLIVAN, SHARON, 'Aborigines of the uplands of New South Wales', in *The Aborigines of New South Wales, National Parks and Wildlife*, vol. 2, no. 5

—— 'Central aspects of material culture of the Aborigines of Richmond', *Armidale Historical Society Journal*, vol. 1, no. 1, August 1965

THOMSON, D., *Bindibu Country*, Nelson, Melbourne, 1975

THORNE, A. G., 'Morphological contrasts in Pleistocene Australians', in Kirk, R. L., and Thorne, A. G., *The Origin of the Australians*, Australian Institute of Aboriginal Studies, Canberra, 1976

TINDALE, NORMAN, 'Aboriginal net making', *Mankind*, vol. 4, May, 1951

TREZISE, P. J., 'Rock art of south-east Cape York', *Australian Institute of Aboriginal Studies Bulletin*, no. 24; Canberra, 1971

—— *Rock Art of South-East Cape York*, Australian Institute of Aboriginal Studies, Canberra, 1971

UCKO, P. J. (ed.), *Form in Indigenous Art*, Australian Institute of Aboriginal Studies, Canberra, 1977

VERBRUGGE, A. R., *Hand Figuration in Primitive Australia*, Editions Ophrys, Fondation Universitare de Belgique, 1970

WALKER, G. W., *The Life and Labours of G. W. Walker*, London, 1862

WALLACE, P. and N., *Killing Me Softly*, Nelson, Melbourne, 1977

WARNER, W. L., *A Black Civilization*, Harper, New York, 1937

WEST, ALAN L., *Australian Aboriginal Cordage and Single-Element Fabric Structures*, unpublished MA thesis, La Trobe University, Victoria, 1980

WHITE, J. P. and O'CONNELL, J. F., *A Prehistory of Australia, New Guinea and Sahul*, Academic Press, Sydney, 1982

WILLIAMS, N., 'Aboriginal art at Yirrkala, the introduction and development of marketing' in Graburn, N., *Ethnic and Tourist Arts*, University of California Press, Berkeley, 1976

WRIGHT, B. J., 'The art of the rock engravers', in R. M. Berndt and E. S. Phillips (ed.), *The Australian Aboriginal Heritage*, Australian Society for Education Through the Arts in association with Ure Smith, Sydney, 1973

—— *Rock Art of the Pilbara Region, Northwestern Australia*, Australian Institute of Aboriginal Studies, Canberra, 1968

ACKNOWLEDGMENTS

I would like to thank all the people who helped me prepare this book, particularly Kerry Steinberg for assistance in research and art selection, and my mother, Carmel Pepperell, who typed the manuscript and kept me and the book on schedule. I would also like to thank Reg and Maggie Morrison for their welcome company and cooperation on field work. All photographs in the book were taken by Reg Morrison unless otherwise indicated.

Thanks are due to the following for hospitality and help in the field.

Amata: Pat d'Aranjo, Peter Yates, Walter Pukutuwara, Topsy Tjulata, Nellie Patterson. Amoongana: Maudie Booth. Aurukun: Jeannie Adams, Arkapenya, Lou Yunkaporta. Bathurst Island: Mick and Chris Reid, Declan Apuatimi and Eddie Puruntatameri. Maningrida: Luke Taylor, Charles Godjuwa, George Gawarun, Johnny Bulu Bulun and James Mowanjul. Papunya: Daphne Williams, Paddy Carroll, Two Bob Tjungurrayi, Don Tjungurrayi, Entalura Nangala, Alastair Burns, Ada Andy Napaltjarri. Ramingining: John Mundine, Dianne Moon, David Malangi, Gindjimirr, Ganbada. Yirrkala: Wandjuk Marika and family, Steve and Lil Fox.

I must also thank Margaret West, Curator of Anthropology at the Northern Territory Museum of Arts and Sciences, and Kate Sutcliffe of the Queensland Archaeology Branch, D.A.I.A., for the loan of transparencies of Queensland rock engraving and painting. The staff of all museums and galleries spent much time in helping with research and photography, and to them I am most grateful.

Ian Primrose was particularly helpful with research on rock art, and Heidi Herbert gave me much useful photographic advice.

I must express my gratitude to Lisa Kem, who acted as a personal assistant and who kept the family going while I was travelling. I would especially like to thank my husband David and children Joseph and Samuel for their generous love and support throughout this project.

Finally, I must acknowledge a very real and lasting debt of gratitude to my Aboriginal teachers and the families who adopted me, painstakingly teaching me from the beginning, reorientating me to life and art. In every way this involvement has been the most rewarding aspect of my total education and that of my family.

Additional Photographic Credits

Archeology Branch. Queensland Department of Aboriginal and Islander Advancement: pp. 14, 137, 141, 142, 147, 148, 149, 162; p. 163 top and bottom, p. 168. Jennifer Isaacs: p. 64 bottom, p. 132. Tom Nell: pp. 78, 79.

INDEX
Illustrations indicated by italics